Demise of the Common Law

The Story Behind America's Legislative Anarchy.

Ed Blanton

Penors Word Press, Inc
Las Vegas, Nevada.
www.PenorSword.com

Demise of the Common Law

SUGGESTED CATALOGING DATA
Blanton, Edward. Demise of the Common Law

Summary: Autobiography of Edward L. Blanton Jr. which details the decline of the academic standards in American law schools and the subsequent abuse of the litigation process, aided and abetted by legislative corruption and graft.

1. Common Law. 2. Legislation. 3. Corruption. 4. Litigation. 5. Judiciary. 6. Lawyers. I. Title.

Cover Acknowledgements: Adapted from several contributors to Wikimedia Commons. No endorsement is implied.

Book Design and Production: Studio Kazinski, Helsinki, Finland.

ISBN: 978-0-9797320-7-2 (Print)
Published by Penors Word Press, Inc.
Printed in the United States of America.

www.PenorSword.com

Table of Contents

"The end of a thing is better than its beginning..."

Solomon. (Ecclesiastes 7:8)

Introduction

Although born in a Harper Lee world, I lived my adult life in the Baltimore-Washington metroplex. My story would not be instructive but for the state and national leaders, many of whom were close friends, with whom I worked. I graduated from law school when law schools taught law instead of litigation and dispute resolution. As an idealistic young man, I chose to work in a state where corruption has been a way of life for so long few know the difference between right and wrong.

I turned to politics and did no better, so I put down my sword and picked up my pen, not to expose, indict or condemn but to inform. This memoir shares what I learned from those with whom I worked. We live in an enthralled society, and even worse, we have lost the common law of England.

With the insight old age bestows, many things I did without thinking, or shrank from doing because I chose to live my life free of the publicity the media impose on those who work in the public spotlight, contributed to the loss of the common law, the 'dumbing down' of the Maryland judiciary, and the decline of the Republican party.

Had I stepped up to the plate and suffered the consequences instead of retreating to my own private Eden, the profession to which I dedicated my life would be more to my liking. If you persevere to the end, you will see why I begin by suggesting steps you should take to alleviate the damage I did. I do this because time is of the essence.

As a military officer overseas, a teacher, a legislative and judicial advisor, a lawyer, a politician and pro-bono community activist, a trustee of private charities, a director of a publicly held corporation and a trustee of tax-exempt charitable organizations, I had access to public servants at both the local, state and national level.

The critical reader will note how, when and where I failed and why I see myself as the last lawyer. The insightful will read between the lines and detect the factual basis for the conclusions I reached, but more importantly, the ones I hesitate to suggest because I can not prove them in a court of law beyond a reasonable doubt. You need to be aware, however, of the effortless way things are done.

We now live in a world where public schools no longer educate, they indoctrinate. Legislators no longer legislate, they delegate. Courts no longer adjudicate; they abdicate their responsibility to decide, deferring to the bureaucrats who enthrall us and the second and third year law students who do the work the judges are paid to do.

The oligarchy in Washington decide how we are to be indoctrinated, imposing their will on us through unions, accreditation committees and legislative enactments that ordain what is required of us. By oligarchy I refer to the leadership of both major parties, as tight a band of confederates as the sacred band of Thebes, with similar proclivities.

They alone—the five hundred thirty-five congressmen in Washington and one hundred ninety-two legislators in Annapolis and eight in Baltimore County—decide what we must do, think, be and pay. Our part-time legislators, jurists and executives ordain we support them for the rest of their lives with multiple pensions earned at every level of so-called public service for the little they do for us and the much they do for themselves, pretending to represent us while actually representing themselves at our expense.

It may well be too late to save the national government, and maybe we ought not try. I live in a house, now over three hundred years old, that was here before the federal government came into existence, and it is becoming increasingly likely it will be here after the national government is replaced or scaled back to an affordable level. The impact of the overhaul on Maryland and Virginia will be severe, not if it happens, but when, for happen it must.

The only part of it we absolutely have to have is what we started with in 1789—the State, Treasury and War Departments. The rest of it is a luxury we can no longer afford, and keeping it will destroy us. States can better decide how to educate their children and provide police, fire and health services. When government pretends it is doing anything more, it is lying, because it can not. Even worse, it enthralls us, eroding our freedom and diminishing the quality of our lives.

When we had no national government before 1774, the people interested in order formed political committees to fight for independence and adopt rules to live by. By and large English in thought, the document they wrote was not a Constitution in the English sense; but a set of by-laws under which the national government operates. When the first one didn't work, the states elected delegates to a national convention to create a second.

In 1788, wise men insisted upon adding to the constitution ten amendments incorporating the English concept of God-given rights enshrined in England's unwritten Constitution derived from the Magna Charta and the Common Law of England, which dates from 1189. It is no accident that liberty first flourished where the Common Law took root.

For years former Maryland Governor William Donald Schaefer and I were entrusted with the perpetuation of a committee formed in 1945 that vetted candidates for executive, legislative and judicial offices through questionnaires and personal interviews, the sole purpose of which was to separate and recommend to voters the fit from the unfit, the authentic from the phony, and those who sought to serve from those who sought to be served. We got good government at the local level for forty years before I tired of it and passed it on to others who let it die. Start there, and until you have it up and running, here are some steps to take to preserve what little freedom you still have. Remember, government is not the enemy, but big government is.

Never elect a lawyer to a legislative body, whether it be the county council, the state legislature or the Congress of the United States. Use your ballot to impose term limits. Never vote for an incumbent. Never vote for a sitting or appointed judge or "Yes" to retain an appellate court judge in office. Keep them rotating out of office and off the bench.

Insist upon the election rather than appointment of school boards, with the parents in each school district deciding what is to be taught and how much they are to be taxed to support their children's education. Schools work best when parents are involved.

Insist the lawyer you retain studied law instead of litigation. Make sure his or her degree is from a Jesuit, conservative Roman Catholic or Christian law school that teaches equity as well as law. Deny corporate America the right to indoctrinate the federal judiciary.

Revise the 1789 law creating the federal judiciary by adopting the German model for appointing rather than electing judges, beginning with internships as law clerks and administrative judges and promoting the most able up the judicial ladder. A professional judiciary, insulated from politics and corporate seduction and indoctrination is essential to the restoration of ordered liberty.

To loosen the economic chains, forbid the management of publicly held corporations to nominate directors. Formation of proxy committees to vet candidates is essential if the boards are to serve the stockholders instead of the executives who convert corporate wealth to management wealth.

Create mutual savings banks, savings and loan associations and insurance companies to originate mortgages, fixing responsibility for credit decisions on the originator. Impose fiduciary duty standards applicable to trustees on corporate management and directors in lieu of the 'sound business judgment' rule.

Insist law schools teach and require proficiency in equity, trusts, property, future interests, corporations, taxation, accounting, conflict of laws and ethics before awarding a degree or allowing anyone to take the bar examination. Restore law libraries, legal research and deductive reasoning instead of Lexis-Nexis/Google-like searches. Here is why this is urgent.

The "financial crisis" of 2007 began in July of that year and continued through the first week of March, 2009. There was in fact no financial crisis. Ben Bernanke, Hank Paulson and Timothy Geithner, in their ignorance, convinced the 545 there was, because Wall Street lawyers and those representing the Federal Reserve Banks, the Securities and Exchange Commission, the Federal Trade Commission, FNMA, Freddie Mac, the FHA, the Congress and the Department of Justice were ignorant of the law.

In 1957, I learned in my freshman class in contracts that a gambling contract is void as a matter of public policy. Neither party can turn to a court of law to enforce it. During the summer of 1958, I took a course in insurance law, and I learned that insurance is *not* interstate commerce. An insurance contract *is* a gambling contract. I bet I will die; the insurer bets I will live. I bet my house will burn down; the insurer bets it won't.

Insurance contracts, notwithstanding their gambling character, are enforced in the courts because they are tightly regulated by the Insurance Commissioner of each state which prescribes the exact terms and the amount to be bet by each party. If the Insurance Commissioner does not approve the contract, it is a crime to sell it. Insurance is gambling that does not violate public policy only because it is *regulated* gambling.

A credit default swap is a gambling contract. A lender fears he will not be paid, so he pays a fee which he calls a premium to a gambler who bets that he will be paid. The gamblers are not, as you might suspect, necessarily an insurance company like AIG, the principal offender. They are also your bank, an offshoot of a regulated utility once known as the Baltimore Gas and Electric Company and later as Constellation Energy, your brokerage firm, or the trustees of your pension plan, the state retirement system or TIAA-CREF. Not being insurance contracts subject to regulation and enforcement, credit default swaps are unenforceable gambling contracts. Ergo, no crisis: just lost bets no one can enforce, no systemic risk, and the bankruptcy courts instead of the taxpayers efficiently clean up the mess.

Yet, the Chairman of the Federal Reserve Bank Ben Bernanke and his minion, Timothy Geithner, backed by a Goldman Sachs Secretary of the Treasury, terrified a naïve President and a clueless Congress into underwriting unenforceable gambling contracts to the tune of trillions of dollars. A "trumped-up" financial crisis honored unenforceable gambling debts and paid them off with taxpayer money, enriching the wrongdoer in violation of the ancient equity maxim that miscreants may not profit from their wrongs.

In August 2008, I was startled by an overnight decline of fifty percent in the price of shares of Constellation Energy, a significant holding of a trust of which I was trustee. The holding company, the brainchild of my childhood friend and sailing buddy Benard Trueschler, was created to bamboozle the Public Service Commission. Reviewing the notes the company's accountants appended to its certified financial statements included in the annual report for the past three years, I found that the company, then run by an 'investment' banker who probably did not know the difference between a watt and a volt, was party to credit default swaps obligating it to pay amounts triple its entire net worth.

The Board of Directors, all stalwarts of the local community, allowed the CEO to gamble with the stockholders equity. Stockholders bailed out in droves, but the CEO negotiated himself a bonus of $18,000,000 payable to his family trust by a predatory corporation launching a rescue effort. If the deal did not go through, the company would pay, with money that belonged not to the investment banker CEO but to the hapless stockholders, $400,000,000, which the company will collect, by means of its legislatively bestowed monopoly, from the enthralled citizens of Maryland who buy their electricity or natural gas from its wholly owned subsidiary. That is larceny-after-trust, and it is an indictable offense. There is no Maryland prosecutor who can make the case and the United States Attorney, a creature of the Department of Justice, can not act without the consent of the clueless Attorney General.

There are others, ranging from county-council persons to the 535 members of Congress and the Senate, who appropriate public funds to their plush retirement plans, as well as corporate managers, CEO's, and Directors who help themselves to stock-holder wealth, should be held to fiduciary standards, together with CEO's and Boards of eleemosynary institutions, if there is a lawyer left in America who knows that such things existed.

In 2010, Congress, apparently ignorant of the Supreme Court decision that held insurance was not interstate commerce, passed a 2,700 page bill regulating health insurance predicated upon its right to regulate interstate commerce. Can anyone today even find the case that held that insurance is not interstate commerce? The same Congress reduced the social security "tax" as part of a stimulus package, unaware that the Supreme Court sustained the Social Security System in 1937 predicated on the fee deducted from employee pay being an insurance premium and not a tax.

If it had been a tax, it would have been unconstitutional, and the Supreme Court made that plain. But today's lawyers and today's legislators have no collective memory. Why? Because law schools no longer teach law. They teach litigation and give law students credit for aiding and abetting the abdication of judicial responsibility by interning as law clerks.

We are where we are because more than a century ago, a Columbia University professor named John Dewey set out to achieve social justice through government. Two things stood in his way: the best public school system in the world and a government committed to the rule of the Common Law of England. The Maryland Constitution provides that the people of Maryland are entitled to the protection of the Common Law of England as well as the statutes of England in force on July 4, 1776.

John Dewey's dream of taking over public education in America was accomplished in the early nineteen fifties, when the supporters of public education finally gained control of accreditation associations of colleges and secondary schools. Ironically this was just three years before a long fight by African Americans to open up access and admission to these very schools, only to find their victory was pyrrhic, for the public schools had already embarked on a long, downhill descent into mediocrity from which they will never recover. Increased funding does not help; it makes the problem worse.

In the eight years between my graduation from Baltimore Polytechnic in 1949 and my return to the public schools as a mathematics teacher in 1957-1959 in the same school system, the signs were everywhere. Teachers had become babysitters, and tenure depended upon not confronting trouble makers and passing every student, whether or not he or she could read or solve $x+2=6$.

Dewey's disciples expanded their control to colleges and universities, both public and private. I graduated from law school at the University of Maryland in 1960, the same year the proponents of critical legal education (known as the "crits") seized control of the faculties at Harvard and Stanford law schools. With the exception of a dozen or so law schools, every law school in America now teaches that the law is not about justice but dispute resolution. There is no right or wrong; just good argument and bad argument. Crit infested law schools teach the adversary system and litigation. They do not teach law, and judges see a fraud on the court as 'good lawyering.'

People yearn for justice. Disputes can be settled with guns and knives. But the law is supposed to settle conflict based upon fixed and unalterable rules to which all adhere. We live in an age without the rule of law, for the law is lost, buried in books no longer on the shelves but supposedly in the computer data base. Law libraries in county court houses are replaced by computers. Legal research by tutored minds is a lost art.

Maryland is the canary in the coal mine. In 2009 the adult population was 4,160,620. The Department of Labor, Licensing and Regulation posits that 3,030,064 Maryland residents were employable, of which 954,064 were on Federal, state or local payrolls; another 695,336 were over age 65 (potentially recipients of Federal social security checks); 854,345 were receiving disability payments and 7.1% were unemployed and receiving unemployment benefits. Do the math: 2,718,940 adults in Maryland are beholden in one way or another to government largesse for all or part of their income, collected from the 1,441,660 adults working in the private sector. The enthralled minority are taxed to support the mendicant majority.

Voting results in the 2010 general election in the three Federal District bedroom counties and Baltimore City and County –where the majority of government workers and mendicants live—were heavily Democrat; the remaining eighteen counties were heavily Republican. Is it any surprise that Maryland taxpayers are facing even more burdensome tax increases from a legislature controlled by the Democrat party, regularly meeting in special sessions to increase taxes semiannually?

Fifty years ago the chief judge on the Maryland Court of Appeals, who was in fact a lawyer and not a bureaucrat, opined that no man and his property were safe as long as the Maryland Legislature is in session. True, but laws passed by city and county councils, state legislatures and the Congress can be repealed by their successors. Bureaucracies running amuck need not be funded and government workers can be fired and their pay and retirement benefits reduced. Can it be done peacefully when the majority is on the dole? As consigliore of the Maryland Republican party for quarter century, I don't think so.

A vastly scaled down national government is the only way to free us from the military-industrial complex President Eisenhower warned us about in 1960. We must control spending by bringing government employee salaries and pensions into parity with private employment. Pensions part time legislators vote themselves and the bureaucrats they employ should be abolished and those enacting them banished from public office.

Maryland is a lost cause, and it appears that Virginia will soon follow. Between Washington in the northeast, the Navy in the southeast and the Valley in the west populated by students, the Old Dominion is near enthrallment by the mendicant majority. We can no longer free ourselves, and we must appeal to the voters of the remaining forty-eight states for help. How? By curtailing the power of the national government.

Western governments, such as our own, have made promises beyond their means. Debts that can not be paid are discharged by bankruptcy, and when a nation defaults, the government inevitably collapses and must be replaced. Such was the case at the end of the American Civil War. The Confederate South was a nation defeated in war, left without an effective government and impoverished by financial collapse. There was land and labor to work it but no capital to pay wages. The South invented share cropping, and it is still in use today. American ingenuity is turning back to a variation—bartering and issuance of local scrip. That is what we will all soon face.

"You are a young man who will make your mark on the world."

—Mayor Theodore Roosevelt McKeldin,
August, 1945

A Challenge

At the close of a summer day I sit alone warmed by the fading sun sinking behind a wall of dark-green evergreens framed by the light-green grape vine embracing the fence around my tennis court. The same light-green seeps between the shadows on the gently sloping lawn sweeping down to the fence beyond which my horse grazes, swishing his tail and flexing his shoulder muscles to deflect late-lingering flies.

In front of me, tall evergreens beside a white, Chinese-Chippendale fence reflect in the still, pale blue water of the pool, beyond which three distinct clumps of trees stretch skyward. The nearest, shading Rattlesnake Run, grow just beyond the far fence of my pasture. Midway up the hill the tops of a large stand of pine hide the pond impeding the flow from the spring which, a century ago, supplied water to my house. A majestic blue heron rises above the trees, large flapping wings slowly propelling him to his accustomed perch on a branch of a dead honey locust tree.

Beyond the pine encircled pond is the deciduous forest on the hills at the foot of Long Green Valley, green now but soon to display the rich earth tones of autumn. The dissonant chorus of bird calls, frantically protecting their chosen space in the gathering gloom, diminish as the sun sinks, now just a golden glow in the trees between me and the hayfield. I await the quiet night at peace with the familiar scene where I like to sit at the end of my day.

The house behind me is more than three-hundred years old, and a half-century of work has left me spent, but I trust my stewardship will keep this pleasant prospect as it now is for others to enjoy for centuries to come, if indeed those who come after me to this place have centuries to come. It is because I fear they do not that I am writing this memoir. It is a confession of my complicity in your enthrallment. Thrall is a synonym for slave and it was I who may have put you there by the things I did and the things I failed to do.

I am old now, past eighty, but I came here as a young man in 1965 with my pregnant wife and two children, not knowing then I would stay so long or that my life would take the course it did. I came into the world far from here, too long ago to remember, in a house not unlike the one behind me, owned by my mother in North Carolina, overlooking the pond that gave Hope Mills its name.

My mother marched in the vanguard of modern American women, employed at age eighteen by the Southern Bell Telephone Company to go into surrounding towns and rent space for a switchboard, hire and train young women to be telephone operators, politely asking the fortunate few who could afford them "Number, Please" and plugging the line with the lit light into the hole with an unlit light assigned to the person being called.

She inherited the house in which I was born from her father, whose picture hangs in the house behind me now known as *Avondell.* My grandfather, John Bunyan Bullard, was dead at twenty-four, beloved and mourned by a large family of siblings who fought over his possessions. My mother was two when he died, and but ten when her mother followed, after which she lived with my great aunt Johanna, my grandfather's older sister, on the campus of Trinity College in Durham, now known as Duke University.

My father lied about his age to join the United States Navy in 1916 and served as the radio operator on the *USS Arizona,* sailing through the Panama Canal to Peru and Hawai*i*. He won the Pacific fleet light-weight boxing championship. He married my mother in 1926 and they moved into my mother's house overlooking Hope Mills, with twenty-two bird dogs belonging to my father and the army officers who hunted quail and played polo with him. My father trained the dogs for field trials in Tennessee, where they did so well they were often stolen by traveling men from South Carolina who plague me still, wanting to paint my neighbor's barn.

There were Lumbee Indians on my mother's farm, and three of them worked in the house. One was my nurse until my mother discovered her chewing my food and transferring it from her mouth to mine as a robin feeds her young. I have the vaguest recollection of watching the laundry being done outdoors, wood fires under three large black pots: one for soaking, one for boiling the clothes in soap, and the third for rinsing. I watched clothes moved from pot to pot with wooden ladles, then hung on lines to dry, flapping wildly in the wind.

I have not a lot of memories there, for I was taken to Vero Beach until it was time for me to start to school. I became a law-breaker early, filling the cups in the greens on the golf course beside our house with sand I found in the traps, and drinking home-brewed beer made by the German grounds-keeper who discouraged my play and protected me from irate putters.

Florida was not a healthy place in the 1930's, and my mother and my sister Millie came down with malaria. Mountain air and no mosquitoes were prescribed, and my father moved us to Princeton, West Virginia. The snow was over my head, and being marooned was a welcome respite until a chattering neighbor cleared a path to our door. I dropped a piece of coal a dump-truck left in an outbuilding on the head of a boy I did not like. He survived, but I feared for my own life after the switch I was sent to cut for my whipping proved too limber to break.

When the curative mountain water had been drunk, the pure air breathed and the tropical malaise overcome, we returned to North Carolina, not to the house where I was born, for it had been reduced to ashes on a cold, wind-swept

November night when the housekeeper went to bed before it was safe to close the damper in the fireplace. She put the ashes, some still red, in a cardboard box on the wooden porch just outside the door.

The house where my ancestors entertained their Connecticut cousin in Sherman's army was no more. You may read about it in my novel *Grasping the Wind: the Worth of a Word.* So we lived for a few months in a boarding house on Bogue Sound in Morehead City. It was there I began my day as I still do with orange juice and fresh chilled cantaloupe. It was also there I learned to sail cat-boats in the safe waters of the sound, separated from the white-capped waves of the Atlantic by a spit of sand on which I often beached my boat and waded ashore to find starfish and sand dollars to stuff in my overall pockets.

An ideal summer passed quickly, and the house my father rented in New Bern was ready for us in September. It was here I abandoned my criminal ways to start life afresh. It was just in time, for it was while living in the bungalow on National Avenue that I first attracted the attention of the trash collectors and a girl who liked me.

New Bern sits on the point of land where the Neuse and Trent Rivers come together, not, as they say in Charleston, to form the Atlantic Ocean but just to make a bigger Neuse River. Having been captured early on by the Yankees in the War Between the States, who held it in spite of heroic efforts by the Confederates to get it back, the houses and churches were not burned and the once-upon-a-time royal capital of North Carolina was and is still a charming town.

I started my schooling at the Riverside School, to which I walked every day from my house near the cemetery for the Union dead. I passed the house of Representative Graham Barden, and I heard my father tell my mother that he was chairman of a Congressional Committee in Washington that parceled out tax dollars to those who voted for his party. He had a daughter named Aggie, and she, not yet old enough to go to Riverside, played in her yard under the watchful eye of her nurse.

I heard Adolph Hitler shouting on the radio in far off Germany, but I had no idea what upset him so. A friend of my father's was going into a risky business, and he wanted my mother to put up ten thousand dollars for ten percent of it. I heard this as I sat at a small table in the kitchen, eating my supper with my younger sister Faye. The door to the butler's pantry was open, as well as the door to the dining room, so my mother could make sure we ate our peas and used our knives and forks.

The business was going to market "Pepsi" concocted by a local druggist. My mother was certain a copy-cat drink would not be a success. We drank beer and wine, and "soft-drinks"—which my Negro friends called "dope"—were not found in our pantry. My mother wrote lyrics to sad love songs, which she later heard on the radio after her agent took them as his own, set them to music and released them on big, black seventy-eight rpm phonograph records.

There was going to be a celebration of the first English settlement in America on Roanoke Island in 1587. One wing of Governor Tryon's palace still survived in New Bern, and it was decided that Aggie Barden and I would lead a troop of other children in a minuet on the lawn in front of the palace. I did not know Aggie, but I was told she had made it a condition of her participation that I be her partner. You may read about Tryon Palace in my novel *Tory Terror.*

I endured black, patent-leather shoes, long-white socks, blue-silk knickers, a lacy shirt and blue-silk jacket from which my doily like sleeves and collar stuck out. We practiced the dance forever to make sure every step was in sync with the music. My teacher sang the words and hummed the tune as she taught us the steps. The urge to drag Aggie to the Neuse River and drown her came to me more than once. To avoid practice I hid behind the garage sitting on a pile of boards, only to be turned in by our neighbor's servants, who wanted to know why that little white boy was sitting behind the garage all morning.

There was a lot of cork floating in the Neuse. It was used to line the caps of the Pepsi bottles. Some pieces were big enough to use as boogey-boards. Bereft of my beloved cat-boat, I paddled around the Neuse on chunks of cork whenever I found the river free of the water moccasins that crawled in the caves my older sister's boyfriends dug in the fields next to Mrs. Hartsell's garden, which she modeled on the kitchen garden at Tryon Palace.

It was not the Tryon Palace garden that attracted me, but the library in the surviving wing, with its leather-backed law books from the eighteenth century which the Governor used to decide what was right and what was wrong. Now I model my garden after hers and my library after his. And it was from there that I set out to make my life's work righting wrongs to atone for my criminal past.

My mother tried to right wrongs as best she could. I was often called down from the pecan tree in the backyard to the kitchen table to eat dinner with visitors, white hair crowning their chocolate faces, telling me how things were when they were my age, before the Yankees set them free. At first I thought they were distant relatives, for they were introduced as Auntie this and Uncle that. My mother explained the titles were a sign of respect because they were enduring to the end, as St. Paul urged us all to do. They shared their faith-based wisdom with us. My mother told me the South had lost a war, and we all had to stick together to work our way out of it.

I had one aunt who was real, a half-sister of my mother, who was going to college in South Carolina. She came to visit and it was never Christmas until the taxi dropped her off at our door to laugh the night away. She said the driver told her the Christmas tree in our dining room window was the prettiest one in town. Aunt Ethel walked us to the First Presbyterian Church where kind ladies gave us red-mesh stockings filled with penny candy on Christmas Eve.

Every night before bed-time my mother called us to the alcove by the piano to read from Hurlburt's "Story of the Bible" after which she asked questions to make sure we had listened. I knew there were places called Jericho and Jerusalem before I knew there was a city called New York.

I liked maps and studied them, so I could find my way home if I was ever lost. There were maps of the places she read about. I knew Galilee was north of Jerusalem but the disciples were always going up to Jerusalem. I thought they didn't know north from south, for the two most important things I had learned was north was up and south was down. When I went to Israel as an old man, I realized "up" referred to altitude in a vertical, not a horizontal sense.

The rants from Hitler were heard more often but there was less fear in the house when my mother listened to fireside chats from a man named Roosevelt, a name that sounded like the stuff my Sunday hat was made of. He was a Yankee, a good one we could trust, like the cousins who stopped by her house near Hope Mills for dinner while my father's ancestors set up an ambush at Bentonville.

I thought Roosevelt was a salesman, like my mother's cousin who astonished me one day by driving up to our house with a Ball canning jar, all lit up and big enough to climb into, stuck in the rumble seat of his car, with peaches as big as beach balls stuffed inside. My mother said his car reminded her of the white Chrysler convertible she drove until my father, lost it in the same poker game in which he won a pair of polo ponies. Too bad Pinehurst was so close to Hope Mills.

Just as school was about to start there were maps on the dining room table and talk of a place called Hickory. It was all the way across the state, and there were more Republicans there than Democrats. We had to go there because there was more money there. My sisters and I sat in the bed of a pick-up truck all the way from the salty tidewaters of the Neuse to the clear cold waters of the Catawba, teaming with bass, crappies and perch.

We shared a huge Victorian house with rounded towers, porches and balconies on a hill at the end of Seventeenth Street with an old lady who spent the winter in Ft. Lauderdale, Florida. She promised me oranges and alligators when she returned in the spring. My laughing Aunt visited us here as well. She said there were more millionaires per capita in Hickory than any other city in America, including New York and Hollywood. When I doubted it she explained 'per capita' to me, my first introduction to the idea that figures don't lie but liar's figure. It's the basis for equal pay and equal opportunity.

I walked everyday to the Oakwood School, and if we finished our work on time, our teacher read from 'The Secret Garden." It snowed in Hickory, but my mother had hot chocolate and warm oatmeal cookies waiting when I got home if I waited patiently until she heard the end of a radio program called 'My Son and I.' It made her cry, but so did the lyrics she wrote, more so when she heard them on the radio.

There was a row of cabins behind our house, and a large barn between the house and the cabins was being converted into a house for Sam and Hannah Jackson, who reminded me of my New Bern Aunties and Uncles. All of the rooms were being finished in knotty pine which I helped brush with stain. Sam wore suspenders and was almost as dignified as Hannah, who wore elbow length gloves like my mother's and broad brimmed hats when they went to the Baptist church. At Easter, Sam filled a galvanized wash tub full of dyed Easter eggs for me and the children from the cabins.

On Saturdays the selling ladies came up the hill with fruit, vegetables, and cookies that melted in your mouth, sold from the back of an ancient roofed-over pick-up with a scales dangling from the back. My mouth watered as I watched the scale with some fear, for things were sold by the pound and money was scarce. I heard my father tell my mother he was down to his last dime. So I went out to pick as many blackberries as I could carry, and my mother made them into a pie.

A few days later, I walked down the hill to pick up the newspaper and the bold-black headline said "France Falls." There was a map, and I looked at it and found that Belgium, Holland and Luxembourg had fallen as well; to something Hitler had called 'panzers.' The phony war had suddenly become real, so I looked at the date to make sure I remembered it was May 10, 1940.

On Saturdays I took a nickel and went to the double-feature at the theatre with Harvey Geitner and Joe Petree. We saw a cartoon, an installment of the "Green Hornet", and two movies with Guy Madison, Bob Steele or John Wayne always getting the bad guys in the end so we could go home happy. The "News of the Day" showed London being bombed and German paratroopers falling on Crete.

Harvey was in my class at Oakwood, and we roamed the woods and streams behind his house catching snakes, prettier than and not as mean as the cotton-mouths in the Neuse. There were beautifully decorated copperheads that were nearly inert, the laziest snake I ever saw, as well as king snakes, blue racers, and timber rattlers. A hall in Harvey's basement was lined with wooden cages with wire-screen lids and sides. We lifted the lids and dropped the snakes inside, feeding them a live mouse or a live frog once a week.

To catch them we sharpened the ends of a forked stick with our pen knives. I penned their heads to the ground while Harvey grabbed them by the tail. When I pulled up my stick with one hand, he dropped them into a burlap bag I held open with my other hand and the stick. When we got too many, we would match up an unwanted rattler with a king snake in the sandy road between the Shuford's swimming pool and Harvey's house. The king snake always won, and I feared I might be back sliding to my criminal past. So I studied my Westminster Catechism all the harder, got gold stars from my Sunday school teacher covering the numbers of all the questions, and I was rewarded with a New Testament from the First Presbyterian Church.

In the fall my father bought a new car, a Pontiac—blue on the doors and gray on the roof—the first two-tone car I had ever seen. He bought some bird-dogs and assembled a portable fence for them. Sam found a young man living in one of the cabins to bring two mules and plow a large garden behind our house for my mother. I helped her prepare the soil, plant the seeds and dig out the weeds. I still garden far more than I should.

I wanted chickens, and there was a shed in the orchard where they could stay, so my father got a portable fence, taller than the one he made for his bird dogs, to keep my chickens safe from predators. They were all white, until my mother cut their heads off to fry them for Sunday dinner, which had to be finished on Saturday after my double-features, for no work could be done on Sunday. I went to my chicken coop to get eggs for the cold potato salad we ate with the chicken. A black snake curled up in one of the nests had swallowed an egg I didn't get to quick enough.

Our Republican neighbors were voting for a man named Wendell Willkie. Their son Joe told me that Roosevelt was trying for a third term so he could become dictator of America just like Hitler in Germany. Their cook was a Republican woman named Bill, who called me and Joe in from our hiding place under the fig trees by shouting "Hot Biscuits" out the kitchen door. When I asked her if she wanted Roosevelt to be a dictator she said her people were Republicans and they were going to help the white folks put a stop to the Democrats trying to destroy America. It cheered me up to know we were all in it together.

In the spring of 1941 I had a chicken sitting on eggs, and I looked forward to seeing the little chicks emerge. But I came down with the mumps, missed some school days, and before I was well the trees were green, the sky blue, and the chicks pullets. It was the only time I was ever sick in bed until my internist had to give me up to surgeries. I was not sick then, just recovering from being knifed.

One Sunday afternoon after Thanksgiving my mother drove me and my three sisters in the two-tone Pontiac east to Statesville to bring my father home. My mother's song 'Someday Sweetheart' was playing on the car radio when it was interrupted by a special news bulletin. The Japanese, who made cheap toys and tiny tea sets for my little sister, had bombed Pearl Harbor.

My father went to Raleigh to see about getting back in the navy to teach the Japanese not to attack on Sunday morning when everybody was in church. The *Arizona* was sunk and with it the plaque honoring my father as a Pacific Fleet boxing champion. I knew then why I always got boxing gloves and punching bags for Christmas when what I wanted most was a Red Ryder Daisy air rifle and a Bowie knife.

There were firecrackers at Christmas as usual, war or no war. My sisters got new bicycles, which I knew they would because I watched them being delivered to Sam's house for safekeeping. When he brought them up to the house on Christmas morning two girls from the cabins were trying them out to make sure they worked right. They came into the house with their little brothers and sisters to help my sister Faye play with her toys.

We passed around a basket of dried fruit, exotic salted nuts and candy in a large wicker basket left at the house by Mr. Jones, the furniture maker for whom my father worked. The boys wanted to put the Daisy to work on the birds in the pine grove next door, so I went out to show them how well I could aim. There was quite a crowd in the backyard, firecrackers being tossed about—dangerously close I thought—so I took the fellow who liked me best down the hill to find a target.

Drury pointed out a bird perched on a limb and I took aim, allowed a bit for windage and fired. The bird fell and when I picked it up, its little yellow and black head tilted lifelessly over my thumb. I gave the gun to my accomplice and told him he could keep it, sinking my head against his musty chest to hide my tears when he hugged me. That New Testament I worked so hard to get had not done me much good, for I had killed a bird I did not eat, a cardinal sin in my father's eyes.

The Japanese had bought up all the scrap metal in America and used it to make tanks, battleships and airplanes. With our fleet sunk we needed to find any they had missed. Joe, Harvey, his cousins from the Canal Zone and Drury formed the "Junior Marines" and went into the fields and barns, even under the cabins, to get all the scrap we could lay our hands on. We made a huge pile of it in somebody's yard, and the photographer from the newspaper took our picture, wrote down our names and printed them in the paper. I was surprised I was such a little waif, as I was sure I was almost grown and ready to become a real marine.

After Christmas my mother decided I was too old to share a room with my little sister, so we moved to a brick house on 12th Avenue, not far from a wholesale warehouse, where I could buy a box of twenty-four candy bars for eighty cents and sell them for five cents each, netting a profit, if I gave none away and resisted the temptation to eat some, of forty cents. I envisioned great wealth from this scheme, and I knocked on many a door and ruined many a tooth.

On Halloween my mother celebrated my eleventh birthday in the party room at the Coca Cola plant, inviting my fifth grade class, including my rivals for the affection of Phyllis Matheson. She could tear your heart out when she sang "O Holy Night" at our Christmas program at Oakwood. The war had turned with the route of the Desert Fox in North Africa and the sinking of the carriers that attacked Pearl Harbor in the battle of Midway.

My father came home for Christmas and announced we would be going up North when school was out. Johnny Cauble helped me and my sister make a Memorial Park by the creek that separated our house from his. She knew nothing of snakes and I had to grab her hand as she reached for an ugly fellow, coiled and ready to strike, sitting on the bottom of the creek glaring at her. Cotton-mouth moccasins were not welcome in the rock garden we were building as a good-bye present to North Carolina.

Jimmy Jones lived behind our house with his grandmother on our side of the creek. His uncle had taught him about sex and we crawled under his house before I left so I could learn what he knew, but his grandmother heard us laughing and sent me home. I wondered if people could tell when you knew how babies were made. I was afraid to look at my mother when she read from Hurlburt's that night because she might see that I had lost my innocence.

My older sisters, who dated boys on the high school football team, did not want to go on the train with us when we left, and it was only when my mother promised they could comeback in the fall to finish school that they went at all.

Baltimore was a different world, not at all like North Carolina, but there was no polio epidemic like the one that came to Hickory as we were leaving. Polio had crippled Roosevelt, a man greatly loved in Maryland. I got a job right away delivering newspapers for a friend of my fathers, who had two sons who read the Bible every night before going to bed.

Johnny was sixteen and attended Baltimore City College, where he was the Maryland Scholastic diving champion. I liked his older brother David who lived in West Virginia with his grandmother. He always hit a home run in the bottom of the seventh inning to win the softball game. David went on overnight camping trips with my Boy Scout troop. He could whistle loud enough to be heard a block away and he let me hold his tee shirt when he played softball.

Summer ended and David went back to Marshall College and I started to school at William Paca P.S.#83, a big brick building in the city surrounded by tiny houses with white marble steps which were scrubbed clean every morning. The windows had landscapes painted on the screens, and there was a bakery that smelled like heaven on every corner that did not have a bar selling National Bohemian Beer. The school building was old and smelled like books. The Vice-Principal looked at my report card and sent me to the class of Miss Kathleen Moore, who was a Virginian like my father's family.

Yankee children had strange names I had never heard before, smelled like garlic and played with a black and white ball they called soccer, bouncing it off their heads and never touching it with their hands. Miss Moore had a reading ladder and moved my name up a notch every time I read another book, and when I got to the top she gave me Pearl Buck's 'The Good Earth' to keep. She did not know I had read all thirty books in the Rover Boy series, and most of those about Tom Swift, a fictional hero a lot like David Conner was a real one.

It snowed a foot on Thanksgiving, and my papers were heavier with all the Christmas advertising. I was afraid the weight would pull my head off and the melting snow soaked my socks so bad my feet blistered, but David's father counted on me to keep the papers dry and put them inside the customer's door. I could not let him down, so I missed Thanksgiving dinner. My mother saved me a glass of port to warm me back up when I came home half-frozen.

The war was going better but the Germans kept sinking our convoys so they were launching a Liberty ship a day at the Bethlehem and Fairfield yards in Baltimore. They needed help making bombers in Middle River, so my mother learned how to make them. There was no place to make a Memorial Park so we collected odds and ends and joined with some Pennsylvanians to pretend we were making airplane parts until we were told the place where we played was contaminated and we better stay away from it.

My mother did not have much time to shop but I went with her on Christmas Eve to the heart of the city to shop at O'Neills, Hutzlers, and Stewarts department stores, trying to find a doll for my little sister, but there were none left. I have never before or since seen stores as empty as they were in 1943, and the money I had saved to buy gifts was useless. I knew it was better to have money and nothing to buy with it than having something to buy and not having any money.

Even food was rationed, and we had blue and red buttons we used to buy meat, butter, eggs and sugar. There was also a coupon for gasoline, but the letter on the windshield of my father's 1942 Oldsmobile allowed us some extra because my parents were helping win the war.

An older boy delivered the morning paper for Mr. Conner, and on June 6, 1944 just before sunrise he woke me up crying "Extra, Extra, read all about it." There was an invasion of France underway, and the maps on the front page had arrows pointing to the place where men were dying. That was the day Miss Moore told me that the principal wanted me to go to a school named after Robert E. Lee on Cathedral Street where I could finish school more quickly if my parents would give me money for public transportation.

I had learned to make my own way in the world besides delivering newspapers. I collected beer and soda bottles, took them to a liquor store that gave me two cents for small ones and five cents for large ones. I borrowed a lawn mower from the rental office and cut the small lawns in my neighborhood for a quarter if inside and fifty cents if it were a corner house. I paid for my own school lunches and my carfare, so I told her I would go.

My scout troop, lead by Mr. Kirby, camped out in Chinquapin Park and later that summer we went to Camp Horseshoe on the Octoraro Creek, up near the Pennsylvania border. I was at home paddling canoes in snake infested waters. The Maryland snakes are not fierce and they swim away instead of swimming after you. My troop leader told me they were not poisonous like the snakes Harvey and I caught. They call them water moccasins but they are just snakes that swim. We sang a dumb song at meals, trying to drown out boys from other cabins, about "our ears being made of leather and flapping in windy weather because we were from Hemlock don't you see."

Later the Scouts had a Jamboree in Patterson Park and Mayor Theodore Roosevelt McKeldin came to pass out signed pictures of himself. If I were going to spend my life righting wrongs I would have to be a politician, so I watched to see how it is done. When all the pictures were given out the Mayor turned around and looked right at me. He knew I was watching him. He was a big man and he walked over to the fence I was leaning against, picked me up and sat me on it. He asked me who I was, where I was from, and what I was doing. So I made a note to ask voters about themselves, get them talking, a great ice breaker.

I told him where I was starting junior high next week and he tapped me on the shoulder and told me I was going to make my mark on the world. I asked him not to tell anybody because other boys were already jealous. When he asked me why that was, I told him I could run faster than any of them, had better grades, more girl-friends and an older friend who played football, basketball and baseball for his college. I did not want it to get any worse. He promised not to tell anybody, and with a happy shake of his head walked over to the next troop, looking back at me and laughing so hard he forgot to give me his picture.

My junior high was on Cathedral Street opposite the Rathskeller. The building was old and creaky but the teachers were not. Boy's Latin school was a block away. When I went to Mercy Hospital to have my tonsils removed, a priest and two nuns holding burning candles were standing at the foot of my bed when I awoke. I feared I might be in heaven already.

Bruce Hornstein found out about my belated circumcision when I bled on my white gym shorts while performing on the pommel horse. Gilbert Hurwitz told me my eyes were hypnotic, and he liked looking at them because they were always changing color. I was afraid of what he might see because I knew my eyes were the windows to my soul.

The war ended in 1945 so delivering the afternoon paper was boring without the daily maps of the shrinking Third Reich on the front page. When I started to high school at Baltimore Polytechnic Institute in September 1946 I bid my customers farewell. They were all in agreement I should put my education above all else if I wanted to make my mark on the world.

Without knowing if I could afford it I signed up for the college preparatory course. The school was modeled after the Naval Academy in Annapolis, combining practical engineering and drafting courses with college level mathematics, physics, and mechanics. The latter were easy for me, but no matter how high my I.Q, my mechanical aptitude tested off the bottom of the scale. I was not good engineering material.

Kind classmates like Charlie Gerwig and Vernon Brooks helped me through pattern making, metal crafting, blacksmithing and machine shop. We put our wooden patterns in molds, pounded wet sand around them, removed the pattern, melted the metal and poured it into the mold to bring out a casting exactly like the wooden pattern with which we began. It was the only place in the school where I felt at home.

My grandfather Bullard's Connecticut cousins had a large foundry they used to make artillery for the army, and my mother showed me some stock in their company with her maiden name on it which my father did not know about. I elected to pursue electrical engineering where I had nothing to make, just parts to assemble, to complete my laboratory work.

Having run all my life as fast as I could I tried out for track in my junior year and broke my left arm playing football in November. I was a half-back and I liked vaulting over the tacklers, until some wise guy reached up, grabbed my ankle and pulled me back to earth. I missed some fundamental lectures in algebra, got but forty percent on my exam and had to attend summer school to make up what I missed.

Johnny Conner went to Duke where he became the Southern Conference diving champion, and both he and his brother David went into the air force to fly jet planes when he graduated from Marshall. In December, I took an examination to attend the Naval Academy in Annapolis, but flunked the eye examination because I was near-sighted, after which I was fitted for glasses to wear at movies and in classrooms.

My family was adamant that Davidson College, a Presbyterian school near Charlotte was the only place I could go to college. I asked Dr. Chamberlain, the Presbyterian minister who drove me and my blue-nose friends to Washington to attend youth meetings to write a letter of recommendation. He, too, had told me I was destined to make my mark, and he was as angry as a pea-turkey hen when the college said I couldn't come. He made them so ashamed they offered me a partial scholarship.

Partial would not do, however, and Miss Kathleen Moore, my sixth grade teacher who attended the church where our youth groups met sent me to the Rotary Club for an interest-free student loan. The loan committee had two members from the Franklin Street Presbyterian Church, and their minister of fifty years was Dr. Harris Kirk. His grand-son, Elliott Verner, was a freshman at Davidson. Next to David Conner, I admired Elliott more than anybody else. The committee was kind enough to lend me four hundred dollars.

Unlike loans for college these days, I had to pay my loan back before I graduated. It was a good thing the tuition was only three hundred dollars a year. I returned to the state of my birth to find out where and when and how I was going to make my mark.

Here is a clue. There is a lot I know that I will take to my grave, so I ask that you rely on your skill as a detective to know where and when I learned things I have omitted to protect friends, many of whom are no longer here. I am not seeking to condemn but to inform. If you follow the facts to their logical conclusion, you will see quite clearly when we lost our liberty and became thralls.

"How did you ruin your life?"
"I didn't go to Davidson"

Middle Tennessee State graduate,
February, 1955

At College and University

At age seventeen I got off a bus in Davidson, North Carolina, took one look, decided I hated the place and took the next bus to Mooresville, seven miles north where I called my laughing Aunt Ethel. She took me in, gave me a pep talk, and sent me back the next morning.

Davidson was all-male, rigidly controlled by the Southern Presbyterian Church. There was no drinking of alcohol on or off campus, an hour of chapel every morning except Saturday and mandatory Vespers on Sunday night in the college church. The student body was predominately southern and disappeared on Saturday afternoon, leaving a hand full of out-of-state students alone in deserted dormitories.

The next morning I was still determined not to stay, but a preppy classmate sitting next to me was so excited about being there, I decided to give it another day or two. As freshmen we ate in the college dining-hall, where Mr. Spence served us grapefruit every morning with our orange juice, eggs, bacon and toast.

Everyone belonged to a fraternity after the first semester, but assuming I was a Yankee, the North Carolina students did not know me, although my mother had told me plenty about their fathers, many of whom she had dated. I automatically became a member of the Campus Club, a holding place for those who could not afford a fraternity or who had yet to make up their minds. Sigma Chi had sprung from its ranks the year before I arrived and Alpha Tau Omega during my freshman year.

We participated fully in all intramural sports, from touch football, track, swimming, softball, wrestling and the inter-fraternity sing each spring, a competitive songfest in which we had to sing the alma mater, a classical religious piece, and a Broadway musical number. George F. Bason, a graduate of the Hill School, was our musical director. At graduation, George was class salutatorian, going on to Harvard Law, joining a Wall Street law firm before being appointed a Bankruptcy Judge in Washington, where he authored one of the longest legal opinions I ever read.

I roomed with two Floridians my freshmen year in Old East. Joel Mattison was a Phi Gam and a sophomore, while Allan Garrison, a Kappa Alpha, was a George F. Baker scholar from Lake Wales, Florida. Joel later became a doctor and worked at Lamborene with Dr. Albert Schweitzer where he found a wife. Allan, as a physicist, later worked with my brother-in-law, James J. Gallagher when Jim was Director of Science at Georgia Tech.

Everyone was enrolled in Army Reserve Officers Training Corps the first two years and the outbreak of the UN sponsored police action to repel the invasion of South Korea at the end of my freshman year gave it more importance, for a lucky fifty of us would move on to get commissions, thereby gaining deferral from the draft until we graduated and were commissioned second lieutenants of infantry in the Army Reserve.

During the summer I worked as a laborer in the pipe mill at Sparrows Point, alternating shifts every week. The United Steel Workers of America represented the employees and there was a tug-of-war between the Union's agent to get me in and the Bethlehem plant management to keep me out. I caved and joined when a load of pipe was dropped from a crane on the spot where I was sweeping the floor. The shift foreman had seen it coming and forewarned me. A worker in a union plant who doesn't carry a union card puts his life at risk.

As a sophomore, I roomed with W. Tucker Blaine, Jr. in Rumple, the oldest dorm on the campus. Donald Schreiber, who later became President of Union Theological Seminary, called it an "arsenal of culture", a term I now apply to my house in Glen Arm. Tucker's father founded a general insurance agency in Houston in 1910 when the city had fewer than ten thousand residents. He was a director of Houston Natural Gas, later known as Enron. So much old Baltimore money was invested in the company a special car was added to the train in Baltimore to take directors and stockholders to the annual meetings in Houston.

The director I knew best was Fred Singley, a Baltimore lawyer who later became a judge on the Court of Appeals. The Singleys and the Blaines were close friends, and Mrs. Singley attended my church. Fred told me the only time he walked into the Court of Appeals without butterflies in his stomach was the day he was sworn in as a judge on Maryland's highest court.

Tucker did not make it into third-year ROTC, so he transferred to the University of Houston where he was commissioned in the Quartermaster Corps. He was sent to Korea as an assistant S-4 after the armistice.

We were told when we arrived at Davidson in 1949 to look at the person on either side of us in our assigned chapel seats. If I were there four years later, neither of the men on either side of me would be. That was painfully true, for only a third of us endured to the end, as our numbers dwindled from 375 to 118 before we graduated.

In those days, America's colleges and high schools were among the world's best. That is, sorry to say, no longer true. In 1953, Davidson bragged about its homogeneity, its rigid adherence to academic standards and its Rhodes Scholars. Today it brags about its diversity, its selectivity and its mediocrity. Everybody graduates with high marks, but if they have had a Rhodes after our class graduated I would be pleasantly surprised.

I continued working for Bethlehem Steel following my junior year as an expediter at the cold-rolled, steel sheet mill. I worked the day shift, making sure orders were filled on time and accurately. Orders were deemed filled as long as the delivery weight was plus or minus ten percent. The temper and thickness had to be correct, however, and my job was to take steel from an over order, send it to be re-tempered or re-rolled and add it to a short order. While working in the comfort of an air-conditioned office, I did get out into the plant to locate the over order and re-tag it with instructions for the mill to carry out.

Bill Bivins and Tyler Berry, both pre-law students from Tennessee, were my closest college friends. Bill and I were in ROTC, and he later became the chief justice of New Mexico. Tyler was in the naval reserve, which required him to hitchhike to Charlotte once a week for drills. He was my assigned partner in accounting lab, and our friendship lasted until his death. He was a Sigma Chi, and when I became President of the Campus Club at the end of our junior year, his brothers joked that the Sigs were the only fraternity on campus with two Presidents.

Tyler and I did everything together, including our senior papers in Dr. Lilly's 18th Century prose class, an elective Bill, Tyler and I took just to test our mettle against the most demanding teacher on the Davidson faculty. Our joint effort earned us both high marks, and Dr. Lilly's praise. At our Tenth Class Reunion, Dr. Lilly told my wife about our effort. At our Fiftieth Class Reunion, I gave our original papers with Dr. Lilly's hand-written comments to Davidson's then President, Robert Vagt, who promised to put them in the college archives.

In the summer of 1952 Bill Bivins and I went to Fort Benning for six-weeks of orchestrated hell designed to teach us how tough it could be on enlisted men when officers do not know what they are doing. My debate opponent in the Eumanean Literary Society, John Ottley, from Atlanta, Georgia, was given a new Studebaker silver sports car for his twenty-first birthday. We used it to explore Phoenix City, Alabama, where we were rescued from a confrontation with a bunch of red-necks who thought we were 'too damn pretty to be army officers' by Sergeant Penley—a Cherokee assigned to the Davidson ROTC faculty—who extracted us from our first combat with no serious casualties. The rednecks must have focused on Ottley, who was strikingly handsome drunk or sober.

We were rewarded with a three-day pass, and Bill, Angus Andrews and I drove to Panama City to swim in the Gulf of Mexico. We stopped at Angus's house in Defuniak Springs to mooch lunch from his mother. As we were leaving, the door from the kitchen opened, and Angus's younger brother, Doug, appeared. I thought I knew him but I could not place him. We did not speak but when school started in September, I was playing basketball in Johnston Gym with Tyler and his Sig buddies. Someone leapfrogged over me, a BMOC, and when I came up ready to swing, it was Doug's smiling face I was about to punch. He grinned and said, "I know you. You were the guy in my dining room." Our friendship endured until his far too early death.

When we graduated on June 1, 1953 I was commissioned second lieutenant in the United States Army Reserve. The UN police action in Korea was three years old, and I and forty-nine of my classmates expected to be leading infantry platoons in Korea within six months. The likelihood of our being alive a month later was slim indeed, so graduation was a day of mixed emotions.

Charlie "Choo'Choo" Justice and Art Weiner had come to Davidson to recruit business majors for Burlington Industries, Inc. They had offered me a job as an executive trainee, although they knew I had to report to the Infantry School at Fort Benning on September 1, 1953. After a brief return to Baltimore, I took a Greyhound bus to Burlington, North Carolina and rented a room on Fountain Place from a widow named Brown. A less recent graduate of North Carolina State College of Agriculture and Engineering in Raleigh was also renting a room in the same house. He was selling fertilizer for American Cyanamid. He had a car, which we used to drive out to the highway restaurants for supper.

I worked nine to five learning the ins and outs of a textile mill, working an ancient electromechanical, Marchant calculator to compute the efficiencies of various departments based upon mountains of numerical data submitted to me on forms completed by the department heads. Once a month I submitted a report of my own, explaining what I was learning from my experience.

For a few weeks all went well until older employees in the plant began urging me to escape at all costs. They did not like the company, distrusted it, and assured me there were better ways for me to make a living. The plant was fascinating, but not as impressive as the huge steel mills at Sparrows Point in Maryland. I was told the stock of the company was a nickel a share in the1930's.

My mother had a cousin who was a lawyer in Burlington. His name was Barnie Patrick Jones, son of my great aunt Johanna. My landlord was interested in my family connection and quizzed me about Pat endlessly as we sat in the swing on her front porch sipping iced tea on humid summer nights. Pat's daughter was an accomplished equestrian, and upon his death he left his law library to my cousin Charles Allan Herndon in Baltimore.

Mrs. Brown was also interested in the fact Mrs. RalphHolt, mother of my Davidson classmate of the same name, invited me home to dinner after church on Sundays. Mrs. Holt missed Ralph, who had joined the navy, so I substituted for him at table. Ralph's father had sold the mill in which I worked to Burlington some years before, and opened new mills of his own making hosiery in Burlington. The Holt Mills were automated and the old timers assured me they were a better place to work. I thought they were just trying to get rid of me.

A few weeks after I arrived in Burlington, I received a letter from Dr. Robert Calhoun Provine confirming my acceptance at Vanderbilt University in September, all expenses paid courtesy of the Ford Foundation, to earn a Master of Arts in Teaching degree through a cooperative program with the then independent George Peabody College for Teachers. One of my teachers, Dr. Ostwalt wanted to nominate me, knowing I was Korea bound and had no real interest in going, because he wanted to nominate Tyler's room-mate, Maxwell Devane, in 1954. He said he would not be asked, however, if he did not nominate someone each year.

The signing of a truce in the Korean conflict lessened the Army's need for replacement lieutenants and the Army advised there would be no difficulty in postponing my return to Fort Benning until the following year. In September, I caught an airplane to Nashville, Tennessee to begin graduate study. There were twenty-nine students from other states taking part in the program, including two I immediately liked, Judy Adams and Betty Mundy.

Drinking alcohol was grounds for expulsion at Davidson. The first day on campus at Vanderbilt, a waiter in a white jacket met me at the door with a silver tray of old-fashion cocktails when I attended a reception at the home of one of my professors. At a lawn party at another professor's house the next night, I was served a gin and tonic. Although in later life I switched from gin to vodka, to this day the only cocktails I drink, other than Southsides served at the point-to-point races in North Baltimore County every spring and fall, are those two.

My roommate at Vanderbilt was Allan Parent, later Dean of the Episcopal Seminary in Alexandria, Virginia. Betty Mundy was a Sweetbriar grad, a beautiful brunette, majoring in French, who taught me to sing "April in Portugal" in French. When I took her to see "The Student Prince" she taught me to sing "Gardeamus Igitur" in Latin. My younger sister Faye was dating a midshipman named Derald Beal with a 4.0 average at the Naval Academy, and he had taught me some bawdy navy tunes about girls from Sweetbriar and Hood. I offered them as the best I could do.

Judy Adams, a University of Georgia graduate was my best friend. She was a dark blonde, sharp-faced girl who reminded me of my sister Faye. Judy was not pretty, but buoyant, entertaining, fun to be with and therefore attractive. She wrote and produced a sequel to "Gone with the Wind" her junior year at the University of Georgia in which the principal characters were Butt Retler and Harlot O'Scara. She was promptly elected president of the student body. Nashville was known as the Athens of the South, and Betty, Judy and I often sat on the steps of a replica of the Parthenon to eat ice cream sandwiches.

My soul-mate at Vanderbilt was Peter F. Walker, a non-Ford Fellow completing a PhD in history. Rumor had it Pete had been twice expelled from a Baptist College in Mississippi of which his father was president. He joined the Marines, rose quickly to the rank of Captain and earned a medal rescuing people from an earthquake in Greece. He was older than I, darkly handsome, with salt and pepper hair, independently wealthy by graduate student standards, living in a house and having a snappy convertible automobile. He attributed his readily available wallet to contributions he was making to a sperm bank, fearing his unknown offspring might be born with linoleum hair.

When my Davidson soul mate Tyler Berry, who lived near Franklin, Tennessee, came home on leave, he borrowed his uncle's Cadillac, and Betty and I did a double-date with Judy and Tyler. Pete often took me out to a local pub for supper and a beer, which was not served on campus in those days. One night Allen and I were discussing *Brown v Board of Education* in our third-floor room. We heard Pete calling from the stairwell. Allen frowned, having made it clear he thought Pete was a bad influence on me, shook his head and said, "Don't answer."

Just as we thought he had gone away, Pete strode in, picked me up and carried me out. Allen grabbed the telephone to call the police, but I assured him Pete meant me no harm. Carrying me down three flights of stairs, he dropped me in the front seat of his convertible. He was just lonely, and wanted to have someone to talk to at supper. Pete let me drive the car home, and when he was satisfied I could pass, I took the driver's test in Nashville in his car. Although I had flunked every driver's test I took in Maryland, I passed easily in Tennessee, which had no parallel parking, still something I rarely get right,

Peter took a fancy to Judy's room-mate; a girl from North Carolina named Gwen Hamer. Because Judy and I were in the same classes and studied together in the Joint University Library, we often ate together in the dining hall. Pete asked me to enlist Judy's help in finding a way to get him together with Gwen. Our plan was for me to take a table, Judy would bring Gwen to the table we shared, Pete would stop by, and I was to insist he join us.

Pete lived alone, in a two-story house near the campus. Being a decorated hero and a good-looking guy, his parties were legendary and well-attended. It was August and graduation was but a week away. Things went well and Pete invited the three of us to the party that night, asking for our help in setting things up. Gwen declined, but Judy, who was in on the plot, quickly accepted, insisting they needed to get started right away. When I walked through Pete's front door at five, he and Judy were standing at the top of the stairs embracing. Judy grinned at me with that "cat that ate the canary" look of hers, and told me to be the first to congratulate them on their engagement. I said they were both crazy as hell because they had just met at noon.

I was ticked because I thought Pete was bored and his intentions toward Judy, my surrogate sister, were less than honorable. A week later Judy and I received our Master's and hugged Pete good-bye. A couple of months later I received an invitation to their wedding in December which I could not attend because I had to report to Fort Benning on November 29, 1954 to begin my two years of active duty.

Some years later, Pete's dissertation on the behavior of the population of Vicksburg under siege in 1863 was published as a book and reviewed in the Baltimore *Sun*. The reviewer gave it high marks, suggesting that, in the event of atomic war, America's current population would behave no better and perhaps much worse than the people of that fortified city. Americans of today do not share the unity of purpose that motivated the American South during the War for Southern Independence. Dr. Walker became Professor of History at the University of North Carolina at Chapel Hill, where one of my nephews took his course.

My mother had sold her farm near Hope Mills and she gave me a 1954 Ford Custom car, forest green in color, for graduation. Returning to Baltimore in September, I taught seventh grade mathematics at Hamilton Junior High School. The school was well-run, the staff professional and the children were a real joy.

A polo-playing friend of my father's, Colonel Larry Gaines, visited us at Thanksgiving. He was still in the army, counseling me to remember that my superior officers "put their pants on the same way you do—one leg at a time". His advice served me well. I heard him tell my father that when the army found out what they had, they would try and keep me.

During my training at Benning, I was told I set a record for doing "sit-ups." I was just trying to compensate for my inability to do more than the minimum required "pull-ups". I had fractured my wrist in three places playing football in high school, and I was worried that it would break again. My limited knowledge of anatomy failed to inform that it was muscle, not bone, which did the heavy lifting in a "pull-up".

Being in the army, without a war, was great fun, playing soldiers full-time, with life-sized toys and getting paid for it. I was at Benning less than a month when I went home for Christmas, returning early to go to New Orleans with several other members of my BIOC to celebrate the New Year.

Walking into Louie Prima's "500" I recognized a Davidson grad, who assumed I was there for the 1955 Sugar Bowl contest between Navy and LSU. When he learned I didn't have tickets, he told me to stop by the Roosevelt Hotel in the morning and he would give me enough tickets for me and my friends. When I asked for his room number, the desk clerk gave me a floor number. His family had booked the entire floor, and his extended Delta family and their servants were everywhere, the doors to all the rooms open and a floor-wide party in progress. Along with the tickets, we were served champagne and Cajun food catered by a famous New Orleans eatery called Maylie's.

Three of my Davidson friends were stationed at Fort Benning permanently. William White, a year ahead of me, and my classmates Larry J. Dagenhart, and Bill Bivins. They invited me to the Officer's Club for supper, a privilege no other member of my BIOC class shared. There were also long week-ends in New Orleans and Atlanta with them and a young officer I did not know from Middle Tennessee State University. One night as we were returning to Fort Benning from Atlanta in Bill White's car, the lieutenant from MTSU started crying while sitting between me and Bill Bivins. I asked if there was anything I could do, but he just cried the more, insisting it was too late, he had already ruined his life.

Puzzled, I asked, "What did you do to ruin your life?"

"I didn't go to Davidson."

Between sobs he blurted out that we four shared a common culture and years of experiences he could never have. We were as close as brothers and he felt like a complete outsider. The people, places and events we shared bound us together. We laughed about happenings and people he would never know. He could never be one of us, and he wanted to be one of us in the worst way. He was an outsider, as I, as a freshman, had once been. He was right, for it was better to be in than out.

I insisted whatever he thought he had lost was ephemeral and replaceable. The Davidson that was, like the golden age of Athens or the Camelot of King Arthur, lasted but a few brief years and then was gone forever. It was, like beauty, in the eye of the beholder. You had to be there. Thomas Wolfe taught us that you can't go home again, for time is a river, forever flowing, constantly changing while remaining the same.

"When they find out what they have, they will want to keep him."

—Colonel Larry Gaines to my father,
November, 1954

Abroad in the Army

In late April I was assigned to the 10th Infantry Regiment in Gablingen, Germany. I turned my Ford over to the Army at Camp Kilmer, New Jersey, and took a chartered flight to Frankfurt, stopping off in Gander, Newfoundland and Shannon, Ireland to refuel. Several other officers from my BIOC drew similar orders, and we set out, by train, for Augsburg. A little knowledge being a dangerous thing, I did not anticipate the care with which the Army was looking after us and after being in the hands of the tactical officers at Benning, my level of trust was non-existent. Why, I wondered, did my ticket say Augsburg when the Regiment was in Gablingen?

Having studied German at Davidson and being tutored by Kurt Beidenkopf, an exchange student who lived next door and later became President of Saxony, I enquired about the location of Gablingen. As it was famous as the first jet airbase established by the Luftwaffe, my fellow passengers knew where it was. They insisted I did not want to go to Augsburg, however, as the base was north of that city, just beyond the autobahn from Stuttgart to Munich. They told me where I could change to another train, which would stop in Gablingen, as the express I was on would not.

Another skeptical officer traveling with me, also ordered to report to Gablingen, followed me off the train. We boarded a local, and when we got off the train in Gablingen, we were bewildered. Our official reception committee waited in vain for us at the Bahnhof in Augsburg. We were met by a mangy dog and an old woman who was startled to see two fresh-face, American army officers get off a dusty local train carrying their own duffel bags.

She pointed toward the Kaserne, across the tracks and some distance away. She summoned a taxi, which drove around the airfield and discharged us at the gate in late afternoon. The guards were also surprised, for we were not expected until tomorrow, as our escort had planned to put us up in Augsburg at the "Drei Mohren" Hotel for the night, give us an orientation tour of Augsburg, and bring us out to the Regimental Headquarters at Gablingen the following morning.

Somewhere along the way some clerk in an army personnel office confused my 201 file with one belonging to someone else. My MA degree from Vanderbilt was magically transformed into a MA from Cornell's School of Hotel

Management, about which I knew less than nothing. I was assigned to duty as "Assistant Adjutant General" of the Tenth Infantry Regiment of the Fifth Infantry Division, with authority to sign orders on behalf of the Regimental Commander. A secondary responsibility was the Officer's Club in Gablingen, two enlisted men's clubs—one in Gablingen and another at Infanterie Kaserne in Augsburg—and a NCO Club, also in Augsburg.

My primary duty was Regimental Courts and Boards Officer, with an office in the Headquarters Building. Four lawyers, all specialists with an E-4 grade, worked in the office, doubling as typists, preparing forms, orders, and transcripts of testimony when they were not busy teaching me military justice at the summary and special courts martial level.

The Tenth Regiment's first battalion, its headquarters and headquarters company, medical company and tank company were all located at Gablingen. The Second and Third Battalions were stationed in Augsburg at Infanterie Kaserne, along with the rest of the Regiment. My company commander was Captain Dietrich, the hero of the novel "Devils in Baggy Pants", a story about the 101st Airborne Division's drop into Normandy on D-Day eleven years earlier. If we could get an orchestra to play "Lili Marlene" our captain would cry.

We often urged it on unsuspecting musicians because the tears mellowed him and made him love us more. He headed many of my courts martial, where I served as prosecutor, armed with CID reports summarizing witness testimony, although one of my watchful, enlisted lawyers sat at my side keeping track of the elements of proof and prompting me whenever any were missing.

The transcripts were not verbatim and were prepared by the lawyers who technically worked for me although in reality I worked for them. As members of the bar, if the testimony was missing, they would not supply it. They reported only the facts testified to in the hearing. The transcripts were reviewed at division level by members of the Judge Advocate General's Corps, and the Division Commander would not approve the sentence imposed by the special court martial unless the testimony supported the verdict of the court.

A month later my car arrived, and I took a train to Bremerhaven to pick it up. I stopped overnight on my return through the British Zone at Kassel, where the Army maintained a transitory billet for officers journeying from the American Zone to the ports in the north, where a different German dialect, known as "Güte Deutsch" was spoken. Hitler's autobahn was incomplete North of Kassel, but from there south it was finished. Driving on it was a thrilling experience, and I wondered then and I still wonder why American highways are so poorly engineered.

Three day passes were easy to get, and because I often began prosecuting cases at 1300 and continued until 2100 in the evening, I took as many as I could. The 10th was to be rotated to Fort Ord, California in less than a year, and most of the Headquarters staff was trying to see as much of Europe as they could. Vienna, Paris and Venice were less than an eight hour drive from Augsburg, and I took a bus or drove my Ford to those cities at every opportunity.

Munich was but a twenty-five minute drive from Gablingen, and I explored every nook and cranny it had to offer, my most frequent destination being the

"Haus de Kunst", a splendid and undamaged art gallery located in the Tiergarten. It served as an opulent Officers Club long after the occupation ended on May 5, 1955 when West Germany assumed control of its own affairs with a provisional government at Bonn.

My Regimental Commander was Colonel Ace Collins. The commander of the First Battalion was Major Peter McDowell, a survivor of Merrill's Marauders in Burma during World War II. He chaired most of my more serious courts martial if the offender was not a member of his battalion. When the trial was over and the record prepared, I delivered the blue-bound transcripts formalizing the proceedings to Colonel Collins for his signature before sending it up to division JAG. Ace would frequently ask questions about the case, anxious to make sure we had done our work properly and the sentence imposed was just.

Not long after I arrived a sergeant in C Company was discovered performing fellatio on a private in his platoon. The learned lawyers in my office were correct in their use of the language of the law, and the verb fellate rather than the more crude Anglo-Saxon or American vernacular was used in preparing the Section 209 discharge papers. As Ace read them I stood nervously by his desk with a hand full of other cases he needed to review. He was a West Pointer, and I became weak-kneed when he asked me what fellatio meant.

In imbuing a love of English prose to Davidson students, Dr. Lilly mentioned the *Satyricon* of Petronius Arbiter as one of the books Miss Julia Pasmore, the College Librarian for whom I worked, kept locked away in a vault of rare books, beyond the reach of innocents like us. Naturally I retrieved it and Tyler and I sat up all night to read it, and fragmentary as it was, we added the verb fellate and the noun fellatio to our vocabulary. Struggling for a way to explain it without success for what seemed an eternity, I finally asked the Colonel if he knew what the term "blow job" meant. Startled and red-faced, he assured me he did, the look of disgust on his face I hoped was not directed at me for having brought it up. I assured him that was the act the terms fellate and fellatio described, and he quickly signed his name and tossed the file back to me as if I and the file were contaminated.

Shortly before the 5th Division rotated to Fort Ord, Colonel Collins called me into his office and asked who had written the brief history of the 10th Infantry Regiment which was printed on the back of the menus in the clubs I supervised, all of which were staffed by German or Displaced Person employees, hired by my overall German manager Herr. Kurt Rudolph. I confessed with some fear, but breathed a lot easier when he told me he thought it was exceptionally well-written. If you are already bored, blame him, because he was the one who instilled in me a desire to write.

What he critiqued was the absence of ice-cream, milk shakes and ice-cream sodas from our available refreshment offerings. My clubs were what the government refers to as non-appropriated funds, and they operated like independent businesses, subject however to Inspector General audit. Kurt was incredulous when I told him to order the equipment to stock and prepare them. Some months later he told me he had actually sold one milkshake, no ice-cream sodas but lots of ice cream. I did not let "Ace" know the men were making beer floats with it. The most popular drink sold was a "French 75", a brandy in a shot glass dropped into a stein of German beer, the "Rabbit's brew" made in Augsburg known as "Hasenbrau."

Kurt was part Swiss and part German with a bit of Italian mixed in. He was a playboy with great social connections. When he dumped his girl friends, which he did regularly, they would cry on my shoulder. I got a lot of dates that way.

One of my duties, rigidly enforced by Ace, was to go to Munich three days each month to preview the vaudeville acts we hired to play in our clubs on the week-end. I had to make sure that my Boston-born commanding officer was not offended by any risqué or borderline pornographic acts or speech in any of the acts I booked for my clubs. Vaudeville had a longer life in Germany than America, and many of the acts were those of expatriate Americans.

My favorite group was the Hansen Quartet, billed the "TV Quartet" in my clubs. It consisted of two men, trained to sing opera and two women, both named Inge, one a blonde and the other a brunette. Their theme song was "I love Paris" whether on German television or performing live. The blond-haired girl was Inge Mashke. I had difficulty initially persuading her to go out with me, because her family did not want her dating an American soldier.

Munich was her home and after meeting her parents, and describing to her father, a former naval officer, the paper I wrote at Vanderbilt on the fight in the United States Senate during Woodrow Wilson's first term to create an American flag maritime fleet, I was welcomed into his society. From that fight, which began a hundred years ago in a Baltimore armory, America began its descent into socialism, begun by a Princeton professor and extended in 2008 by a Chicago Law School adjunct instructor whose knowledge of the American Constitution is limited to equal rights guaranteed by the Fourteenth Amendment, which is the only aspect of "Con law' he taught.

Wagner's opera, "Reinzi" was being performed at the Red Gate, part of the medieval wall around the inner city of Augsburg. In a letter to Iain Wilson, my Bible Professor at Davidson who later came to Baltimore as pastor of the Franklin Street Presbyterian Church which I attended, I mentioned having heard it and I thought the music was very stirring. He said he hoped it didn't have the same effect on me it had on Adolph Hitler, who wrote in "Mein Kampf" that his dreams of world conquest first came to him while attending a performance of that opera. Iain was not the only Davidson professor of mine to relocate to Baltimore. Dr Charles Eberhardt was teaching at Towson University, and his wife, Dorothy, later taught two of my children at the St. James Academy in Monkton.

Kurt Rudolph introduced me to German friends who drove racecars, pushed bobsleds at the 1956 winter Olympics in Cortina d'Ampezzo and bred European champion Irish setters. One day Kurt and I drove southeast from Augsburg toward Memmingen, trying to locate their kennel. Kurt was multi-lingual, but we found dialects in that part of Bavaria that reminded me of "Germelshausen", the Bavarian Brigadoon, a novella my German professor at Davidson used as a teaching tool.

After kilometer upon kilometer on dirt paths winding through the low-lying hills listening to Kurt fuming at the "stupid peasants" who could not understand a word either of us uttered, we reached our destination without their help and I became the proud owner of a full-brother to the European champion, a tall, dark-red Irish setter named "Die Abs von Hermanshorst zu Neidereiden".

A member of the Bavarian "Land Staats-polizei" who lived in Gersthofen, a small collection of farm houses beyond the fence which surrounded Gablingen kaserne, kept him for me. He fed him a raw egg weekly, and his coat shone like silk. He responded well to commands he was taught in German. To keep him loyal to me, Abs received no affection from his German trainer. When I came to see him, he was so happy he pissed on my highly-polished boots while licking me in the face, while Herr and Frau Gruber smiled approvingly. When I completed my tour of duty I was assigned to the USNS Rose as Executive Officer en route to New York, so I could not take Absel with me.

I gave a power of attorney to my driver, Spec 4 Norman Weber, a tall, blonde, German born in New York before the war. His father, an investment banker at Warburg, took him back to Germany in 1939, where he was strafed in 1945 by an American fighter pilot as the war was ending. He had a scar on his knee to prove it. Weber returned to the United States to claim his citizenship courtesy of his enlistment in the Army, and an American girl he met at Fort Campbell later came to Munich to marry him. As his best man, it was my job to whisk her away during the reception, to teach him to treat her with constant attention. His uncle, a Panzer veteran, did his best to convince me America should let West Germany build our tanks.

When his enlistment was up, Norman was going to bring the dog to me in Baltimore. I never saw the dog again. He was hit by an automobile when Weber stopped for a rest break on the autobahn. Later, when he visited me in Baltimore, Norman spoke of "Abs" in the present tense. His English was better than that, and I hope Abs had a happy life with someone who loved him even more than I did.

In December, 1955, the Fifth Division began its rotation to Fort Ord. As Major McDowell, Lieutenant Dan Blocker and I had just arrived eight months before, we were to be reassigned to other units stationed in Germany. The Eleventh Airborne Division from Fort Campbell, Kentucky, was to replace us, and advance parties of officers and enlisted men began arriving to be briefed and familiarized with the way we did things in USAEUR.

I was assigned to meet two officers in Augsburg, bring them out to Gablingen to spend the week-end showing them around the Kaserne, the location of the ammunition dump, a hangar that could be used to pack parachutes, the BOQ, the Officers Club, and anything else they wanted to know. They looked like twins, both well over six feet tall, blonde, blue-eyed, regular army airborne, Ranger first lieutenants. I still wore a gold bar, not having served the mandatory eighteen months necessary for automatic, unless you were a bad actor, promotion. Their names were Rasmussen and Fisher.

I did not ask first names nor did I care where they came from. I resented giving up my week-end plans, and I don't think I ever looked either in the eye or did anything other than drive, answer questions as succinctly as possible, and point out landmarks they needed to remember. I put them in the BOQ most distant from mine and breathed a sigh of relief when Sunday taps was played.

Christmas in Germany was a grand experience. I spent it with Lieutenants Al Halliday, Wade Herring and John Kane and four girls who worked in the USO Club in Gablingen. They had an apartment in Augsburg, and Wade arrived with a deer he had shot illegally, dressing it in their bathtub. It ruined Christmas, but New Years was more fun because it was followed by "Fasching," a month-long, pre-Lenten party that becomes progressively more insane with each passing night.

More paratroopers were descending on us, not from the air but from Frankfurt, including the executive officer, Colonel Royce and his jeep driver. The latter spent the day doing nothing but waiting, most of it in my office. Fraternization between officers and enlisted men, taboo in the battalions, was less rigidly enforced at headquarters where cooperation and interaction is constant. After all, it was an office like any other except we wore costumes and were extremely polite.

Halliday went with me to some of these parties, where I frequently saw Kurt and his friends. Not unusual, because Kurt was the one who invited me, told me what to wear and what to bring. Colonel Royce's driver begged me to let him bring his buddy with us to the Tuesday night finale. They showed up in civilian clothes and waited by my car at the BOQ. Like most of the jumpers, they were tall, good-looking young men, and Al thought girls would be drawn to them. I needed no help, for I was dating one of Kurt's cast-offs, a Wittelsbach no less.

The party was at the Hoheblasse, a country place beside the Lech River where the white-water canoeing took place during the ill-fated Munich Olympics in 1972. My nickname throughout the regiment was the "Law west of the Lech". Kurt handed me a bottle of champagne in an ice bucket and urged us to follow him upstairs. The last thing I remember was going up the steps; a descending Bavarian grabbed the bottle, took a swig and dropped it back in the bucket.

The next thing I recall is driving the four of us home in my Ford through a thick fog. The ground had been covered with heavy snow since Thanksgiving. I could see the street lights high above the fog. The street was wide but I did not recognize it. I started to go a bit faster when I saw the Hercules fountain dead ahead, where it had been for the last five hundred years in the center of Augsburg's famed Maximillianstrasse. The snow was banked around the base, and I thought I had missed it. But a polished, white-round stone at each point of the octagonal base was buried in the snow, and the left-front of my car ran hard against one of them. I was cut badly under my chin and required hospitalization.

When I was released later that morning and reported in, Colonel Royce raised his eyebrows, told me he had read the accident report and knew his driver was a passenger in my car. He told me I was lucky I had missed the artery; otherwise I would have bled to death in the snow. Warning me not to encourage his driver to lead a dissolute life, he reminded me officers are supposed to set a good example.

I don't know what the Colonel said to his driver, but the lad never set foot in my office again. Colonel Royce had me transferred to his command effective April 1, 1956, the day the last of the Fifth Division left Augsburg, to perform the same duties in the 188th Airborne Infantry Regiment I was performing in the 10th Infantry. He also launched a determined effort to bring me into the army as a regular, rather than a reserve, officer.

"Harry, this gentlemen asked what sort of review Mr. Churchill received on his latest book. Can you believe it?"

—Clerk in a London book shop,
August, 1956

"The Law West of the Lech."

In March 1956, more jumpers arrived, gradually replacing the 10th Regiment. They were the "Screaming Eagles" of the 188th Airborne Infantry. The officers were, unless newly minted, combat veterans of World War II and Korea as were most of the non-commissioned officers. The troops were barely old enough to drink three-point-two beer at Fort Campbell, and did not realize German beer was at least twenty-four proof, eight times the alcoholic content.

After a few beers in Augsburg Gasthauser the young jumpers were out of control. They crowded my prosecutorial docket. In desperation I asked Ace, who commanded the hybrid regiment, if I could set up a court composed solely of airborne officers to deal with their problem. He told me to draw it up and sign it. I selected five officers, headed by a major, two captains and two lieutenants. In a spiteful mood, I named lieutenants Fisher and Rasmussen as trial and defense counsel, thinking they deserved a humanizing diversion. I scheduled my courtroom in the basement of the headquarters building, on Tuesdays and Thursdays for airborne miscreants, and I kept it for my own cases the rest of the week.

Prisoners from our division were held in Dachau or Crailsheim, depending upon their status. A Sergeant Muldoon—red-haired, Irish and thick limbed—had decided to single handedly crush a group of young paratroopers who were out of control. He was arrested by the Military Police and locked up at Dachau. Just before my lawyers left for Fort Ord, Specialist Fleckner, the most mature of them, came in to plead Muldoon's case. He insisted Sergeant Muldoon, a storied combat veteran, was doing God's work and should be sitting by his peat-burning fireplace with an Irish setter at his feet. He knew me far too well, I fear, for he convinced me Muldoon did not deserve to be court-martialed.

We called for my jeep, and on the way to Munich I read the CID reports as we sped down the autobahn. Bavaria is such a beautiful and well-manicured piece of Europe, I was surprised to see that the same was true of Dachau. Just west of Munich and slightly north of the autobahn, the prison was nestled in a beautiful little valley between low-lying hills thick with tall evergreens through which a small stream meandered. I would never have guessed anyone would build an infamous death camp in such a beautiful valley.

When the military police brought Sergeant Muldoon out, I found that he was deep in his cups when the fracas began. He had tried to reason with the young paratroopers, but they were beyond reason. In desperation, he decided they were better off unconscious, where they could do less damage to German-American relations. At the time I was pushing the 10th's role as "ambassadors of good will to the people of the West German Republic" and Muldoon so saw himself, having bought into my menu story line and taking it seriously. I was shocked to find my writing made me complicit in his crime.

He had a Bavarian wife, or "schatzy". Feeling responsible, I brought him back to Gablingen, told Ace about my role in Muldoon's crime, and persuaded him, as convening authority, to opt for Article 15 discipline. So Muldoon bid me adieu a few days later, docked with but ten days pay. I walked to the rail head within the kaserne to say farewell to Ace, my lawyers, and the friends I had made in the ten months I had been part of one of the oldest and proudest of America's military regiments.

Neither Dan Blocker nor I were leaving, because Colonel Royce, the executive officer of the Screaming Eagles and his adjutant, Major Hauer, hi-jacked both of us, two 'straight-legs,' into their booted world. I remained as regimental assistant adjutant, courts and boards' officer and club officer. Dan was retained as assistant supply officer. Colonel Sammy Homan, a tall, rural Southerner compared to the urbane Ace Collins, was the regimental commander or S.6.

Numbers were used on our telephone extensions as well as our radio call-signs. In the 10th the majority of the officers were reserve; in the 188th, they were all regular army officers. Late one Friday afternoon, as I was looking forward to a weekend with Kurt and his von Furstenburg and my Wittelsbach girlfriend at her country house overlooking the Lech, Dan appeared in my door and asked if I had seen the order to move the regiment from Gablingen and Augsburg to Grafenwöehr, a large training area on the Czech border where they were to rehearse battle order scenarios in the event the Soviets came through the Fulda pass.

Drawing fuel, ammunition, food and supplies from Army depots requires orders. The regiment was supposed to depart at 0600 Monday morning, and even although we were both newly minted first lieutenants, there was no one in authority over us to be found anywhere. How they planned to move the regiment through Germany to the Czech border without authorization was, as Churchill might have phrased it, a mystery wrapped in an enigma.

Remembering we had moved the 10th to Grafenwöehr for winter training in December, 1955, I rooted through my files and found ten, single-spaced, mimeographed pages fourteen inches long. It had been signed by Dan and me, and no one else, in our capacities as assistant S-1 and S-4 of the 10th. We collared some typists, and replicated the order, substituting roster names, dates, and unit designations wherever applicable. The order we used as a model was the product of planning and input by the entire regimental staff under normal circumstances, but we had no input from anyone so we winged it.

We didn't know what training the jumpers had in mind, but they were going to do exactly what the 10th had done six months earlier in the snow. As we proofread the stencils, shaking our heads in disbelief at our ingenuity, we crossed our fingers, signed our names, had the orders mimeographed and distributed throughout the chain of command.

On Monday morning, the entire regiment fell out on our schedule and followed the route we directed, arrived safely, and no one ever questioned how it came to be. As regular army officers, they did what they were told to do, from the regimental commander on down. Every officer on regimental staff assumed that some other officer in authority had supervised the preparation of the order.

Dan and I left for a four-week leave through Europe that took us to France, England, Holland, Denmark, and Sweden. We had the leave accrued, they didn't need either of us at Grafenwöehr, so I prepared our orders, signed them and nobody questioned that either. Even in the savvy 10th, when alerts were sounded, we —as excess staff officers —fell out in full combat gear with nothing to do and no place to go, so we sat on the floor of our BOQ waiting for the Russians. It was embarrassing. No way was I going to do that for two weeks.

We found lodging through the USO in the Marble Arch section of London, a pleasant walk through Hyde Park to Buckingham Palace. We mastered the Underground routes, ate pot-pies in greasy spoon restaurants, and did our Christmas shopping six months early. I found a copy of Churchill's "History of the English-Speaking People" and bought it, amusing the English clerk when I asked what kind of review the famed man had received. They thought it an inane question, and made no effort to disguise their glee.

They refused to sell me a four-volume, leather bound 1774 edition of Blackstone's "Commentaries on the Laws of England", which served as the foundation of American law, because "entirely too much of our heritage is going across the Atlantic, never to return." The books had been used as texts by law students at Cambridge, and I found marginal notes and hand-written crib sheets stuffed between the pages. For several days I stalked the shop, and as soon as the proprietor left, I came in, wearing civvies, and approached a young clerk, faked a British accent, bought the books and paid for them with British pounds. I arranged for their shipment to Baltimore at the post office, where they still have a prominent place in my library sixty years later.

We took the boat train from Harwich to the Hook of Holland, and continued through the night playing chess with a Dutch forester. A few days in Amsterdam were followed by another trip by ferry to Copenhagen, where we had rooms reserved on a street remarkably reminiscent of East 33rd Street between Memorial Stadium and Lake Montebello, the section of Baltimore where my parents lived. Even the city buses looked the same.

Leaning over the rail of the ship looking toward the distant shore, we were approached by a well-dressed, middle-aged man who spoke to us in a language I did not recognize. French rather than English being the diplomatic idiom at that time, I responded in French. We conversed until he asked me where I lived, and I told him near Augsburg in Bavaria. He began speaking German, and after a few minutes discovered we were American officers on leave from an "Americanisch fallschirmyeager division" fortunate enough to be stationed in Bavaria. He switched to English, and although he was a Swede and had first addressed us in Danish because he thought we were Danes, he followed our choice of language flawlessly until he had us penned down. But getting penned down by him was the last thing either of us wanted, so we thanked him for the compliment and set out on our own as soon as we docked within sight of the little mermaid who graces Copenhagen's harbor.

I made the mistake of falling hopelessly in love with a blue-gray eyed, blond American Express guide, and drug Dan along on every tour she worked during the next three days, nights and early mornings. Tivoli, Sternbourg, or Hamlet's castle, the summer gardens, the markets, Malmö, Sweden, the palace for the changing of the guard, nightclubs and a concert, but the only thing I remember is her. She must have been an angel, as my camera had no picture of her, although I aimed it at no one else.

When I returned to Gablingen, my Commanding Officer wanted to see me, I thought to thank me for my preventing his regiment from starving to death in Grafenwöehr. He told me instead that our regiment had the lowest rating in the entire division for military justice, and he wanted to know why. Without the four lawyers I had previously I was having difficulty teaching the people assigned to me how to do their work. Even worse, the sergeant who was supposed to assist me had never reported for duty, having been charged with sodomy and perverted practice, and his victims may have been my clerks, which would result in their discharge as well.

Colonel Homan, whom everyone called Sammy, asked what he could do to help, as there were no enlisted lawyers in the division, much less our regiment. I asked him to send me every enlisted man with an IQ over 120 who could type, and I would address the problem and fix it. The next morning the Regimental Sergeant-major, an impressive Alpha male if ever one lived, walked into my office, sharply saluted, and invited me outside. Twenty young paratroopers trembling with fear were standing at attention, certain their most secret sins had been found out.

Expecting to be court-martialed, they had difficulty answering my questions, which were designed to make them relax and reveal their intellect and personalities. After walking through the two ranks, I picked the four who seemed most articulate and relaxed. They were re-assigned to Headquarters and Headquarters Company immediately and reported to my office.

Stories about the Regimental Sergeant-Major preceded him and explained the young trooper's anxiety. A sergeant in first battalion had spoken disrespectfully to him on the telephone, so he asked the non-com to hold the phone for a minute. He ran outside, commandeered a jeep, drove to the company headquarters, looked around the room to see who was holding a telephone, and decked the offending and surprised non-com.

Before he left, Specialist Fleckner had taught me the trick of winning points at JAG. I cut an order of instructions to trial and defense counsel requiring them to be ready for trial within eight days after charges were preferred. The only exception was if defense counsel requested, in writing, additional time to prepare a defense. Those days did not count against us, and once the boots understood the ground rules we moved from last to first so fast Sammy tried to give me a medal. The division commander could not bring himself to approve a medal for a non-jumper, so he gave me a Certificate of Achievement instead. Sammy and Major Hauer, who was my immediate superior, both apologized.

My bright young typists quickly mastered the elements of proof and the art of preparing transcripts. But storm clouds gathered, for none of the young paratroopers had yet learned the potency of German beer. The entire division was confined to base, week-ends included, for several months, to preserve amity between Bonn and Washington, while they learned the difference.

The way the order was written convinced me it did not apply to me or Dan, as we were non-jumpers, referred to as "straight legs" by the non-commissioned officers, almost all of whom had more than a hundred jumps to their credit, many of them in combat. Their chests were covered with "salad" and they wore their wings proudly.

Colonel Royce insisted I go into the field with the regiment, and with Weber driving my jeep and two clerks in the back seat, we pulled a trailer loaded with our typewriters, forms and office supplies as well as our radio and gear. I liked this better than sitting in an empty building. In combat clothes, my pants were bloused in my boots, just like theirs. When at Gablingen I worked in Eisenhower jacket and matching pants. At social events, unless dress blues were specified, we wore "pinks and greens," the World War II uniform so familiar to viewers of "Twelve O'Clock High."

When I stopped by the NCO club at Infanterie Kaserne in Augsburg to hear Inge sing, the non-coms swarmed around me, a ready listener to their stories. I had two pairs of wings pinned to my chest by battle-hardened non-coms who wept in their beer as they told me their stories, saying I reminded them of another lieutenant they had served with during the war. They wanted me to be a part of their unit, so I guess pinning their wings on my uniform made me one of them. I was convinced they were as enamored of Inge as I was, having seen me with her several times before.

While Dan and I were in London, we had seen large groups of British soldiers, dressed in combat fatigues, carrying their weapons on trains, leaving to join with the French to seize the Suez Canal. Gamal Abdel-Nasser was the object of their displeasure. We were on heightened alert, and there were rumors that the Soviets might seize the moment. I decided to take a trip to Berlin, and secured passage on a train through East Germany. The windows of the railway car were covered with olive drab, army blankets, and the train was not allowed to move during daylight.

West Berlin was alive and vibrant, prosperous and well-lit. East Berlin was rampant with bombed-out buildings or massive, gray concrete apartment complexes. Russian war memorials were well-maintained and guarded by heavily-armed troops, who did not like to have their picture taken. Berlin was the perfect place to contrast communism and capitalism.

When I got back to Gablingen, the jumpers were excited about plans to parachute into Egypt and take up positions between the Egyptians and the Anglo-French forces with designs on the waterway. President Eisenhower annoyed President DeGaulle considerably with this threat, which is what it turned out to be. I told Major Hauer, my immediate boss, that I would be happy to keep the home fires burning while they were away, but he assured me they would not go anywhere without me.

I reminded him I did not jump, being one of two "straight legs" in his regiment. Not to worry, because he had set up a jump school right next to my BOQ, and I was to get two days of training on the thirty-four foot tower they built in my absence, two days of jumping from an aircraft at twelve hundred feet, after which I could blouse my boots and legally wear my gift wings.

Jumping into the Sinai desert did not appeal to me at all. I would lose my identity if not my life in this greatly anticipated adventure. But the American bluff worked. The threat of our descending in their midst cowed the Anglo-French, and the situation was defused without our help. Not to waste our readiness, we went to Hohenfels, our other training area, to play war games.

Colonel Royce had arranged for me to go to Munich to take a test to see if I was intelligent enough for a regular army commission. The test was scheduled for the day after we left for Hohenfels, and that morning I was sitting in my jeep talking to Weber. A helicopter was circling overhead, and grabbing my field glasses I saw Colonel Royce shaking his fist at me. Landing in a nearby field, he strode toward me, demanding to know why I was not in Munich. I said I wasn't ordered to go and I had no way to get to Munich. He drove my jeep with me in it to his helicopter, and told the pilot to fly me to the kaserne in Munich where the test was scheduled.

We landed in a cobble-stoned courtyard. Inside, I found the test about to be administered by Lieutenant Robert Wearn, one of my ROTC classmates at Davidson. Every other officer in the room was dressed in the new green uniform we had just been authorized to wear. I was in baggy, combat fatigues. At the end of the testing, Bob announced that for the first time ever someone in our group had made a perfect score, answering all of the questions correctly and finishing within the time allotted. It was, unfortunately, me, the one guy in the room who had absolutely no intention of becoming a regular army officer.

A few weeks later my orders arrived to travel to Ft. Hamilton, New York to be discharged on November 29, 1956. Because I was to go aboard the USNS *Rose*, I needed to get an early start. I could travel to Bremerhaven in my Ford, and bring it with me on the *Rose* to New York. The ship stopped for a day in Southhampton, England where I was surprised to see gaily colored Christmas lights throughout the town. In Germany, the year before, all Christmas lights were white. Only beer and wine gardens had colored lights.

As Executive Officer of the *Rose* I was scheduled to make a tour of the ship with one of the naval officers. He told me that, a year earlier, he had made the same trip at the same time of year, and as the ship passed Land's End, the North Atlantic was roiling. As he put it, it looked like the floor rushed up past his head.

A few minutes later I had the same sensation as we descended the stairs below deck. I abandoned my orientation tour and rushed to my cabin, nauseous. The next morning I tried to venture out, but on deck mountainous waves higher than the *Rose* were on all sides. I fell back in my bunk, hoping my life would end and with it my misery.

The next morning, a retired admiral entered my cabin, saying he had heard there was a sick puppy in need of help. He had a thermos of black coffee, a package of saltines, an apple and a paring knife. He encouraged me to shave, get my cover, and walk the decks with him. The ocean was more restive, the sun was coming up, and it looked like a good day. He fed me the apple and crackers as we walked the deck, and then gave me the black coffee. My mal-de-mere left, and, not having eaten for three days, I was dehydrated and ravenously hungry. I thanked the admiral and joined him at his table the next day, which was Thanksgiving.

As we drew near New York, the temperature dropped and we could no longer walk the deck in shirt sleeves. I stood by the rail and watched the skyscrapers of New York emerge from the sea. The next day I picked up my car at the Brooklyn Navy Yard and was discharged at Fort Hamilton. I had to wait another day to have some paper work completed, draw my final paycheck and per diem, and pick up my Veterans Administration eligibility paper.

Judy Garland was performing on Broadway, and thinking I would never be in New York again, I asked two of my shipmates to go with me. We had dinner beforehand at a small restaurant near the theater. The show was a real extravaganza, the shows I previewed and booked for my clubs in Germany paling in comparison.

It was good to be back in America. The next day I collected my car at the Brooklyn Naval Yard and drove down the New Jersey Turnpike to Baltimore. When I reached the road to Middle River, I knew I was getting close, because I had walked that distance eleven years earlier completing my fourteen mile hike as a boy scout. I had just turned twenty-five.

"We take the oldest, wisest and most respected man in the community, and he decides who lives and who dies."

Jack Joseph Craparo,
August, 1959

When Law Schools Taught Law

Within a week of arriving home from Germany, I was teaching mathematics at Baltimore's new vocational, technical high school on Hillen Road, a few blocks south of the row house bought with money saved while in Germany. My contract with the Army required six additional years in the active reserve or the Maryland National Guard. I chose the latter.

The school was named after Otto Mergenthaler, the inventor of the linotype machine, a way station between the printing press and the computer. Robert Mergenthaler taught linotype printing there and he was also the company commander of Headquarters and Headquarters Company of the 175th Infantry Regiment of the 29th Infantry Division. He appointed me to be his executive officer and I attended drills once a week in the Fifth Regiment Armory on Howard Street in Baltimore. We also spent a week-end at the armory once a month, and two weeks at summer camp, either at Indiantown Gap in Pennsylvania or Camp A.P. Hill in Virginia.

In the summer of 1957, while taking courses in modern European novel and Russian history at Johns Hopkins, I took the foreign service examination, passed it, and later traveled to Washington to be interviewed by a committee. Unfortunately, my interview was scheduled on the day Vice-President Nixon's car was attacked in Venezuela by an angry mob. I was asked why I thought that happened, and I suggested the disparity of wealth between the Americas fomented anger and resentment among the less fortunate. The Democrat gave me his endorsement, but the two Republicans turned me down, explaining that I attributed America's wealth to economic advantages instead of sound government policy.

In September I tried to register for night classes at the University of Maryland law school. I was informed I had neither applied nor been accepted. The Registrar, sympathetic to my panic, suggested a meeting with the Dean. At four o'clock the next day, his secretary handed me a slip of paper. The Dean was in the Law Review office in the basement, and when I knocked on the door, Dean Roger Howell, a kindly and scholarly man, came out and offered me a seat on a metal trash can. He sat on another while I pled my case.

My record at Davidson was good enough to get a Ford Fellowship to Vanderbilt and I had always tested in the highest percentile on every competitive test I took. I had been away from Maryland for eight years and I did not know I needed to apply for admission in order to take night classes. The Dean, as sympathetic as the Registrar, allowed me to complete an application which he approved subject to my transcripts from Davidson and Vanderbilt verifying what I had told him.

I drove up Charles Street to Curlanders and bought my text books, and the next night I went to class. The ram-rod straight lieutenant I assigned to a military court-martial in Gablingen had resigned his regular army commission to go to law school. His name was Edward J. Fisher, III; a graduate of Gettysburg College. He was also in the National Guard, serving in the 115th Infantry Regiment in the Catonsville Armory.

The younger brother of my Davidson classmate, Angus Andrews, was also in my class. Doug and I had formed an instant bond at his house in the summer of 1952 while I was attending Ft. Benning as a ROTC cadet. Doug was stationed at NSA in nearby Ft. Meade, and he and his wife Ruby had two children. Doug, Ed and I became members of Taney Senate of the Delta Theta Phi legal fraternity.

Teaching mathematics to two hundred seventy high school students, divided into seven classes, was hard work. The City's investment justified entrance requirements geared to the innate learning ability of the students. In other words, the student body was selected, which motivated me to make certain they learned what they needed to know. I taught students interested in radio, television and electronics general mathematics, algebra, trigonometry and geometry.

The students were a joy most of the time, a pain some of the time and a challenge all of the time. I would go home mentally, physically and emotionally exhausted. I cared about them and played tennis with some of them on the courts in front of the school. They would tire in the second set just as I was getting a second wind. But I was twenty-six and they were teenagers, some taller and heavier, and I had to constantly remind myself they were still children.

Doug had a set of keys to the Judge Advocate General's library at Ft, Meade. The JAG officers were willing tutors, and my week-ends were spent with Doug and Ruby taking advantage of the library and the advice of the army lawyers. Having our own private law library, larger than that of the law school, was a big assist. When I replaced my 1954 Ford with a 1957 model, Doug stuck his head inside, breathed deeply to take in the new-car smell, insisting there was nothing else on the planet that smelled as good.

Doug's grandfather had been Chairman of the Senate Armed Services Committee when Pearl Harbor was attacked in 1941, and he died of a heart attack on the Capitol steps the next day. Almost all of my enduring friendships were instantaneous, and the Reverend William Iain Girdwood Wilson, a dour Scot who arrived at Davidson College to teach me freshman Bible in 1949, was another such friend. He was a Royal Army chaplain, evacuated from Dunkerque in 1940 and landing on the Normandy beach on June 6, 1944. He was working with the World Council of Churches in the Netherlands, putting families back together after World

War II when he was persuaded to come to America to teach at Davidson.

While I was at Vanderbilt, Iain had been called to Baltimore to succeed Dr. Harris Kirk as the minister at the Franklin Street Presbyterian Church. Fearful he might not accept, I caught a plane from Nashville to Charlotte to add my voice to those making the call. Stuart Plummer, another Davidson classmate, had come to Baltimore as Iain's assistant. Stu was a Sigma Chi and he had a bachelor pad at Kirk House. Although we had not been close at Davidson, I was glad to have him in Baltimore.

My cousin, Charles Allan Herndon, was already a lawyer and the Atlantic Refining Company's weatherman on WBAL-TV. He had to be at the station on North Charles Street by 10:15 to don the uniform pump attendants then wore and prepare his broadcast. He also attended my church, and Iain, Charlie, Stu and I often met at the Peabody Book Shop on Charles Street in Baltimore, putting to good use the time between the end of my law school night classes and Charlie's go at weather forecasting. When Al promised snow and none fell, he hired an airplane and sprinkled the WBAL building with Kellogg frosted flakes.

During the summer and on week-ends, I continued my high school and college custom of sailing with Bernie Treuschler and Charlie on a twenty-eight foot, glued together wooden sloop they kept at Arnie Gay's boatyard on Northeast Creek in Annapolis. The boat had an eight foot, fixed keel, and sailing it without charts in the shallow waters of the bay was hazardous. Outside the entrance to Annapolis Harbor, as we were returning tired and hungry from an all-day trip, I felt a slight tug, followed by a surprisingly light tiller. I pushed it to the left, nothing happened. So I pulled it toward me, again nothing happened.

We had lost the rudder due to electrolysis in the slightly-salty bay water. Bernie, who was an engineer and should have remained an engineer, attached an outboard motor to an extension designed for that purpose, and we got back to the boatyard, fish-tailing all the way with the small rudder provided by the motor. *Pagaille* was well-named and fun to sail because she could heel over so far we often vacated the deck, sitting on the side of the hull grasping the rail to avoid falling across the deck into the water on the far side, where the far rail was literally underwater. I never knew another boat that could do that.

In the summer of 1958 I went to Chapel Hill to take insurance law and federal income taxation at Carolina. Allen Strand, who played on the Davidson tennis team, was in graduate school there. His Davidson room mate, my friend Bill Bivins, had led a platoon of chrome-helmeted, white-gloved and white shoelaced soldiers known as the burial detail at Ft. Benning. I brought him up to date on Bill's military service and did my best to improve his social skills, sharing with him the crash course I had in male-female interaction at Vanderbilt and Augsburg.

After two years of teaching and attending night school, I gave up teaching to become a full-time student. In order to graduate in three years, I needed to complete two required courses in conflict of laws and constitutional law. The only summer school in the country offering both was Stetson, in St. Petersburg,

Florida. I enrolled, packed my Ford and drove to Sunbury, North Carolina to deliver some things to Estelle Edwards, a student at Peabody Conservatory in Baltimore who was put in my pew one Sunday morning by Wilbur Plitt, the chief usher who was troubled by my singularity.

Wilbur was a successful businessman and the pews at the Franklin Street Presbyterian Church were rented on an annual basis. All of the ushers wore morning coats every Sunday, and Wilbur escorted every attractive, unattended female to the pew in front of me, behind me or beside me, seeking my approval. I signaled my acceptance of his latest offering, confident Estelle was the girl I was going to marry.

Although she beat a hasty retreat after the service ended, I managed to track her down at a program for young people Sunday evening. At that time Estelle lived at 102 West Monument Street, and when I called I was met at the door by a butler who escorted me to see Mrs. Pleasants. I introduced myself, and submitted to a lengthy interrogation before she allowed the butler to take me to the fourth floor in the elevator, where Estelle and Irene, her Hong Kong roommate, lived.

Estelle and I began dating and Dr. James Frost, a Princeton graduate and Johns Hopkins pathologist who also attended Franklin Street, telephoned her while I was in her apartment. Jack and I were friends, and we discussed our mutual interest one Friday night sitting on the floor of his apartment at Hampton House drinking bourbon. Estelle had come to Franklin Street as a substitute organist, liked Iain's sermons and came back often to hear him.

One of the purposes of my delivery, I was certain, was to allow Estelle's family to meet me. After a brief visit, I drove on to Orlando, Florida, where my sister Jean, who had married a Hopkins physicist, was living to spend the night and have Sunday dinner with her before going on to St. Petersburg. She had a huge dog named 'Paintbrush' and while my brother-in-law was opening a bottle of wine, Paint stole a slab of London broil from the grill, depriving me of a mouth-watering dinner.

That night, in one of those dreams that warn you of the future, I saw a roster posted on the law school bulletin board showing J. Craparo as my roommate. The Stetson law school was built around an old, Moorish-style, Gulf Coast hotel. When I arrived there late the next day I found an envelope glued to the Registrar's office door with my name on it. The key inside let me into a room with two beds, one by the window, fully made, and another by the wall, with nothing on it but a mattress.

I unpacked my bags and read the front page of the local newspaper, headlining the marriage of Sal Traficanti's daughter to a law student, with a picture of two ominous guards posted outside his house. Exhausted, I fell asleep, only to be awakened in the middle of the night by a slightly drunk but strikingly handsome young man wearing a white dinner jacket. Surprised by my presence, he demanded to know why I was sleeping on his bed spread. I let him know, with equal force, that having found my bed unmade and no way of acquiring sheets and pillow cases on a Sunday night, I covered the mattress with the washable bedspread the college told me to bring. My assailant, who looked like the movie actor Glenn Ford, became belligerent and moved toward me. I jumped out of bed, stepped toward him, my face inches from his.

"Hear me out. I bought this bedspread at Sears, Roebuck in Baltimore because the college told me to bring one they could launder. I took it out of my suitcase and put it on the bed. It's my bedspread, so shut the bleep up. You're drunk. Get in bed and sleep it off."

He froze, stared for a minute, as if trying to decide how best to kill me, while I was deciding which of the seven ways I had been taught to kill a man with my bare hands I should use in defense. A smile crossed his face. He went to the closet, opened the door and pulled a bedspread from the top shelf identical to the one I had on my bed. He started laughing, kissed me on both cheeks and said he liked my spunk. He said he had been to his roommate's wedding. I picked up the paper, showed it to him, and asked, "This one by any chance?"

The bed I had for the summer belonged to the law student who had married into the Traficanti family, and my room mate had introduced them. His name was Jack Joseph Craparo, as I had been forewarned. He was born in Detroit and had come to Florida to be Rocky Marciano's sparring partner. But Sal had taken him in as a surrogate son, to replace the arrogant lieutenant in Tank Company I had disliked so intensely at Gablingen.

Jack worked at the Sunshine Park Racetrack as an auditor. He was divorced, had custody of a five-year old son named Jackie who lived with his mother in Tampa. Upon graduation, Jack became consigliore to the Traficanti family. Knowledge of our long-distant but close friendship by my political friends and fellow lawyers later caused them to dub me consigliore of the Maryland Republican party.

Our classes met from seven to eleven, interrupted by breakfast in the fountain courtyard for students and faculty alike. When Jack discovered we were both born on October 31, 1931, our friendship was sealed. He watched me like a hawk, never letting me out of his sight. He kept track of every similarity in thought, habit or deed, convinced we were long-lost soul-mates like those described in Plato's *Symposium.*

In Professor Eugene Scholes conflicts class, and Justice James T. Brand's constitutional law class, we sat side-by-side. Judge Brand, former Chief Justice of Oregon, had presided over the trial of the German Judiciary in Nürnburg, portrayed in a movie version by Spencer Tracy. Judge Brand looked more like Woodrow Wilson. When the Supreme Court approved warrantless health searches in *Frank v Maryland* I sat in front of his desk appalled. Dissenting, Justice Frankfurter had written "One rebel a year is not too great a price to pay for the preservation of our civil liberties." Justice Brand cautioned, "Mr. Blanton, you should never let your judgment as a literary man sway your judgment as a lawyer."

Jack was determined to make me as tanned as he was, and from 11:30 to twelve every morning he insisted I jog with him on the white sand beach, convinced I would tan if he could keep me covered with sweat. Being the first "cracker" friend he had ever had, I only turned deeper shades of red.

After lunch, we studied in the air-conditioned library until the afternoon thunder storm passed, after which it was cool enough to venture outside. Ingemar Johanssen was challenging Floyd Patterson for the heavyweight title that summer. I was sure the Swede was going to win, and Jack asked me how many "beans" I had on me. I had eighty dollars. He picked up the telephone, talked in Italian for a few minutes, after which he told me he had put my money on the Swede.

The next day he came back from Sal's house—he went there to study twice a week—and threw a wad of bills on my bed and said, "Your man won. The odds were four to one." My money never left my pocket. I suppose he would have asked for it if I had lost. But it was enough money for the two of us to eat out at the best restaurants in the Tampa Bay area for the rest of the summer session.

Two weeks later when Jack was at Sal's, and seeing me alone, Harvey Firestone invited me to dinner. He did not like Jack, and he warned me about the damage I was doing to my reputation by hanging out with a Mafioso. The law school had assigned me to his room and I had no intention of turning my back on so devoted a friend. Harvey had injured himself playing jai halai, having been struck in the head by the flying object they fling around in that sport. He had lost the full use of an arm and a leg, but his mind was sharp and his intentions were good.

I was benefiting greatly from Jack's relationship with Sal, for Jack had access to a beautiful, ocean-going cabin cruiser which belonged to the family. We drove up to a house on the beach in Jack's convertible, he called out in Italian, and a deeply-tanned, black-haired, young man emerged from the second floor and tossed down some keys. Jack scooped them up, and we were off into the Gulf for the week-end on a fully-stocked boat where we could talk freely. He insisted his society, as he called it, was superior to mine.

"In your society, any dumb lawyer with a friend who is a politician, both of them too dishonest and too incompetent to practice law successfully, is put on the bench and he can decide who lives and who dies. In my society, we take the oldest, wisest and most respected man we know, and we put him in charge to decide who lives and who dies. Now you tell me who has the better system."

It was a point I could not argue and win. Although I was a sailor, I enjoyed those trips on what Bernie and Charlie called a 'stink pot" with Jack, talking and admiring the Gulf. Jack assured me if I ever needed his help, I was to let him know, with the understanding I would never be obligated to his "family" as they understand obligations. Any favor he might do for me was based solely on our friendship, free of any obligation to him or anyone else.

Knowing I would never call on him for help, I was truly overwhelmed. Jack was convinced he had learned more about himself from watching me for six weeks than he had learned in his entire lifetime. He told me he now knew what he would have been like had he been born a cracker, and seeing me was like seeing himself living a completely different life in an altogether different world.

I flew back to Baltimore to interview for a clerkship in Baltimore during my senior year in law school. Judge Harlan was astonished at my deep-red sunburn which was perpetual but no longer painful. His clerks had scored the highest grade on the bar exam for the past two years, and I wanted to make it three in a row. He found me wanting but hired one on my classmates, David Bowers, instead.

When back at Stetson, I found there was to be a dinner dance following the end of classes. Jack's current date was a mermaid in the Wicki-Wacki Springs underwater mermaid show. She had often swum by the window where we were spending our gambling winnings on dinner, waving at us as she passed. Jack insisted I invite Estelle, who was spending the summer with her parents in North Carolina. I declined, but he insisted.

Jack wanted to meet her to make sure, as he put it, that she deserved me. If she did, he insisted, she would get on an airplane and be there. Wild horses couldn't keep her away. And if she didn't want me bad enough to show up, she didn't love me enough to marry me, and he wasn't going to let her have me. I began to worry about his possessiveness, but I relented and called her. She thought I had taken leave of my senses and flatly refused to come. Jack laughed, decided she was the right girl for me. "She's as spunky as you are. "But it was ignorance, not spunk that had me toe-to-toe with Rocky Marsiano's sparring partner the morning we met.

Before I resumed my classes at the University of Maryland in September, I was invited to Kitty Hawk, North Carolina as a house guest by Estelle's parents, where a wider group of her family and friends had an opportunity to meet me, and for me to meet them. That trip initiated a tradition which has continued ever since, as there has not been a year thereafter that we did not spend a week or two on the Outer Banks.

At her Masters recital at Peabody Conservatory Estelle played a piano sonata by the Russian composer, Dmitri Kabalevsky. Her teacher was Don Julio Esteban. When my wife-to-be was presented with bouquets of roses, I became curiously jealous, resolving to send her some of my own at the first opportunity, which did not arise until Valentine's Day.

I ordered the roses delivered on Saturday, following a dinner date scheduled for Friday the thirteenth. But a blizzard of epic proportions was predicted for the week-end, and the florist, anticipating disaster, made the delivery before I arrived at the apartment Estelle was sharing with Tinka Knopf at 12 E. Madison Street in Baltimore. The roses served their purpose, and before I left in the blizzard, we not only had agreed to become one, we had tentatively set the date for August 13, 1960, exactly six months later.

Before she went home for spring break, I scraped together enough money to buy her an engagement ring at Sam'l Kirk & Son, not what I wanted, but all I could afford. My only source of income was my National Guard check, barely enough to get by. I knew I could teach school after we were married and I made arrangements to return to teaching mathematics at Gwynn's Falls Junior High School in September before we got married. Lucky it was for me that young males certified to teach math in Maryland were hard to come by.

At the request of Estelle's mother, I compiled a list of names and addresses of family and friends to whom wedding invitations should be sent. Long distance telephone calls needed to be made in many cases to get names and current addresses correct. When we had all of the information I typed the list and mailed it to Estelle. In the days before copy machines, copies were not possible without carbon paper, and my typing was not good enough for one piece of paper, much less two.

About a month later, Estelle called to say she had lost the list and asked me to send another. Compiling the list had taken days of effort, and I did not know what had happened to the notes I had used to type the original. I told my mother I was going to call off the wedding. She threatened to shoot me. Knowing she used to hunt quail on horseback with my father, and that she was a crack shot, I decided that a life of misery was preferable to no life at all. We spent another three days preparing a second list when I should have been preparing for the bar exam.

I formed a study group to read and synopsize the last eight published volumes of the Maryland reports. Pat Rogan and I took the preparatory course offered by Ronnie Siskind, where we practiced reading, analyzing and writing answers to practice questions in twelve minutes. Norman Burke, class valedictorian and Editor of the Maryland Law Review, and Ed Fisher, my military acquaintance from Gablingen, took the Ginsburg course, which provided comprehensive outlines and summaries of Maryland black letter law. The split between the "case study" approach and the "memorize the rules" approach to the training of lawyers was just beginning.

As infantry officers, Ed Fisher and I had been taught that preparation was the key to survival. The bar exam was scheduled for July, the very time Ed and I were expected to be in Indiantown Gap. We were assigned alternative duty to teach at the Maryland National Guard's officer's candidate school. As executive officer of the Headquarters and Headquarters Company, however, I was assigned the additional duty of picking up the payroll for the Dandy Fifth at Fort Holabird, Maryland, then a facility run by the Army Quartermaster Corps, the branch responsible for feeding, equipping and paying the troops.

I was given a jeep, two guards, and four clips of ammunition for my Forty-Five. The payroll was about a hundred thousand dollars, for enlisted personnel only, all of whom were paid in cash. I signed for the money after counting it, put it in a large white-cloth moneybag, and took it to the Officer's Club at the Fifth Regiment Armory in Baltimore, site of the 1912 Democrat convention. Woodrow Wilson had attended Davidson for a year and later Johns Hopkins. He drove to Baltimore to listen to Dr. Harris Kirk's sermons at the Franklin Street church in Baltimore when he was President.

I found a broom closet, lifted up a pair of mops sitting in a galvanized scrub bucket, dropped the cash into the bucket, and put the mops back on top of it. I opened my books and my notes and studied for the bar, sitting in the chair Woodrow Wilson allegedly sat in through more than two-hundred fifty roll-calls before the convention settled on him as their nominee for President, a harbinger of the fights to come in the United State Senate over the progressive agenda which laid the ground work for Franklin Roosevelt and Barack Obama to build on twenty and ninety-five years later.

On the Thursday before the bar exam was to begin on Monday, Estelle called. She thought I had already taken the bar exam and she had come to Baltimore to complete our wedding plans, now scheduled for the Philadelphia Methodist Church in Sunbury, North Carolina. I decided to close my books and be kind to the poor girl who thought I was the love of her life. We went out to dinner, and as I drove her back to her apartment, we heard John F. Kennedy accepting his party's nomination for President from the Cow Palace in San Francisco on the car radio. There's a better story about that later.

My cousin Charlie had married Carole Mae Smith, of Norfolk, Virginia in 1958. Callie had spent five years in France as an editor for Vogue magazine. Martha Stewart she was not, but she invited us to their house in Roland Park for dinner on Sunday. Charlie was mixing gimlets, frosty green and tasty, serving them shortly after we arrived at five o'clock. I had not yet learned the three rules of drinking—never drink anything that tastes good, you can't see through or which has an umbrella stuck in it.

Before Callie served dinner at ten, I was in a world of my own, having listened to endless renditions of Mabel Mercer singing "Don't Cry Young Lovers" from the "King and I" and the duet from the first act of Bizet's "Pearl Fishers." Early the next morning, I dropped Estelle off and managed to find my way back to Northwood to get some sleep. Not much, however, for lights kept whirling around in my head even with my eyes closed.

Drowsy and disheveled, I got to the War Memorial Building, across the square from City Hall to take the bar exam at nine. I sat on a metal chair at a rickety card table giving every indication of collapsing momentarily. By pushing down with my toes, I could elevate my knees high enough to support the table, keeping it level enough to write my answers. I was doing just great until half past ten, when I began to feel clammy, a slight head-ache was getting worse by the minute and I detected a hint of nausea. It was like a reprise of my 1956 sea sickness.

Never having had a hang-over before I decided my best move was to remain rip-roaring drunk until five o'clock the following day, at which time I could get on with my hang-over. When the morning session adjourned, I took off for a bar on Baltimore Street that served lunch. I drank two doubles with my lunch and returned to my rickety table, balancing it on my knees, happily writing answers in a world of my own. Oddly, my memory was keen and words were flowing from my pen. Not only was I remembering the names of the cases but the volume and page numbers as well.

My sister Millie was entertaining my family at a cook-out at her house that night to meet my betrothed. I had stopped by Madison Street to pick Estelle up on the way home from the bar exam. I continued drinking as I had the night before, checking to make sure I was still in control and no sign of the greatly-to-be-feared hang-over emergent. The next morning, I took my orange juice with vodka. Somehow in cleaning up, the tables were rearranged, and someone else had to suffer with my rickety table.

I made it through the morning, and at lunch, I was back to Baltimore Street for two more doubles, vodka this time, to disguise the smell. When five o'clock came, the ordeal ended and I avoided friends anxious to compare answers, fearing they might find out just how irresponsible I had become.

Ed Fisher and I were on active duty that summer at the MDANG officer's candidate school in Pikesville. I realized he deserved more attention than I had given him thus far, for I had unknowingly influenced his life. He had not decided to go to law school until I assigned him to serve as defense counsel on the special court martial I had set up in Gablingen to prosecute the paratroopers clogging my court docket.

"There are two truths I know about people you need to keep in mind. They are always less honest than you think they are, and they are always kinder than you think they are."

The Honorable John Worth Kern,
August, 1962

Working With a Wise Judge

Doug Andrews and I left Baltimore to spend four days at the edge of the Dismal Swamp attending breakfasts, brunches, lunches, teas, and dinners. Doug was to be best man while Ed Fisher, my cousin Charlie, and Estelle's foster brother, Thomas Edward Muncy, would be ushers at my wedding. Estelle's sorority, Mu Phi Alpha, attended en masse and brought their musical instruments with them to supplement the church organ.

I made but one request, the Intermezzo from Mascagni's opera, Cavalleria Rusticana. I first heard it in Augsburg in 1955 at the Ludwigsbau, the temporary home of the opera while the grand building on Maximilian Strasse, designed by Adolph Hitler, was being restored. Estelle's music-savvy friends snickered because the underlying theme of the opera was Othello-like, homicidal jealousy. But the musical theme the night before Easter sunrise was ethereal, and sounded quite proper with "Jesu Joy of Man's Desiring" and "Sheep May Safely Graze," two selections of Estelle's.

The stringed instruments filled the Sunbury Methodist Church with a glorious sound. Estelle's friends had traveled though Europe with her in 1956, with their instruments in tow, to Les aux d'Aire, Switzerland, to live among natives who believed lying flat on mother earth gazing heavenward invigorated and restored the body. Strangely, it does. That was the summer Dan Blocker and I were also traveling through northern Europe, but Estelle and I have compared notes to make sure we had not crossed paths earlier.

Doug Andrews and my father-in-law became fast friends, sharing the same country sense of humor. They were having a wonderful time, and however worried Mr. Edwards may have justifiably been in entrusting his daughter to me, he was convinced anybody who had Doug Andrews for a friend could not be all bad. On the afternoon of the wedding, I confessed to Doug I had locked the keys to my Ford in the trunk along with the shoes I was supposed to wear in the wedding.

Fearing my constant assurances that I was all right were a cover I was certain to lose when Estelle started down the aisle and convinced he would have to chase me down and drag me back to the altar, Doug welcomed my mindless state, certain I was manifesting passive resistance to my imminent demise. He removed the rear seat, retrieved the keys and my shoes. The delay allowed Estelle to get to the church before we did, likely the last time she was ever on time for anything.

The reception was across the street from the church on the lawn of the Edwards family home on a very hot afternoon. Champagne was served, a first at a social event in Gates County, but Estelle and I were so busy talking and posing for pictures we had nothing to eat or drink. I remember nothing that happened that afternoon, but photographic evidence abounds to attest to the fact we were married.

During the reception, my white Ford was inscribed with raunchy phrases in black shoe polish, and as soon as Estelle and I could get away, we changed into our street clothes, grabbed our bags and took off through a shower of rice. Our first stop was a car wash in Suffolk. Our second was a Dairy Queen on Route 32 north of Suffolk. Our third was the Williamsburg Inn. If we had dinner I don't remember it. Alone in our room, Estelle discovered she had forgotten the keys to her suitcase. I called a bellhop who arrived with tools adequate to the task of prying it open. We quickly decided we could live with broken locks better than an unconsummated marriage.

The next day we drove to Charlottesville and from there to Roanoke, spending our nights in hotels with old family ties. Our second week was in a small mountain cabin at Lake Fontana, in the Great Smokies, where we shared our dinner with a black bear, not because we wanted to, but because he invaded our boat and refused to leave. We took in a Paul Green pageant, "Horn in the West" in the Cherokee reservation between North Carolina and Tennessee.

For the third week we had the Kitty Hawk cottage to ourselves, and I helped Estelle close it down for the winter. The apartment I had rented at 3 East Read Street would not be available for another week, so Estelle and I moved back into her old room at 12 East Madison, a block away through Love Grove Alley. Her new roommate, Francis Motyca, was already back in residence, and sharing our home with her began that day.

My promotion to captain in the Maryland National Guard was coupled with a reassignment as Heavy Weapons platoon leader of Combat Support Company. Instead of the Fifth Regiment Armory, I was now stationed at the Dundalk Armory. My platoon consisted of sections of 4.2 inch mortars and 106mm recoilless rifles, jeep mounted anti-tank guns which were dangerous and lethal fore and aft.

Colonel Roger S. Whiteford, the hero of St. Lô, had been replaced by Colonel Thomas McNeil, and his position was in jeopardy due to the poor performance of the 175th Infantry under his leadership. It was my good fortune to have inherited a superb group of exceptional and well-trained young men who knew their duty and performed it well. They saved him without any help from me. I watched them, liked what I saw and stayed out of their way. Of seventeen exceptional ratings given our battle group that summer, sixteen were earned, not by me, but by the platoon I was lucky enough to have.

When we moved into our apartment, we furnished it with a cherry dresser from my bedroom at the Lochwood Road house and a vinyl sleep sofa from my study, covered with a gray slip cover. My mother loaned us a drop-leaf dining table and two chairs. I bought a box spring and a mattress from Sears. That was it, day one, although we had two sets of china, silver, crystal and all the gifts we received when we were married.

In the next few months we hung some pictures and added an oriental rug, a coffee table and a small writing desk. Shortly after we moved in, Estelle's bought a baby grand piano and we ordered a china closet from a craftsman in Virginia who had duplicated some chairs and crafted a similar china closet for my cousin Charlie and his wife Callie.

We stood in line for hours to vote for John F. Kennedy and watched the returns late into the night on a television set with a 'rabbit ears' antenna I bought for the occasion. On our trips to Sunbury, I picked up firewood from Estelle's father, which I kept in the trunk of my Ford, parked in a space assigned to us behind the house. There was a marble fireplace in our living room, separated from our bedroom by pocket doors. We kept them open at night if we had a fire, and when it blazed up in the middle of the night before burning itself out, we watched the shadows dance on the ceiling. Our children, the first being conceived in that apartment, still want fires blazing in the fireplaces at Avondell when they come home in winter.

As I was teaching my favorite class of ninth graders at the Gwynn's Falls Middle School in late November, a message was handed to me. Estelle had called with the results of the bar examination, and I had passed with a score of 256. At home, my parents received a call from Ronnie Siskind, my mentor in preparation, who told me I had received the highest grade, she thought, ever. She urged me to keep the letter I received from Governor Millard Tawes and the newspaper articles, and whenever I felt depressed, take them out and read them. I had them framed and hung near my desk.

The law school also called, wanting to know if I would accept an immediate opening to clerk for Judge John Worth Kern, Chief Judge of the United States Tax Court in Washington. I went over for an interview, and I was hired with the understanding that I begin on January 2, 1961. The newspapers published other good news. Ed Fisher, Pat Rogan, and Norman Burke joined me in the top five finishers on the bar exam. Ed and Norman were already clerking for judges on the Maryland Court of Appeals.

One of my wife's close friends at Peabody was Vicki Adelberg, who had married my law school classmate, David Rudow. Unaware of my means but impressed with the result, they invited us to their house for a champagne reception. We have been friends ever since. My preparation notes were in great demand, and they have yet to find their way back to me.

I started to work in Washington in January, 1961. The President picked as his Secretary of State Dean Rusk, a Rhodes Scholar from Davidson that *Time* magazine called the chairman of the American establishment, whatever that was. My office was on the second floor of the Internal Revenue Building between 10th and 12th Streets and Pennsylvania and Constitution Avenues, directly across the hall from that of Judge Kern, whose father had been a Senator from Indiana and the Democrat candidate for Vice President in 1908.

While a professor at Indiana University, the judge—pushed into politics by his students—was elected Mayor of Indianapolis. Like Franklin Roosevelt, he had been crippled as a child and pulled himself around on crutches. He was a kind but tough employer. His prose was simple, beautiful and precise, and no matter how hard I try, I can not emulate it. He had to rewrite almost everything I gave him, so it was very unfulfilling work on my part. My two years as his clerk, although I was called an "attorney-advisor", convinced me I did not ever want to be a judge, a monastic existence, sitting alone in a room, reading and writing day after day.

I commuted to Washington daily on the B & O Railroad, buying a monthly pass for forty dollars. I often shared my seat with Jervis Langdon, who was also an elder in the Franklin Street Presbyterian Church and president of the B&O. His uncle was Samuel Clemens, better known as Mark Twain. Jervis and his wife lived on Gibson Island. I knew it well, for my sister Jean had dated Dr. Marshall Sanford, a Hopkins cardiac surgeon who anchored his forty-eight foot sloop *Windigo* in front of a house he owned there. As a colonel in the army, a rank awarded all railroad presidents when the government seized the railroads during World War II, Jervis worked on his military correspondence courses on his way to meetings at the Interstate Commerce Commission. He was striving to keep the favorable freight rates from Baltimore to the mid-west, the loss of which has since effectively shut down the Port of Baltimore. None of the railroad employees on the train knew who he was, and he wanted to keep it that way, so he could better experience what his paying customers endured if he suffered along with them.

I enjoyed strolling around Washington during my lunch breaks, and many mornings as Jervy and I walked from Union Station the lamp posts were decorated with foreign flags. There would be two flags and a notice on my desk advising that the President and Mrs. Kennedy were to meet a foreign head of state at National Airport and drive them back into the city in an open car across the 14th Street Bridge. In exchange for an extra half-hour for lunch we were expected to line the route from the bridge to the White House, waving our flags in welcome. The President was less than eight feet away, smiling, safe and waving from an open car. Dallas ended that forever.

Working in Washington allowed me to attend Davidson alumni meetings. Dean Rusk noticed my name tag, and assumed I was the son of his Professor of Military Science and Tactics at Davidson when he was a student. No matter how hard I tried, I could not dissuade him from insisting I was the son of his mentor. I became his companion of choice at alumni events. He insisted I call him Dean, and we became friends. He confided that his job was impossible.

"Why do you say that?"

"A hundred years ago, if there were a war or revolution in Africa or South America, it would be months before we found out about it. Today, news is instantaneous and I am expected to have a response and a policy initiative ready overnight."

Dean played basketball at Davidson, and he was recruiting players from the prolific Washington suburbs for Lefty Driesell's Davidson team. To my amazement, I once saw him, in overcoat and hat, sink a three-pointer from mid-court. He was an effective recruiter and Davidson briefly became a basketball power, making it to the NCAA finals.

Dean knew Dr. Paul Crane, another elder at Franklin Street Presbyterian, who also attended Davidson. Paul was a medical missionary to South Korea, a special responsibility of the Southern Presbyterian Church. He established Korea's first hospital, and he told me cultural differences mandated the terminally ill had to be rushed in a speeding ambulance, not to the hospital, but home to die surrounded by their kin.

Paul was called upon to translate when President Syngman Rhee came to America to meet with President Kennedy. Later, when Lyndon Johnson was President, Paul gave Dean a copy of John Baillee's "Book of Daily Prayers," which Dean passed on to President Johnson. Lyndon referred to it in a Barbara Walters interview. Iain Wilson had continued Dr. Kirk's practice of giving a copy to every member of the church upon their acceptance by the Session.

In the office adjacent to mine, Judge Russell Train's law clerks shared an office where Herbert Chabot from Maryland, who later became a Tax Court judge himself, and John Totz from Texas talked endlessly, playing with their cases and exploring the far reaches of the opinions they were working on. When I could stand it no longer, I would interrupt to distil their arguments.

One Friday, they had been at it all week, trying to find logic where none exists, in the area of personal holding company income and that of Subchapter S corporations. We were supposed to have lunch together, so I interrupted them a half-hour early to suggest they analogize income to sex, with an active participant and a passive participant. If a taxpayer did not have to do anything but own property to get income from it, it was passive income. But if he had to perform a task and exert energy to generate income, then it was active income. They seized upon my analogy with glee, using my words in their draft opinion. Judge Train, the youngest judge on the Court, retained my concept of active and passive income in the opinion and it became part of the tax lexicon, now written into the statutes, regulations and rulings.

Charlie and Callie were also at Kitty Hawk in the summer of 1961, and Estelle and I came in second, behind them, in a cat boat race in Currituck Sound. Afterward, we drove north on the beach from Duck, where the paved road ended, to the Whalehead Club. I jumped out of Charlie's jeep and lifted the cables that blocked the beach at the old Army Air Corps bombing range so we could get through. It was dark when Charlie drove us back to the Kitty Hawk cottage, and the sand sparkled with thousands of scurrying lights as the jeep's head lamps caught the sand fiddlers diving into their holes as we barreled toward them. Getting back to work that September was not easy, for we were having magnificent fall weather.

One beautiful October day I was sitting in Judge Kern's court room, listening to the testimony in some local cases, when his secretary entered and handed him a note. He summoned me to the bench, and handed it to me. My father had suffered a heart attack. I caught an early train back to Baltimore. It appeared he would recover, and after a few days in hospital, he was sent home.

Charlie and Callie let us use his cottage in Southern Shores that November, and we found the Atlantic water warmer then than it had been in August. We walked barefoot on the beach, wearing shorts and a sweater, collecting driftwood for the fireplace. The Outer Banks beaches still had residues of oil left over from torpedoed tankers in World War II, and a barefoot walk necessitated a session with lard and seashells to remove the tar from our feet. At night, the lights from the fishing fleet were visible from the huge picture window in the living room of the Herndon cottage.

Estelle and I planned to spend Christmas Eve and morning with her parents in Sunbury, and drive back to Baltimore to have dinner with my parents. My father was not feeling well, but he was delighted Estelle was pregnant. My mother insisted we have dinner first, but Dr. William Fritz, my father's physician, urged me to take him to the emergency room at Johns Hopkins immediately.

We drove to the hospital, entering from Broadway past the larger than life marble statue of Christ, and checked him in. Two hours later we were approached by an intern or resident who told us my father had died. Undoubtedly he should have gone to the hospital in an ambulance, for his condition was far worse than we knew. My mother insisted we had killed him for the rest of her life. A more cautious physician would surely have sent an ambulance for him.

When I returned to work Judge Kern came into my office and talked at length about life and death and his relationship with his father, a Senator from Indiana who served as Senate majority leader and Vice-President nominee in 1908. The judge called me "Mr. Blanton." His secretary was always "Mrs. Stokes," and his other attorney adviser was "Mr. Parsells." He pretended to be impressed that I was a Presbyterian elder, joking that his own spiritual qualities were so deficient the only office he was qualified to hold in the church was that of trustee. Would that every Presbyterian elder have his spiritual gifts.

A month later Judge Kern called me into his office to read a letter he had written to the President's brother, Robert Kennedy, the Attorney General. Bobby had gone public with his criticism of the membership requirements of the Metropolitan Club; and as Chairman of the Membership Committee, Judge Kern reminded him that he had agreed to abide by the rules of the club when he became a member; there were prescribed methods for resolving member disputes internally; his conduct was in violation of the rules and any further repetition would result in the immediate revocation of his membership. Judge Kern wanted to know what I thought of the letter.

"I think it's a bit strong. But I that's what Bobby is hoping will happen."

Judge Kern smiled. "If you think this letter is a bit strong, you should have seen the letters written by the two other members of my committee. We will send this one."

When Judge Kern reached retirement age, one of his two secretaries moved to an office where she had nothing to do but water her potted plants, read the paper and take coffee breaks. Mr. Parsells was finishing a voluminous left-over opinion in an excess profits case, and I needed a typist to finish my draft opinion in the *Goddard* case. At Judge Kern's direction I took my draft opinion to his former secretary. Having grown accustomed to doing nothing, she was furious we expected her to actually work for the salary, pension and health care the American taxpayers were providing. None of the other women —all discarded secretaries of dead or retired judges warehoused on that hall —had to work. When appointed, a judge may bring his secretaries with him, and once they receive civil service status and benefits, they keep them for life. They live in Maryland and Virginia, vote to keep their benefits, and swell the ranks of the mendicant majority.

As my two year assignment to the Tax Court drew to a close, Judge Kern told me he knew nothing about Baltimore law firms, insisting there was no tax practice there. He encouraged me to work in Washington, Atlanta or Houston, cities where he thought I would have a bright future. He asked Judge Morton Fisher, who was from Baltimore, to take me to lunch at the Metropolitan Club. Judge Fisher confirmed the lack of a thriving tax practice in Baltimore, but if I insisted on working in Baltimore, he told me which firms to avoid.

Judge Kern pushed hard for the Washington firm Arnold & Porter, and sent me to see Caroline Agger, wife of Abe Fortas, on leave from the firm as an associate justice on the Supreme Court. She was an attractive blonde, sitting behind a white, French provincial desk in an office with bountiful, purple velvet draperies, collapsing in heaps under the windows on plush wall to wall carpeting so thick I could have slept on it. She was wearing a tight skirt, an even tighter purple sweater and smoking a cigar. I thought she was trying to scare me, but when I betrayed my disinterest, she summoned Louis Eisenstein. He was a rumpled little genius with a mind I admired. We spent a pleasant afternoon together smoking cigars and pipes and I could almost see myself working with them. I had to force myself to say no.

Abe and Caroline were close friends of Randolph and Muriel Paul, the editors of Mertens, the most reliable of all the tax treatises, which Judge Kern insisted I read before beginning work on a case. When the Pauls went to Washington parties, it was rumored that Caroline went home with Randy and Abe went home with Muriel. I had it on good authority it was more than a rumor. Washington's reputation as 'Baghdad on the Potomac' was deserved, not a place where I wanted to raise my children. Both of my daughters now work there, and so did my son for a few years.

Aware of my interest in politics, and my determination to live in Baltimore, Judge Kern called me into his office. We spent much of the afternoon talking about his father's political career, as well as his own, and Franklin Roosevelt's efforts to get him to run for the Senate in 1938. The President offered him the Vice Presidency in 1940 if he would challenge and defeat Senator Capehart. The previous winter, when Mr. Parsells and I drove out to the Judge's Vauxhall Road residence to help him through the snow, we passed the White House and Mr.

Parsells asked the judge if he ever regretted turning President Roosevelt down back in 1938. Judge Kern grinned and said, "Everyday when I pass this house, I thank God he gave me the good sense to say no."

While on his honeymoon the judge learned he was to teach the course in domestic relations at the Indiana law school upon his return to Indianapolis. His telegram to his law partner urgently requesting a copy of the textbook be sent to his honeymoon hotel lifted eyebrows and fueled jocular speculation at the firm, and the judge assured me he was teased unmercifully when he returned to Indianapolis.

President Roosevelt wanted to prosecute Andrew Mellon, Herbert Hoover's Secretary of the Treasury. The Internal Revenue Service, using the net worth method, assessed civil penalties against him. The Justice Department had hoped the civil case would warrant a criminal action, but Judge Kern, saint that he was, found in favor of the Treasury secretary. He had not committed civil fraud, and he could not be prosecuted. The case against Treasury Secretary Geithner is criminal fraud, and he might yet be prosecuted for it, although his abysmal ignorance of the law might make a good defense.

Ed Fisher completed his clerkship a year earlier than I and he had taken a job with Nick Shriver's firm in Baltimore. Acting on Judge Fisher's advice, I submitted my resume to Wright, Robertson & Dowell and Venable, Baetjer & Howard. My interview with John Wright and Emma Robertson went well, and I was ready to accept any offer they might make. On May 1, 1962 I met with Venable's Norwood Orrick and Frank Murnaghan and discovered they were bringing in, as a tax partner, an established lawyer in Baltimore but they could not tell me who he was. Unwilling to buy a "pig in a poke" as my mother would have said, I sent my resume to Nick Shriver.

Nick hired me on condition I start the first of September. But the taxpayers were already paying me $7,800 a year with health insurance. Nick offered me $5,000 a year, no health insurance, and I was to be treated as a partner, not an employee, working with Charlie Reeves who did their tax and corporate work. Unknown to me, Venable and the Shriver firm were engaged in merger discussions, which would have made the merged firm Baltimore's largest. When I gave my resignation letter to Judge Kern, he gave me more good advice.

"If it should come to pass that you are ever with a law firm and there is a break up—some lawyers want to leave and some want to stay —always throw in your lot with the ones who are leaving. They know things you don't know and they won't tell you why they are leaving. But the ones leaving, in my experience, are always the better lawyers, the bolder lawyers, the ones you will want to be associated with.

If you get into politics—and I think you will succeed when you do —do not automatically reject an invitation from the political machine if one is extended to you. Machines want to stay in power, and they do that by recruiting and supporting able people. Machines are not necessarily bad, most of them are good; and they are a necessary part of the political process."

Leaving so good and wise a man was difficult, but I was, to use Judge Kern's words for me, "a young man in a hurry." I had vacation days accrued, and it was time to go to the outer banks. A horrific storm on Ash Wednesday in March, 1962 had destroyed our cottage at Kitty Hawk but we were offered the use of another in Nags Head owned by close friends of Estelle's family.

Our first child, Ted, had been born in June, and he had trouble breathing in the stiff off-shore winds that sweep the outer banks. I thought he would be a good sailor, for moving with the wind is a lot easier than having it blow in your face. He now keeps his Hobie on his front lawn, and when we speed over Currituck Sound with tautly strung sheets being drenched with water, his children hanging far off the rails to keep us flat, he shouts, "Listen, Dad, she's singing to us."

On my last day in Washington Judge Kern took me to lunch at the Metropolitan Club. There was a lot of love at that table, so thick I could feel it. His parting words were, "I don't know what more I can say, but there are two truths I know about people you need to keep in mind. They are always less honest than you think they are, and they are always kinder than you think they are."

"Don't you dare do that. The secret service will shoot your process server."

Clark Clifford,
April, 1965

"Nick Shriver is the tightest man I know. He gave that kid three raises in two years. He must have something on the ball. How about giving him another look."

Attorney General Finan to Deputy AG Robert Murphy,
June, 1965

A Benevolent Despot

The day after Labor Day in 1962 I associated with the Baltimore law firm Cross & Shriver. My law school classmate, Ed Fisher, had been there for a year as had Benjamin H. Murray, also a member of our class. Nick Shriver was the senior partner, Eben J.D. Cross having left this world for one far better. Thomas D. Washburne and J. Paul Bright were partners. Thomas B Eastman and James J. Fannon were also associates.

Our offices were on the sixth floor of the old Mercantile Safe-Deposit and Trust Building at the corner of Baltimore and Calvert Streets. Although John Wright had been kind enough to offer me a position at Wright, Robertson & Dowell, a firm of equal size with a more impressive office and a substantial tax practice, I had already accepted Nick's offer. The merger discussions with Venable did not work out, and Charlie Reeves had left Nick for Venable. By default, I started out as the tax and corporate guy in the Shriver firm. I wrote short, military style tax memos on every question they threw at me.

Nick was a stern taskmaster and a hard worker. He was also a great teacher, and for that I am grateful. I quickly learned not to get to the office before he did in the morning, or to stay later than he in the evening. To offend in this regard put him in a hyper-critical mood, and no matter what you accomplished on that day, it was not good enough. He was the prime mover in the firm's corporate practice, and he sought tax advice from me on the interesting transactions in which he was involved, taking me along to meetings of corporate boards, late-night negotiating sessions and early-morning court appearances, often in distant counties where he always hired local counsel.

Law firms in those days were austere places. Tile floors, wooden chairs, no pictures except etchings, preferably by Gabrielle Clements, and no upholstery anywhere; here and there a bit of leather, but that was it. It was the same throughout the city, as the only difference between our offices on the sixth floor and

Venable's on the fourteenth was the view outside the window plus a few oriental rugs. I plunged into my work, but from the outset, there was one thing after another to distract me.

Estelle and I had moved from our apartment at 3 East Read Street to my house on Lochwood Road in Northwood shortly before the birth of our son Ted in June, 1962. We arranged for Ted's christening at the Franklin Street Church, and Estelle's family stayed with us that week-end in September. Ted was carried to the Church in the arms of his maternal grand-father, who seemed pleased with him, judging from the broad smile on his face.

Iain Wilson officiated; pleased Estelle and I met in his church. He had been a frequent visitor to our austere apartment on Read Street. Within a month my father-in-law had a disabling stroke and died shortly thereafter. I worked with a North Carolina lawyer and accountant to get the estate tax returns filed.

In early December, I was asked by a lawyer in Florida who was a friend of Doug Andrews to take a deposition of a Maryland witness, which I readily agreed to do. After the deposition, I asked the visiting lawyer from Florida how Doug was doing. The lawyer appeared startled.

"You mean you don't know?"

"Know what."

"I'm sorry. Doug's dead."

I sank back into my seat as if struck by an unseen assailant. His response to my surprised look and "Know what?" was the first of many times I hid my emotions behind a veil of professionalism. Doug and his pilot were flying to Miami from his Florida panhandle law-office. The plane crashed in the Everglades. It was two weeks before the plane and their bodies were recovered. The man I looked upon as a brother, and probably loved more than I would have loved a brother if I had been lucky enough to have one, was suddenly taken, leaving a wife and children behind before his thirtieth birthday. That was just the beginning.

We spent Thanksgiving and Christmas in Sunbury with Estelle's family, trying to get a grip on her father's affairs. The winter passed quickly. Laddie Murray was still competing in the steeplechase races run north of Baltimore in the spring. We cheered him on in the My Lady's Manor race at the St. James Episcopal Church in April. We watched him tack up in the paddock before the Grand National in Butler the following week, and the Hunt Cup a week after that.

Attending these races became part of our life, until the crowds at the Grand National and Hunt Cup grew so large the effort to get there outweighed the fun of being there. We still attend the My Lady's Manor race, relocated from Monkton to Pocock Road in Harford County just south of Ladew Gardens. It is a good way to meet and greet old friends.

In early summer, 1963, when Estelle and I were expecting our second child, Ed Fisher's father died of lung cancer. I attended his Masonic funeral with Nick Shriver, who cautioned me that Masons were "virulently anti-Catholic". The day after his father was buried in early July, Ed Fisher went to the hospital himself. He stayed there for six weeks before he, too, died. The diagnosis, made in January,

1963, was inoperable brain cancer. I haunted the offices of surgeons to no avail; the tumors were far too many to attempt surgery.

Melanoma is a dreadful thing. I visited Ed almost daily. One day I asked him why he did not tell me he was sick, and why he continued working, knowing he was at death's door.

"After you put me on that court-martial in Gablingen, I knew I wanted to be a lawyer. I gave up a lot to go to school again, and when I realized I had so little time left, I decided to be a lawyer as long as I could. If I had told you, it would not have been the same. I could not be the lawyer I wanted to be if everyone was feeling sorry for me."

I suppressed tears, but I knew they were flowing inside in a torrent. We were walking in the hospital hall, and Ed suddenly spun left and slammed into the wall face first. He could no longer control his body; I caught him and helped him back to his room. Within a month he had wasted away, and by mid-August I could lift him with little effort. Two days before he died, I sat by his bed, railing at the unfairness of life, and he whispered, "Everybody's got to die of something. Far better to die with those you love around you than alone on an icy hillside in Korea. That's what we both expected when we were in college. God gave us a reprieve. Enjoy what's left of yours."

At my last visit, he was curled up in a fetal position, helpless and welcoming death. We could not talk, so I held him as long as I could. The next morning his room was empty.

I settled his father's estate and his simultaneously. He left a wife and two daughters. Ed's step-mother, Vivian McDonald Fisher, later told me she asked him before he died what she was going to do, alone in the world so suddenly. He told her "Go see Ed Blanton. He will look after you." I did, for more than forty years. Vivian said Ed's father was aware, as was she, of Ed's diagnosis. She believed his father, who managed the Baltimore office of Retail Credit Co, gave up his own fight against cancer to avoid seeing his son suffer.

Ed's mother had died delivering him. Vivian married Ed's father when Ed was two and she later adopted him. They had borrowed five hundred dollars to buy five shares of Retail Credit's stock in 1930. As a result of stock splits and dividends, that investment left her a wealthy woman when she died three weeks short of her hundredth birthday in 2007. After providing for Ed's two daughters, she endowed scholarships honoring her husband and son at the University of Pittsburgh and Gettysburg College. I insisted upon a third, in her name at her alma mater, James Madison University.

We had no sooner buried Ed than a luncheon meeting of the Maryland Bar Association on the roof garden of the Southern Hotel on Light Street was terminated by the death of President Kennedy in Dallas. Within months, Laddie Murray's wife was killed, taking a jump on a horse in Virginia. Six months later, Laddie succumbed to brain cancer, as a consequence of a steel plate replacing part of his skull following a war injury in Korea. It was a dark time for me, and my grief was not lost on Nick Shriver.

Estates and taxes thread their way through everything in a modern law practice. Nick's first cousin was Sargent Shriver, and he was planning to run for Governor of Maryland in 1966. Nick suggested I take a leave of absence and work in his campaign. I leapt at the idea. It was exactly what I wanted to do. It was a campaign that did not take off, for Sarge accepted an appointment from President Johnson to lead the Peace Corps.

The Shrivers, a German Catholic family from Carroll County, the most Republican county in the state, regarded the Kennedys as shanty Irish rum-runners, and Sarge's marriage to Eunice was an embarrassment to them from a strictly social standpoint. Nick's wife, Melanie, was fascinated by my First Family of Virginia connections. It was all she wanted to talk to me about. She was a Dugan, not Irish, but French, and she shared the Shrivers disdain for the Kennedys. Yet, a legislator friend from Carroll County who knew them well told me that when Nick and Sarge came to Baltimore from Carroll County in the 1930's, they didn't have two dimes between them.

When Sarge dropped out, I sat in my office near the now empty offices of Ed and Laddie. We three had planned to grow old together, and now I had to grow old without them. As the office fount of knowledge for taxes, my memos to the other lawyers prompted more and more meetings in my office, and Nick and Tom began to seek my advice on other matters as well.

Tom Washburne gave me an old file and asked me to see if I could get the case tried or settled. To do that, I needed information from two witnesses in Miami, Florida, so I flew down from National Airport in Washington to take their depositions in February. I had been given a pair of gloves for Christmas which I treasured, and I left them in the cab on my return to Union Station from the airport. When back in Baltimore I dialed the cab company's number on the rotary phones we used in those days to see if the gloves had been turned in by the driver just as Tom came in my office to get a report. His sudden appearance startled me, and I miss-dialed the number. A gruff voice said "Yes." As I started to speak, there was a click and a lovely female voice said, "This is the office of the President. How may I help you?"

Thinking I had the cab company on the line, I asked "The President of what?"

"The President of the United States."

I apologized, and explained that I miss dialed the number. My military experience informed me that I had the number of a telephone on the desk of the President. It was, unfortunately, not my only run-in with Lyndon Johnson, but both were a bit later in my career. My Houston, Texas room mate my sophomore year at Davidson had told me the only reason Texas sent Johnson to Washington was to "get him the hell out of Texas."

Jay Bright decided to redecorate our offices and hired an interior decorator to brighten up the place. The firm charged fifteen dollars an hour for my time, and twenty-five for Nick's. My secretary was paid seventy dollars per week, but that was seventy percent of my pay. I persuaded Nick to up his hourly rate to thirty-five and lift mine to twenty.

Some of the corporate work I did found me working with Patrick Deering from LyBrand, Ross Brothers and Montgomery. One day I was meeting with Pat in our new conference room when Nick joined us. We were having a lot of trouble with an Annapolis lawyer named Mackall Childs, a formidable obstacle to our getting the result we wanted for our client.

Pat left to take a telephone call, and Nick told me he had talked to a law school classmate, Thomas B. Finan, who was Maryland's attorney general. Tom was planning to run for Governor in 1966, and he was looking for a lawyer in Anne Arundel County to fill a vacancy on the bench. I asked Nick if he thought the Attorney General would let me work in his campaign. As we waited for Pat to return, I mused that it would be just dandy if Governor Tawes would appoint Mr. Childs to the bench and get him out of my life.

Nick got that 'deer in the head lights' look on his face, jumped up, muttering what a hell of an idea that was and did the cartoon character "Mexican roadrunner" thing of his back to his office. When he returned he was grinning like a Cheshire cat. He said Tom wanted to interview me for a position as an assistant attorney general, and a few days later, Judge Childs took his seat on the bench, to my great joy and that of our client.

I went over to Mies van der Rohe's masterpiece which in those days we called One Charles Center. I met with Robert Murphy, the deputy attorney general. Bob had joined the Attorney General's office when he graduated from law school handling collections for the University of Maryland hospital. Most of the assistant attorneys general were promising five year associates with the major law firms in Baltimore. Venable had Anthony Carey representing the Comptroller and the State Department of Assessments and Taxation; Piper & Marbury's Jack Cooper had the Insurance Commission; Semmes, Bowen and Semmes's Roger Redden had a potpourri of state clients.

When Tom Finan became attorney general, he picked Bob Murphy as his deputy solely on the basis of seniority. Bob gave me but little time. I told Nick that he had not hired me. Bob later told me that Tom had never questioned any of his hiring decision before, but in my case, Tom had come to him—I suspect after Nick had chewed on his ear—and said "Nick Shriver is the tightest man I know. He gave that kid three raises in two years. He must have something on the ball. How about giving him another look?"

Bob didn't bother. He thought I was a complete and utter nebbish, but he hired me anyway, because he was certain that was what Tom wanted him to do. Bob was kind enough to tell me this a year later, and we remained friendly until his death, when he was then Chief Judge of the Maryland Court of Appeals.

One of my law school teachers, Norman Ramsey, was the managing partner at Semmes, Bowen and Semmes. He called me when he found out I was going to the Attorney General's office on the first of July, 1965 at the magnificent salary of $10,000 per year and asked me to lunch. He wanted me to join his firm as an associate. I was interested in doing that, and I told him I would if they would insert me on the associate's list with the other lawyers who graduated in 1960. I was four years older than most of them, and several of them had served as enlisted men under my command in the Dandy Fifth.

I met Norm's partner, Rig Baldwin, who also wanted me to work at Semmes. They did their best, but later told me I was turned down by one vote. I was welcome in the firm as an associate, but I would have to start, after five years at the bar, at the very bottom of the list. When I told Rig I couldn't do that, he said he had always regretted not having in his biography a posting as an assistant attorney general. I decided to work with Tom Finan as long as I could. Norm later became a federal judge, but returned to Semmes before he died to help Cleve Miller, one of my Dandy Fifth recruits, manage the firm.

As I was leaving Nick Shriver's firm a client asked my help in collecting $5,000 owed him by President Johnson. I called Caroline Agger and asked if she still represented the President. She told me Clark Clifford had that high honor, and when she asked my reason for calling, she said she would talk to Clark. He called the next day and invited me and my client to meet him in his office. En route to Washington on the Baltimore-Washington Parkway, a light plane landed in the back seat of a convertible car, both coming to a stop in front of us. Pilot and driver, as puzzled as we, got out to discuss the oddest of sights, a light plane with its landing gear stuck in the back seat of a convertible.

We arrived at Mr. Clifford's office an hour late. We were met by his receptionist, wearing a ten-gallon hat, mini skirt and leather cow-boy boots. Clark thought my excuse original and ingenious, promising to use it himself the next time he was late. When we sat down in his office he handed me a file containing every newspaper and magazine article about the President's daughter's wedding, with my client's name circled in red. He assured me my client, having played for the President, could command much higher fees in the future. In an effort to impress us with his long association with Presidents from Truman to Johnson, he showed us President's Kennedy's hand-written manuscript of "Profiles in Courage." He said President Kennedy had written it, longhand on a yellow legal pad, balanced on his knees while in hospital.

My client was not a performer but a music teacher. He trained two choirs and wrote a thirty-minute processional for the wedding, held in a Roman Catholic Church the public was not invited to attend. Like lawyers, all he had to sell was his time and talent. Clark suggested I submit an expense account, assuring me that the long-standing tradition of performing for the sheer honor of it would not be disturbed if the White House reimbursed my client's expenses instead of paying his fee.

But my client had commuted to Washington from Baltimore in a school bus with the choir, and when he stayed overnight, he ate and slept as a guest of the priests at the church. Neither my client nor I had any intention of willfully violated 18 USC 1001, which provides for fine and imprisonment for making false statements to the United States government.

The President was to speak at Johns Hopkins University, and I told Clark I intended to have my complaint served on the President by the Sheriff while he was in Baltimore. Clark was horrified and tried to scare me off.

"Don't you dare. The secret service will shoot your process server."

So I asked him to accept service on the President's behalf. He said he would think about it. When I was back in my office, I called Charlie Flowers at the *Sun* and told him I had a funny story that might interest him. His children were students in the Ecumenical Sunday School I superintended. We met for lunch in one of the private rooms at the Hamilton Street Club, and Charlie promised to have a tenacious reporter call me to verify the facts.

When the reporter called, I immediately called Clark, told him I had a reporter on hold, and asked him what I should tell him. Clark said I should tell him that the White House had received the bill and Mrs. Johnson was sending me her check, payable to my client. I asked him if I had his word that what I was instructed to tell the reporter was accurate. When he said I did, I told the reporter the President had decided my client's bill was a private, and not a public, expense and it was being paid by the President personally. Two days later, Lady Bird's check arrived in the morning mail.

Two lawyers I did not know, Bill Manger and Tom Maxwell, invited me to lunch after the press announced my appointment as an assistant attorney general. They were forming a partnership to practice law, and they were going to rent space on the twentieth floor of One Charles Center. I needed a place to meet my private clients, and the convenience of having an office nearby appealed to me. We called the firm Manger, Maxwell and Blanton, and I stayed with them —although I barely knew them —as long as I was an assistant attorney general.

My wife and I learned in July, 1965 we were expecting a third child, and our row house in Northwood had but three bedrooms. We started looking furiously for another place to live. We liked the house Mrs. D.K Este Fisher owned, a replica of the James River plantation Westover adjacent to Sherwood Gardens in Guilford. The house was on the market for $80,000. My offer of $72,000 was rejected.

Blake McFeely's wife was selling real estate, and she encouraged me to look at Avondell, an old stone and log house in Long Green Valley that had been renovated by architect William Stone after it was purchased from Alexander Paul Brown, the Baltimore County Clerk of Court, by a Dr. Vinson in 1945. My sister Faye was familiar with the house, for she had dated Mr. Stone's son and he had shown her through the place when it was being renovated.

Estelle and I both felt at home in it. It reminded me of the house I was born in overlooking the lake at Hope Mills. I still worry that my first offer was immediately accepted. The following week Mrs. Fisher called me to say she would sell me her house on Highfield Road for $72,000. I told her I had just bought another house, and however much I liked hers, I was technically unemployed at the moment and I could not afford both.

We moved into Avondell on our fifth wedding anniversary and the seller left several chilled bottles of white wine on the mantle in the library. More than eight acres of land were part of our new home, as well as a kennel, barn, garage, smoke house, ice house, log kitchen with walk-in fireplace and swimming pool. We also bought antiques and an oriental rug that was large enough for the forty-foot long living room, flanked with fireplaces at both ends.

Our immediate neighbor was Jackson Smith, who lived alone at Greenlea, a Gothic mansion with a windmill that had been built by Dr. Green between our house and Phil Albrecht's landing strip. Mr. Smith called on us that evening, bringing produce from his garden, delighted to have Presbyterian neighbors. He attended the Chestnut Grove church in Jacksonville. He had once sold Packards at the Zell Motor Car Company on Mt. Royal Avenue, before acquiring the *Jeffersonian* newspaper in Towson.

When I assumed my duties as an assistant attorney general on July 1, 1965, I asked Bob Murphy for Paul Cooper's Fiscal Research Bureau and the Baltimore City Elections Board. The Legislature, distrustful of the city's politics, gave representation of that body to the Attorney General. John Sause, whose office was between mine and that of Alan Wilner, was counsel to the Baltimore City police commissioner, another job the Legislature dared not entrust to city politicians.

Bob Sweeney sent me to Annapolis to take over his work with a legislative committee co-chaired by Senator William James and Delegate Stanley Blair that was finalizing a fair election practice act for passage in the 1966 legislative session, limiting political contributions and establishing reporting requirements prior to the primary and general elections. My job was to draft changes in the law with the help of Willard Morris, clerk of the Montgomery County Board of Elections and Vivian Pierson, representing the League of Women Voters, which Willard jokingly referred to as the Plague of Women Vultures.

By Christmas of 1965, our decorator, Karl Graf, had put the living room, hall, library and dining room in a state of readiness to entertain guests. We wanted our friends to meet my boss, so we invited several hundred people to a "meet and greet" event the first week of March, 1966 catered by Peerce M. Lake, a neighbor who owned Peerce's Plantation. But a blizzard of historic proportions arrived on the date of the planned event. No one called and no one came, including the caterer.

When the snow stopped falling and the wind stopped blowing, I went to the garage, jacked up my rear-engine Chevrolet Corvair, put chains on the rear tires and sped out of the garage through the snow, fishtailing around like a motor boat without a rudder, to see if any of the roads were passable. My neighbor, Phil Albrecht—a contractor who installed the swimming pool for the prior owners of Avondell and later prepared the Towson Golf and Country Club's golf course next to Peerce's —had deployed his trucks to help the county plow the roads.

I found Phil in Glen Arm. The snow was so deep on Long Green Pike he had to pole through the drifts to make sure no cars were buried before he could plow. He suggested another route to town. The chains were so noisy on the wet pavement of the Beltway I stopped and took them off. When I got to the office, Tom's campaign rescheduled the event with my wife. When it finally happened, it was a successful evening, and the catering staff at Peerces so competent, it was difficult to tell the next morning that more than a hundred people had been in the house the night before.

"Is your father Ed Blanton, the man who invented Harry Hughes?"

—Thomas Perkins, to my daughter,
October, 1980

A Kind Attorney General

About six months after beginning my job in the State Law Department, Tom Perkins took me to Annapolis for the opening night of the 1966 Maryland legislature. He was returning to Venable as a partner, and I was going to take his place in Annapolis during the session. Although I had worked in the State House before, the legislature was not then in session, and committees in those days met in the basement of the State House, under the steam pipes sitting at ancient grade school desks complete with ink wells and a grooved slot for pencils. The School for the Blind had a concession stand nearby.

Herbert R. O'Conor, Jr., son of a former Governor and United States Senator, was Maryland's bank commissioner. He put me to work on a committee of lawyers and lenders preparing a revision of the Maryland Code regulating interest and other charges lenders could collect without running afoul of the usury laws.

My principal reason for coming to the State Law Department was to work with Dr. Paul Cooper, Director of the Fiscal Research Bureau, on a massive rewrite of Maryland's income tax laws. Tom took me to the trophy room on the first floor of the State House which served as the Attorney General's office when the legislature was in session, gave me a list of numbers I would need, told me where to get supplies and how to use the elevator. The room contained nothing but a desk, a chair and a telephone, but the walls were lined with glass cases filled with regimental colors captured by Maryland regiments as far back as the Revolution. The hall outside was buzzing with legislators, preening for the press and vying for camera time. We went to the second floor balcony in the House chamber to watch the leadership file in.

As people entered the room, Tom told me who they were, what they did, who I could trust and whom I should avoid. The leadership was led to the rostrum by Marvin Mandel, speaker of the House of Delegates and William James, president of the Senate, with both of whom I was already acquainted. Billy James was followed by a tall, handsome man with wavy black hair who seemed comfortable and at ease in his surroundings. I asked Tom,"Who's the guy with Billy James?"

"That's Harry Hughes. You're going to be working with him and Paul Cooper."

"Why is he on the rostrum with Billy and Marvin?"

"He's majority leader of the Senate, and he chairs the Senate Finance Committee."

Years later, Tom would refer to me as the man who invented Harry Hughes. In the ensuing weeks, I went to Annapolis almost every day. When the tourists invaded my office, as they often did, I took my work to a small room in the basement used by Dr. Cooper when the legislature was in session. I shared my idea for a total rewrite of the Maryland income tax law with Dr. Cooper. We were a good team, we could communicate quickly without needing to explain things to one another in detail, and the beginning of the thought was all either of us needed to see where it led.

In early March, my work was completed and Senator Hughes came into Paul's office and asked me if I knew where he could find Dr. Cooper. I said, "He just left to go to your office."

Harry's office was on the first floor of the Court of Appeals building, which was then to the right of the west front of the State House. Harry started to leave, turned around and said "You're Ed Blanton, aren't you?"

"Fraid so."

"Paul told me what a good job you did on this bill. It's important and I appreciate your work."

"It was the reason I came to the Attorney General's office. I wanted to play a part in reforming the state's tax laws."

Harry nodded, looked out the window as he started to leave, spun about and said, "It's going to snow tonight. Are you going to drive back to Baltimore?"

"If it gets too deep, I might stay here."

"I have an extra bed in my room if you can't find anything else. Any plans for dinner?"

"No."

"I'll come by when I'm ready to leave. We can talk about the bill. Answer my questions?"

"Sounds good."

After dinner Hank Cumberland, the state police sergeant assigned to Harry, drove us to a motel on Route 50, where other legislators were hosting the homeless as well. Harry's friends were in and out of the room until midnight, making sleep difficult, but five months later, we were law partners.

The State Law Department was on the twelfth floor and the Center Club was on the twenty-second floor of One Charles Center. Our office was on the twentieth floor. When I was not in Annapolis, I generally spent the entire day, from early morning until late evening, in that building. In Denton, Harry rented offices for us on the second floor of a colonial style bank building. Our firm in Denton was known as Hughes and Blanton. In Baltimore, we practiced under the name Manger, Maxwell, Hughes and Blanton. Assistant-attorneys-general were poorly paid, and we were allowed to have a private practice as long as it did not conflict with our official duties.

When Bob Murphy hired me he let me choose the agencies I wanted to represent. In addition to Fiscal Research, I picked the Bank Commissioner, the Department of Economic Development, the Commissioner of Loan Laws, the Maryland Industrial Development Financing Authority, the Secretary of State, the Baltimore City Elections Board, the Apple Commission, the State Tobacco Warehouse, and the State Board of Agriculture, which doubled as the Board of Trustees of the University of Maryland.

There were fourteen assistants in the Charles Center office, another at the DMV, two at the State Roads Commission, and another at the State Health Department. As the junior assistant, I approved, signed and sealed the bonds every state official had to post prior to assuming office, after checking each bond against a list of approved bonding companies. When I was working in Annapolis, they would pile up on my desk and I would have to return to Baltimore at least once a week to keep the wheels of state government turning. I also had to do my share of habeas corpus proceedings, post conviction proceedings, and criminal appeals reaching us in unprecedented numbers following the decision of the Supreme Court in *Miranda v. Arizona*.

There would be four or five such appeals on my desk every week, consisting of the transcript and the brief filed by the appellant. My job was to prepare the state's brief. The issues raised in these cases were rarely serious and the state's brief could be researched and dictated in less than two hours. The brief would be four, and on rare occasions, six pages long, consisting of the statement of the case, the issue, a summary of the facts, and the state's argument.

Briefs were printed and page proofs from the printer were edited and initialed. This put me in the Court of Appeals at least a dozen times a month, in addition to more complex briefs prepared on behalf of the agencies I represented, which raised important legal issues and required much more time to write. After 1966, the appeals in criminal cases went to the newly created Court of Special Appeals, an abomination that now manhandles civil cases as well.

Unlike his successors, Tom Finan had an ordinary car rather than a limousine assigned to him as Attorney General. The car was usually driven by a state trooper. When Tom was campaigning, assistants volunteered to drive as it was not appropriate for a state trooper to participate in political activity. In October of 1965 I was driving Tom to Annapolis to meet with Governor Tawes. He directed me through the wrought iron gate at the governor's mansion to park in a spot inside the gate. He suggested that if I had difficulty finding a parking space in Annapolis I should use that space. In Baltimore, I had a parking space on Water Street reserved for my car.

In the closing days of the session when I had to be in Annapolis daily, I drove my car through the gate and parked it near the Governor's mansion. One morning a state trooper assigned to the governor's detail followed me to the basement door of the State House and told me I had to move my car. As I ran back across the street, Governor Tawes stuck his head out the window and shouted, "He's okay. He's one of Tom's boys. He can park there."

I looked up and yelled "Thank you, Governor. I really appreciate it." I ran back across the street, as I was already late for my committee meeting. I was never asked to move again.

There was serious opposition to Harry's tax reform bill. Montgomery County, Prince George's County, and Baltimore County led the fight against it. As the larger and wealthier counties, they were suspicious of my motives and my drafting. Dr. Cooper and I spent a lot of time meeting with individual delegates to answer their questions and explain what we were doing.

I had an agenda of my own. As a young lawyer in Nick Shriver's office, I had to prepare a lot of tax returns for clients, including a federal return, a Maryland return and a Baltimore City return. Different laws governed each return. In Maryland earned income was taxed at three per cent. Investment income, however, was taxed at five percent. If the investment income was earned from a Maryland corporation only a percentage of the income received would be taxable on the Maryland return. These percentages often went to five decimal places, and required a lot of work in a world which had no computers and only rudimentary calculating machines.

Each associate did from fifteen to twenty sets of returns, the first step in receiving full responsibility for the wealthy gentry in the valleys of Baltimore County or the gated enclaves in the city where wealth kept a toehold. Returns were done in pencil, typed, the figures checked again after they were typed, and then presented to the clients for signature. Frequently, the client reviewing the completed return would find other deductions to be taken and sometimes other income that needed to be declared. The entire process had to be done a second time, and often a third time. Tax season for young lawyers was a nightmare. Baltimore is an old money town, and that is why there was no worthwhile tax practice there. It is too conservative, and nothing is done unless blessed in advance by lawyers and accountants.

In my world, paying taxes was bad enough. Having to compute them was even worse. I urged a scheme in which the adjusted gross income from the federal return would be reported to the State of Maryland. A few minor adjustments could be made and the state income tax applied uniformly to all income. Senator Hughes was in favor of a graduated income tax that was certainly consistent with the views of his party. I don't think he knew I was a Republican. He was agreeable to a "piggy-back" city and/or county tax limited to no more than fifty percent of the state tax.

When the reform measure actually passed the following year, the counties which led the opposition in the legislature were the very first to adopt a local income tax and quickly move it to the maximum allowed. In subsequent years they have gone back to the legislature to remove the cap imposed on local income taxes. Following the example set by Congress, the income tax has become an instrument of social policy and a means of rewarding campaign contributors. Almost every state in the Union that has an income tax eventually modeled their tax law after the pattern Maryland adopted in 1967.

Father Richard Lawrence and Delegate Thomas Hunter Lowe became my allies in the effort to rewrite the interest and usury laws. There was considerable opposition by the installment lenders, the small-loan law lenders, and the savings and loan industry, all of whom were opposed to tighter controls. My neighbor, Calvert Bregel, owned two S&L's, and he attended these meetings as a representative of the savings and loan industry.

I could never tell whether Herb O'Conor favored or opposed the bill we had prepared. It was a typical committee product making concessions to the lenders in an effort to get an acceptable bill. Senator Paul Dorf, political boss Jack Pollock's son-in-law, told me that I could count on his vote. The day the vote was to be taken, however, Paul pulled me aside and showed me a page from a notebook he kept in his pocket. He told me that the eleven names I saw there were the people who had contributed to his political campaign. Seven of those eleven people were opposed to my bill.

"You can't ask me to turn my back on the people who put me here, Ed?"

"No, Paul, I can't."

I appreciated the fact that he was forthright and I certainly could not fault his thinking. Paul later became a judge on the Circuit Court of Baltimore City, and he has continued to be a friend until his recent death. He left the bench to practice domestic relations law with a firm where I later spent four happy and professionally interesting years as a partner. I later referred domestic relations cases I could not reconcile to Paul for litigation.

On the night prior to the last night of the session, Harry asked me to go before the House Ways and Means Committee and respond to questions from delegates about the provisions of my rewrite of the Maryland income tax laws. Fortunately, Bob Murphy agreed to go with me. I don't think he knew much about the bill, but he knew the Attorney General wanted it passed. He was there to make sure I was not beat up too badly, and to put the committee on notice I was speaking for the current Governor and the man we both hoped would succeed him.

Our bill was important to the Maryland State Teacher's Association and their lobbyist, Robert Dubel, whose knowledge and ability I respected. I recommended him to the Attorney General as a campaign manager. I was unaware that he had already been selected, for Tom just smiled and said nothing when I made the suggestion and offered no cigar.

When I went to dinner that night, I jumped off the wall at the foot of the hill crowned by the State House, and ripped the seam of my pants. My trench coat saved me from an indecent exposure arrest. The House Ways and Means Committee convened just before midnight, after having been in session all day, sitting at our grammar school desks. The questions were led by Meyer Emmanuel, a delegate from Prince George's County, who was also a certified public accountant.

For eight straight hours, until breakfast the next morning, I sat in my ripped pants and trench coat responding to Delegate Emmanuel's questions. It was worse than a Ph.D oral examination in federal and state taxation. Harry later said I had won over most of the opponents, including Delegate Emmanuel and the entire

Prince George's delegation. This put our bill close to the majority needed to pass the House of Delegates.

My interest and usury bill was pending in the Senate and Harry's tax bill was pending in the House. I was working both sides of the hall, doing what I could to round up votes. Ronnie Schrieber, an aide to the governor, invited me to dinner. He had worked in the Attorney General's office and was familiar with Tom's habits. Whenever I asked Tom for something he could not give me, he would look at me, smile, and offer me a cigar, Tom's way of saying no.

When the check arrived, I reached to pick it up. Ronnie grabbed it and handed me a cigar. I knew what was coming. My interest and usury bill was dead, and Ron told me to forget it and devote my time exclusively to my tax bill. I had left Herb O'Conor in the balcony praying, whether for or against my success I did not know.

Ronnie said, "Ed, you're going to lose that bill in the Senate tonight. If Governor Tawes took you over to the State Treasury, opened it up and told you to take everything in it to buy votes, you would be out spent by the people who oppose you. So smoke your cigar, forget the Senate, and work your tax bill for all your worth."

He was right. The bill failed, and we had to work another year to get it right. To make matters worse I went into the House chamber with my cigar, one of the "b'hoys" as the *Sun*'s cartoonist Yardley used to call them, seeking votes for the Cooper-Hughes Tax Reform Bill. I was having some success rounding up doubtful votes and sending them upstairs to talk to Governor Tawes. Louise Gore, a delegate from Montgomery County who was fighting the bill, seized upon the smell of my cigar and asked the Sergeant-at-Arms to bar me from the chamber.

Assistant attorneys-general were allowed on the floor when the legislature was in session, because we were frequently advising and helping members of the House and Senate with their agenda, particularly if our clients were acting as point for them. Someone passed the word along to me and I dumped the cigar. Governor Tawes wanted to talk to Delegate Kemp McDaniel, who was under consideration for an appointment to the Circuit Court of Baltimore County. I went to Kemp's chair, touched him lightly on the arm, and said, "Kemp, Governor Tawes wants to see you upstairs right away." Kemp grabbed the arms of his chair, and said,

"I'm not going. He's going to threaten me with the loss of my robe if I don't vote for this bill."

"Want me to tell him you won't come?"

"You're damned right I do.

Knowing he meant it, I turned away and went to the next name on the list the Governor gave me. But the Sergeant-at-Arms caught up with me and told me that I had to leave, this time for good.

I went upstairs to the Governor's office. He was sitting, with the Speaker of the House, Marvin Mandel and Bob Murphy. There were two other people in the office I did not know. I told the Governor that Kemp refused to budge. The Governor laughed, said Kemp was going to be a great judge, and asked me how many votes we were short. We only needed two more. He was concerned that the effort we were putting on this bill was preventing some other important work from being considered which the legislature needed to finish before midnight. He asked me to talk to Senator Hughes.

I went back downstairs and nothing seemed to be going on in the Senate chamber, where I still had the run of the floor. I sat on a red leather sofa beside Harry's desk. I liked to watch him work. He made the arguments I would have made myself, using the same words I would have used. I hadn't liked anyone as much as I liked Harry since Doug Andrews died. Harry nodded but he was busy chanting bills into law, so I went to my office in the trophy room. It had been totally cleaned out. The only thing I had left was a small copy of the rule book governing legislative proceedings. At about 10:45 Harry sailed through the door.

"I've been looking at the rule book. The legislature adjourns sine die at midnight. In this state we can't stop the clock, and we can't turn it back. We have a lot of stuff that isn't finished. I've got to pull the tax bill."

"I'm afraid so. I've been looking at the rule book, too."

"We are in a bit of a jam. If we can't get this bill passed, and I don't see how we can, there are some things we must do before we adjourn. What a mess. This is going to make me look bad."

"How would you like a special session of the legislature convening tomorrow morning at ten to tie up loose ends?"

Harry looked at me as if I had taken leave of my sanity.

"You can do that?"

Trying to look nonchalant and suppressing a grin I said,"I can't, but Governor Tawes can. He has already told me that if you want it, he will sign a proclamation before we adjourn, calling the legislature back into special session tomorrow morning to do the housekeeping."

"I definitely want it." Harry broke into a broad grin, spun about, and strode out the door, looking as he always did like a tall ship under full sail.

I jumped off the desk and vaulted up the great marble staircase to the governor's office, doing three steps at a time, calling out "Okay, you've got it."

Rushing through the door into the dimly-lit governor's Office, I told him that Harry was agreeable to a special session. He said, "You prepare the proclamation, I'll sign it and 'Hot Dog' will seal it."

So one of the other men in the room was none other than "Hot Dog" Simpkins, the Secretary of State, a client of mine I had yet to meet. I now understood why he and Speaker Mandel were already there. They knew what was going to happen in the House, and they and the Governor were prepared for whatever needed to be done. I turned to Bob Murphy and asked if he had ever prepared a proclamation calling the legislature into special session.

"No, have you?"

"No" I laughed. "Can you type?"

"If I have to."

Never having seen a gubernatorial proclamation before, and not having time or knowing where to look one up, I drew upon my experience as a corporate lawyer to prepare something I thought appropriate. When the governor had first mentioned the prospect of a special session, I had reviewed the constitutional and statutory provisions which govern emergency sessions, and from memory, I began to dictate a series of whereas clauses which ended with a proclamation by the Governor calling the legislature back into session at ten the following morning.

With me talking as if I knew what I was doing and Bob typing, the proclamation was finished with several corrected typographical errors, and I placed it before the Governor and asked "Is this all right?"

The Governor shrugged. "Who cares? You two are my lawyers. Who else could I ask?"

Bob and I laughed as it was signed by the Governor and sealed by the Secretary of State. I rushed it downstairs to Harry who made arrangements to have it read to both houses before they adjourned at midnight.

My first tour of duty with the Maryland Legislature ended. Nothing important to me was on the agenda in the Special Session, as the incomplete matters were housekeeping and budgetary matters which needed patching up as a result of the failure of Cooper-Hughes. I returned to Baltimore to the more mundane aspects of my job.

As a student at Baltimore Polytechnic Institute, my history teacher, Arnold Silverman, had urged me to read Upton Sinclair's novel *The Jungle* and Winston Churchill's *Coniston,* a novel about politics in a New England state where railroads dictated policy and controlled state government. My boyhood interest in corruption in business and politics encouraged me to major in economics at Davidson and to pursue a master's degree at Vanderbilt. I found my job so exciting, however, that I could not wait to get up in the morning, hop in my Corvair and drive to Annapolis.

My first nine months in public service found me living the pages of a novel I had read as a boy. But the people around me and those with whom I worked were real, up-to-date, not made-up people. I doubted that my involvement in the political life of Maryland would ever be more exciting than the ninety days I spent in Annapolis in the winter of 1966. I was living a life portrayed on the pages of Churchill's novels.

"You know what? I have never been paged at a meeting in my life, and your call is the second time tonight it's happened. My life is getting very exciting all of a sudden."

Senator Harry R Hughes,
June, 1966

Accidental Celebrity

In the 1966 gubernatorial primary Tom Finan was opposed by Carlton Sickles, a liberal congressman from Prince George's County; George P. Mahoney, a populist paving contractor; and Clarence Miles, who had brought the St. Louis Browns to Baltimore as the Orioles in 1954. Mr. Mahoney's campaign slogan was "Your Home Is Your Castle" and it was widely believed to have racist overtones.

Although the attorney general had a state trooper assigned to him who often drove the automobile and provided security, the practice was discontinued during the political campaign, and I volunteered to drive Tom on campaign trips. My first trip was to a bank in Prince George's County, and although Tom insisted I go in with him, I was shy and said I would rather wait in the car. I didn't realize I had a fatal political disease —an inability to beg for money. The meeting lasted much longer than anticipated and Tom came out, grinned at me through the window and said, "These guys want to operate on brother Sickles with long knives. You better come in; I want you to hear this."

Our mission was two-fold: to gather campaign funds and to sort out possible allies in the upcoming primary. I think Tom wanted me there as a witness. It was fun sitting at the table with him, and even more fun to participate in the discussion. We succeeded on both points. Peter O'Malley was going to back Tom in Carlton's home county. My optimism grew, because I liked Peter immediately. He was one tough guy.

Having drafted a Maryland version of the Corrupt Practices Act enacted in the 1966 session that took effect on July 1, 1966, I was responsible for compliance, specifically on the part of our campaign but the state as a whole as counsel to the Secretary of State. The law required every campaign to appoint a treasurer and file either with the Secretary of State if the candidate was running statewide or the Board of Elections Supervisors if the campaign was limited to a single county. Campaign contributions were limited to $2,500, corporate contributions were permitted, and the name, address and occupation of every contributor who gave more than fifty dollars must be reported on specified dates to the filing office. All contributions had to be payable to the campaign treasurer.

As the campaign swung into full gear, Bob Murphy and Bob Sweeney spent much of their free time on the campaign. The campaign headquarters was located in a storefront on Baltimore Street. Bob Dubel was the campaign manager, I had his trust and whenever I chose to go, I was welcome in the campaign headquarters. The first evening I was there Bob Murphy pointed out a bleached blond, petulant supporter, and said, "See that guy there. Keep your eye on him."

"Why?"

"He came into the office the other day with a shoebox full of cash he wanted to contribute to the campaign. He's going to get us in trouble. Tom likes him. He worries me."

"Who is he?"

"His name is Charles Flanders. He runs the United Service Bureau."

"What's that?"

"They do investigative credit reports for mortgage lenders."

I sized the guy up, decided I did not like him either, and I would do what I could to make sure he caused us no trouble.

A couple of months later, just before the primary, Charlie came into the State Law Department office complaining about a proposal in the "blue book" that was going to put him out of business. The blue book is a collection of advance bills ready to be introduced at the legislative session. Bob Murphy looked at him, smiled and said,

"Couldn't happen to a nicer guy"

Bob was usually serious but he had a great sense of humor, often making me laugh, so I turned away to hide my glee. Had I known then what I know now what the failure to do mortgage credit reports right would do to our country in 2007 I would have torn my clothes and sat in sack cloth and ashes.

As the filing deadline approached in early July, I asked Harry if he had any interest in being Comptroller. I knew Louie Goldstein, the most astute politician I had ever seen until Bill Clinton and Martin O'Malley came along, was technically on our ticket but he was actually backing George P. Mahoney. I wanted a comptroller candidate of our own. I had helped Hardin Marion, one of my forward observes in the National Guard, organize precincts in Northwood for Joe Tydings when he ran against Louie in 1962 for the Senate. I did not then know Louie well.

Having analyzed the votes in the 1962 campaign, my political instinct told me that Tom, being from Western Maryland, would not do well on the Eastern Shore and Northeast Maryland. I was looking for a way to gain support in those areas, and I invited Billy James, who was already running for Attorney General to meet with me and Harry in my private law office to see if there was a possibility either might run with Tom.

Being more cautious than I, they did not think the idea had any traction. I took my concern to Tom. He said Harry, Danny Brewster and Mac Mathias, the Republican congressman from Western Maryland, had been friends since law school. Their three families vacationed together when they were young sharing the same cottage in Rehoboth. He was sure Harry would not run against Senator Brewster in the Democrat primary in 1968.

I thought Danny was "dead in the water" as a result of recent bad press. I had talked to Harry about his future plans. He knew Mac's plans. He was definitely interested in running for the U.S. Senate. Mac was planning to challenge Danny in the general in 1968, believing that if Danny couldn't keep the job, they should at least keep it in their group. Harry felt the same way. If Harry and Mac ran against each other in the 1968 general, it was a still a "win-win' for the three of them.

Harry knew he could not beat Louie Goldstein, but his tax reform bill would put him in good stead as a candidate for comptroller. It would help Tom in the primary. I told Tom if we promised to back Harry in the Democrat primary against Senator Brewster in 1968, Harry would run with us. Harry was plainly bored where he was, and his most constant comment to me was that for him it was either "up or out."

Tom asked me to set up a luncheon meeting at the Center Club with Harry. Harry's wife, Pat, gave me a telephone number of a hall in Prince George's County where Harry was attending a political event. I called and asked the sponsors to tell Harry that he had an urgent telephone call. When Harry picked up the phone, he said, "You know what? I have never been paged at a meeting in my life, and your call is the second time tonight that it has happened. My life is getting very exciting all of a sudden."

"It's going to get more exciting yet. Tom is on board and wants you to meet us for lunch at noon tomorrow at the Center Club."

"I'll be there."

Before Tom returned to the office the next morning, I had a telephone call from Blake H. McFeely, who was then working for the Gulf Oil Company in Pittsburgh. He was in Baltimore on family matters and wanted to see me. I asked him to meet me in the coffee shop downstairs. That would still leave me time to meet Harry and Tom at noon.

Blake wanted to associate with me as a tax lawyer and look after my growing private practice while I was in the attorney general's office. As a result, my quick meeting with Blake lasted longer than I expected it to and when I went back upstairs, Tom and Harry had gone to lunch without me. Neither broached the subject they were there to discuss. They had a polite lunch, said goodbye and nothing much happened, both giving me the same explanation. I continued to press the point telling Tom that Harry was completely on board and telling Harry that Tom, at least, was interested.

How different things might have been if I had not missed that lunch, not only for Maryland but America as well. So much hinges on small, seemingly innocuous decisions which have implications, not only for the people involved but, for all of us on the planet far into the future. If Tom had won that primary, there may never have been a Governor Agnew or a President Gerald Ford or a President Jimmy Carter. There might have been a President Hughes.

We also needed a candidate for attorney general. On a Monday morning in June, Herb O'Conor came into my office and asked if I had watched a television program the night before. I told him I had. He asked me what single fact stood out most prominently. I replied that eighty percent of the people in Maryland were in favor of school prayer. He asked me if I knew who in Maryland was most closely identified with school prayer. I said, "The City Solicitor, Bill Burch.

"Exactly, my friend. Would you help me move something along?"

"What do you want to move?"

"Putting Bill Burch on Tom's ticket as candidate for attorney general."

"How can I do that?"

Herb was going to call Charlie Whiteford, the political reporter for the Sun Papers. I had run into Charlie in Annapolis and Tom Lowe, who had been working with me hand-in-glove on the interest and usury bill in the previous session, had told me Charlie was the most powerful lobbyist in Annapolis. Surprised, because he was a reporter, I asked Tommy if he got paid for what he did. Tom hit me with his patented look of disgust and said "What do you think?" I took that as a "Yes."

Herb explained that, for whatever reasons, Charlie did not trust him, but he did trust me. I had friends among the editorial staff of the Sun Papers in those days, including the publisher I often met at social events with my wife. The filing deadline was less than a week away and I thought a story in the newspaper about Bill Burch, whether or not it was accurate, would at least motivate Tom and the "Irish Mafia" to get something done.

Herb returned to his office on the same floor as the State Law Department and placed a conference call. Herb told Charlie that we had a scoop for him. Tom Finan was going to name Bill Burch as his candidate for attorney general. Charlie asked me if that is the truth or is this just another of Herb's Machiavellian machinations. I crossed my fingers and said, "The decision's been made. The poll of Maryland voters last night clinched it." I did not know whether or not Bill Burch had even been considered, but I was comfortable in saying the decision had been made because I knew that if it were not Bill Burch, it had to be somebody. Charlie ran the story and I suspect Herb let the cat out of the bag. After all, Bob Sweeney was his law partner.

The next time I went down the hall to the Tom's office, Murphy and Sweeney cornered me and wanted to know what part I had played in the fiasco. I quickly confessed. I told them that we were running out of time, they had not been quick in making a decision, and I decided to make it for them. Tom just looked at me, grinned as he always did, and eventually decided that Bill Burch would be his running mate. At the time, I had never met Bill Burch.

In early August, I began working on the campaign report, spending more time at night in the campaign office on Baltimore Street, collecting the information I would need. As Harry and Tom had never gotten together, we were running what we portrayed as a "Finan, Burch and Goldstein" ticket. I had to interview Louie Goldstein to find out what the state of his campaign was. It was extremely interesting.

Louie pulled some papers from his pocket and told me that he had contributed no money to the campaign himself. "If I am going to give my life to public service, somebody else will have to pay the bills."

The only expenditures he had were mileage on his automobile for which he sought reimbursement. In any event, the mileage expenses were the only things to be claimed and there were no contributions. I took this information back and incorporated it in my report. What a better world we would have if politics were that simple today. We would sure have better government.

I could not pinpoint the origin of a number of checks in the amount of $2,500 for which we had nothing but a name. I asked "the three Bobs" who these people were. At the beginning of the campaign they had agreed not to talk to any political bosses. Most of our money was being raised by the president of United Iron and Metal, a Mr. Levinson, whose son Steve was working hard as a volunteer in the campaign. Steve had just hosted a swimming party for the young volunteers at my house in Glen Arm that very afternoon.

Mr. Levinson told me that the checks, about which I had no information, had come from George Hocker and no one, including him, was going to talk to Hocker, who was a political boss and controlled what was left of the Pollock machine in West Baltimore.

"I didn't take an oath not to talk to George Hocker. Give me his phone number. I'll get the information we need to file on time."

I had never met George Hocker but he was glad to hear from me. We immediately became warm friends and after we met, he always greeted me with a hug every time we ran into each other. I suspected it was because I was the only one from the campaign who publicly acknowledged and thanked him for his help.

Most of the contributors were brewery executives from out of the state. George told them that, if they would contribute to Tom's campaign, he could guarantee no increase in the beer tax in Maryland during the time Tom was in office. The joke, of course, was that the union dominated, Democrat controlled Maryland Legislature, no matter what else it might tax, would never increase the tax on beer. No longer is that true in a state run by Martin O'Malley. But it was true then. George made his assurances in good faith and the money rolled in. I got every name, address, and occupation I needed.

The next week there was a political event at the Village of Cross Keys. Afterward, Bob Murphy made a speech to all of the assistants present at the event and told us that we had to behave ourselves from then until the campaign was over. We had to be careful where we went, what we said, and none of us were to be caught by the police or anyone else "pissing in the street." That did not seem like too much to ask, and there was a lot of sentiment for continuing the party at some safe and out of the way, non-public place.

My wife had taken our three children to our farm in North Carolina, which she often did prior to our traditional end of the summer vacation on the outer banks. The safest place was my house, so we formed a caravan and five or six cars followed me home. We turned on the flood lights at the pool and set up a bar in the kitchen.

My bar closet is esoteric, perhaps exotic, and my co-workers clearly approved. While sitting in my kitchen in a swim suit, Bob told me about Tom intervening on my behalf in 1965 when Nick Shriver sent me over for an interview. Bob decided then and there to put me in charge of the office bar kept locked in a cabinet in Tom's office. We each contributed a few bucks each month, and my job was to keep the cabinet full. My undeserved reputation as a connoisseur of fine wines and exotic drink are traceable to that erroneous entry in my military 201 file back in 1954.

As the campaign heated up, Tom occasionally asked me to fill in for him at speaking engagements when he had a conflict. From other work I was doing for the Commissioner of Loan Laws, I was getting a lot of face time on television. I attended one at the East Wind when Tom was away to make some remarks on his behalf from the head table. Herb O'Conor was part of the receiving line, and he introduced me to Bill Burch.

As soon as he heard my name, Bill grabbed me by the lapels of my suit, and swinging me around, he demanded to know if I was 'the little s.o.b that told Louie Goldstein the comptroller was more important than the attorney general'. My head hit the stone wall in the entry way. I bleed easily, and I touched the back of my head and found blood on my hand. Showing Bill the bloody hand of Ulster, I said,

"I haven't said anything to Louie. I wrote an opinion advising the City elections board that the comptroller's office will appear on the ballot before the office for attorney general. The rule is that the offices appear on the ballot in the order in which they appear in the Constitution. We had an elected comptroller in Maryland long before we had an elected attorney general. The practice of electing attorney generals was fairly recent." I should have added "and ill-advised."

"Why do they call it the 'Finan, Burch and Goldstein' ticket then?"

"Because we only have a candidate for governor and attorney general. Louie's running with Mahoney."

I bit my lip, glanced at Herb and shook my head in disgust as I walked inside. That was the high point of my relationship with Bill. His brother, Claude, was married to a close friend of my wife, and we were social friends and had been for years. After a stint in the wash room to clean up the blood, I sat between the master of ceremonies and the Mayor of Baltimore, Thomas D'Alessandro, III, whose father had been Mayor when I was a child.

My father was once mistaken for the elder mayor when my parents were on a train returning to Baltimore from the Army-Navy game in Philadelphia. I had not seen Tommy since we were teen-agers. His sister Nancy and my sister Faye did not get along, but Tommy was far and away head and shoulders above his troubled siblings, including Nancy, who moved all the way to San Francisco to escape her past.

All evening long, I fought hard not to laugh aloud. No matter what the politician speaking started to say, Tommy would quickly finish his sentence with an inane conclusion but which so completely captured and exposed the speaker and his particular line of blarney, it was hilarious. Tommy was making his comments behind his program so the audience could not see that he was talking. It was a great way to make a bad gig enjoyable, and I hid behind my program so no one would see me laughing, pretending to study my notes.

The summer had been a busy one for me. Tom had given me a file pertaining to John Dallam, the Deputy Commissioner of Loan Laws who was one of my clients. Allegations had been made against Mr. Dallam which, if true, would necessitate his removal from office. I reviewed the file and found no credible evidence in it. In fact, most of the written information in the file was rank hearsay and appeared to have been accumulated during a former investigation which found the charges without foundation. I told Tom there was nothing in the file which worried me, and nothing admissible in a court of law.

I suspected the issue was raised anew because I was helping John with a problem reported to him by the Baltimore City Police Department, and the guilty wanted Tom to persuade me to back off. Used car dealers had borrowed money at high rates of interest they were unable to pay if they conducted business honestly. They advertised used cars for sale for twenty dollars a month, sending buyers to borrow the down payment from small loan companies licensed by Mr. Dallam's department, who could lend up to three hundred dollars at interest rates of forty-two percent per annum with monthly payments of about twenty dollars.

After the buyer signed for the down payment, believing it was the full price of the car, he unknowingly signed a blank retail installment sales contract, which would be completed later by the car dealer. At the end of the first month, the borrower would pay the twenty dollar monthly payment to the small loan company. Shortly thereafter he would receive the completed retail installment sales contract by mail obligating him to pay four or five times that amount monthly to the company that purchased the installment sales contract.

When the victim was unable to pay the dealer would repossess the car and sell it again under similar arrangements. The automobile dealers made kick-backs to loan company employees of twenty-five to fifty dollars per transaction for their help. The hapless borrower would find himself without a car, fully obligated on the small loan as well as a deficiency judgment for more than a thousand dollars in favor of the holder of the installment sale agreement.

This was explained to me by Mr. Dallam, Sergeant Scroggs who had investigated the facts, and Scott Kendall Gibson, an employee in Mr. Dallam's department. They asked me what I could do about it. I pulled the Maryland Code from the shelf, searched around in the index for a few minutes, and advised them to schedule a series of hearings, subpoena witnesses, take their testimony, and if the law had been violated, Mr. Dallam, as the hearing officer, could void the loan. We might also talk to Herb O'Conor, the Bank Commissioner, to void the installment loan. I was glad he was also one on my clients.

The hearings greatly embarrassed the automobile dealers. More importantly, we publicized what was going on in order to provide some protection to the public. The hearings were convened in a conference room at the State Office Building at 301 West Preston Street set up to look like a court room. The Commissioner of Loan Laws had subpoena power, and Mr. Gibson subpoenaed the small loan companies, the retail installment dealers and the used car companies. He also organized the evidence and gave it to me, sitting beside me at counsel table.

Scott was an intelligent guy, and at the end of the first day's hearings we had become friends. My high opinion of him was clinched when he asked me if I had ever heard of a star chamber proceeding. I said I had not only heard of them, I think I have just been a party to one. He later asked me to be godfather to his four children when they were confirmed in the Episcopal Church, a responsibility I happily accepted.

The documents and the witnesses easily proved the allegations made by Sgt. Scroggs and the fraud unit in the Baltimore City Police Department. Mr. Dallam presided over the hearings and I, under Scott's tutelage, produced the evidence. The respondents were represented by counsel and a court reporter recorded the proceedings, as required by the statute. The press was present and our activity received a lot of publicity, not only in the newspapers, but on the local radio and television stations as well.

It was humiliating to see my face on the nightly news, and even worse to hear my voice. But the secretarial staff in the State Law Department thought it was great fun. They teased me unmercifully, insisting they went to sleep nightly with my baritone voice resonating in their ears.

To make matters worse, people I did not know were convinced they knew me, and were often offended when I didn't recognize them. That took some getting used to and I do not think I ever have. Recipients of their fifteen allotted minutes of fame know how precious anonymity is. It had annoyed me when I was with my cousin Charlie or my clients who played for the Colts or Orioles and strangers interrupted our time together to get autographs. The only time my cousin and I could really talk was when we were working on or sailing the *Pagaille* in the middle of the Chesapeake Bay.

Because of my schedule, the hearings would run for a week, we would take a few weeks off to develop further leads, gather more evidence and schedule more hearings. The press began to refer to us as the "off-again-on-again used car investigation." Hearings began in the summer and continued into the fall. Some of the loan companies had appealed our actions under the Administrative Procedure Act to the Superior Court of Baltimore City. It was too late, however, to help the used car dealers. Eleven of the twelve were put out of business by our probe's publicity. Dragging out the investigation was the only way to inform and protect the public.

The loan companies had me followed by a private detective, hoping to find character defects or behavior they could use to blackmail me. Having found nothing, it was suggested that they either entrap me or make accusations I could not refute, falling back on the impossibility of being able to prove a negative. Translated, there was no way I could prove I was not gay or anti-Semitic if they spread either accusation abroad. Rose Shanis, a lady with a heart, rose to my defense and warned them if they dared do such a thing, she would expose them. I didn't know that until years later, when my law firm represented her. Angels come in all shapes, faiths and sizes.

"Seated somewhere in this room is a future attorney general of Maryland—perhaps a governor—and most certainly several judges of the Court of Appeals."

Attorney General Thomas B Finan,
October, 1966

The 1966 Primary Election

During July and August, I took on additional duties that normally would have been performed by Bob Murphy or Bob Sweeney. Television and newspaper coverage of the used car hearings gave me a high profile, and state agencies I did not represent, called me for advice. Because of the unsettled state of leadership—a lame duck governor and uncertainty as to who the next governor would be—political appointees were reluctant to make policy decisions, casting them as legal question so they could ask for advice.

Written opinions had to be countersigned by the attorney general, but there were times when I thought I was single-handedly pressing the buttons and pulling the levers that kept the state government machinery operating.

This did not sit well with Bill Burch. I heard that he had said that the first thing he was going to do when he was sworn in was to "gag that little smart ass." Tom Finan had never objected to what I was doing and, in fact, seemed to be amused by it. He told me not to worry, for he had made it a condition of Bill's acceptance on his ticket that Bill could not, without Tom's permission, fire any of the assistants hired by Tom. That, as I had just found out, meant only me.

Leonard A. A. Siems, chairman of the newly formed Maryland Industrial Development Financing Authority, was one of my clients. Because of a delay in appointing the chairman and members of the board, the agency had never been activated. It had taken offices, however, in the Maryland National Bank Building at 10 Light Street using furniture made in the prison system. MIDFA had been working on a project that required legal assistance.

The law permitted a county or local development company in conjunction with MIDFA to provide loans for the purchase of land and buildings for new industry. We could not move an industry from one county to another, but we could provide financing to bring new industry into the state. Dr. Robert M. Sparks briefed me on just how the project was going to work, giving me documents that had been used by a similar authority in Rhode Island.

I adapted them for use in Maryland, preparing applications, approval procedures, and legal documents that permitted a borrower to take out two loans on his project—one from a bank which would be insured by the State of Maryland for ninety percent of the total cost of land and buildings, and the remainder from the county or local development company which sponsored the project.

John Lutkemeyer, the State Treasurer, sat with Governor Tawes and Louie Goldstein on the Board of Public Works, which approves and signs all state contracts. He was a central figure in The Equitable Trust Company, a state banking institution then located in Baltimore. His son was the Treasurer of Baltimore City. All State and City bank accounts were in that bank. He was on MIDFA's board as well.

At about that time, Frank Allen, Esquire, of the law firm Piper and Marbury, on behalf of the Savings Bank of Baltimore requested an opinion from the bank commissioner authorizing it to have checking accounts. An opinion I wrote was approved by the Attorney General, authorizing savings banks to allow withdrawals from savings accounts by check, but denying them the right to have checking accounts. They could not convert all of their savings accounts into checking accounts, which would have greatly increased the volume of money they could create by making loans based on Federal Reserve requirements.

The Federal Reserve System treated time deposits and demand deposits in banks differently in regulating the money supply. All deposits in a savings bank were considered time deposits. My father-in-law had guided a bank safely through the depression, and mucking around with the alchemy which creates money out of thin air was anathema to me. The Savings Bank of Baltimore appealed to the courts in Baltimore City which necessitated a trial.

Equitable Trust retained Dick Emory to support my position. He found and prepped an expert witness to testify, handing me pages written in longhand on yellow foolscap to guide my examination at the trial. The courtroom quickly filled with spectators, and I asked a young lady sitting behind me with Mr. Lutkemeyer's son what her interest in the case was.

"Are you kidding? This is the establishment versus the establishment. I'm dying to find out how you people behave when you are fighting over big bucks."

Bob Murphy warned me when he read the opinion that Mr. Gray is going to 'come over here and stare at you'. I asked if it would hurt, and Bob said he didn't know, because he did his best to avoid antagonizing him. I don't remember how the matter was decided in the lower court, but I briefed and argued the case in the Maryland Court of Appeals.

The decision added little to what I had said and greatly confused the press. A reporter working on the case called me to find out who won. The Court of Appeals had said quite clearly that savings banks could not have checking accounts, but agreed with us that they may permit depositors to withdraw from their savings accounts by check, which is what we thought they could do.

The difference, which only monetary experts recognize, is that checking accounts are demand deposits and savings accounts are time deposits, subject to different multipliers when the bank computes its reserve requirements. It was reporter ignorance and editorial ineptitude, a malign condition in a world populated by a predominance of public college English majors with little knowledge of economics. The headline read that savings banks could have checking accounts and it was the headline, and not the words in the court's opinion, that mattered. That's what happens when knowledgeable lawyers are extinct.

I expect it was just one of many cases that were decided by the press instead of the courts, and the Savings Bank not only had checking accounts, but eventually became a full fledged bank. The Savings Bank, like all the others then in existence in Baltimore, have disappeared in the vacuum cleaner of mergers and acquisitions. It was then I first began to suspect that the rule of law was in jeopardy. And the rule of law is the only thing that keeps our republic viable. It is no accident that the most stable democracies on our planet are those where the English common law sank deep roots. Without law there is no justice and when there is no justice there is no social stability.

The failure of the Court of Appeals to clarify the issues motivated the mutual savings banks in Maryland to convert into full-fledged banks. I was asked for an opinion as to how that could be done. Their accumulated and undistributed earnings, since inception, belonged to their depositors; admittedly a group that changed over the decades but only the current depositors had legally enforceable claims. The savings banks should be capitalized on that basis, issuing stock to their current depositors for their pro-rata share of the accumulated capital surplus, before issuing any new stock.

That is what they did, and later mutual insurance companies took the same path, as the managerial class in America moved to appropriate to themselves stockholder wealth, running corporations solely for the benefit of management and directors and treating stockholders as a nuisance they had to endure but once a year. They could, and do, shut off the microphones if the protests get out of hand. That, too, will foment discontent in time.

Chief Justice Warren wrote a letter to Attorney General Finan requesting the State of Maryland respond to a petition for certiorari in which a prisoner contended that his appeal to the Maryland Court of Appeals had been dismissed because he had not provided a printed brief. Tom gave me the letter to prepare a response. I checked the Maryland Rules, the code, and Alexander's British Statutes, a compilation of English statutes enacted between 1189 and 1776 never repealed by the Maryland Legislature. I found a provision dating from the thirteenth century requiring the court clerk to provide assistance to poor persons in preparing their papers and filing them in court.

A law student from Vermont was drinking in a Baltimore pub with some of his friends. His wife was with him. Someone in the bar insulted her. The law student slugged the troublemaker, and the miscreant hit his head on a brass rail and died. The law student was charged with manslaughter and convicted. While in prison, his ungrateful wife sued him for divorce. He responded to the divorce petition with a letter to the clerk. The clerk failed to docket his letter as a response and a decree *pro confesso* ending the marriage was issued by the court.

The student's appeal was dismissed because his brief was not printed as required by the rules. If you entered law school after 1960, you need to know that in equity cases, a decree *pro confesso* is a default judgment. The law student filed a petition for certiorari in the Supreme Court, and it was to that petition that the Court asked us to respond. Because the Supreme Court had just decided *Gideon v. Wainwright*, which obligated states to provide counsel at no charge to criminal defendants, Tom feared that the Court might also require the state to provide, at its expense, counsel for, at the very least, prisoners in civil matters, or even worse, for all indigent civil litigants no matter their status.

In the response I pointed out that the ancient British statutes in force at the time of the Declaration of Independence remained in full force in Maryland unless repealed by the Maryland Legislature. The statute authorizing poor litigants to seek help from the clerks of court in preparing their pleadings had not been availed of by the litigant. He also had a cause of action under the Maryland Rules which permitted him to have the order set aside on the grounds of fraud, mistake or irregularity. Since he had not exhausted his various avenues of relief, it was inappropriate for the Supreme Court to grant certiorari in his case.

Several weeks later, Tom called me into his office and gave me a copy of a letter he had received from the Chief Justice thanking him for his assistance in disposing of a troublesome matter. As luck would have it, the wife in that case was represented by a friend of mine who called me a few days later to ask me whether or not his client was, in fact, divorced. I told him I did not know, and that would depend, I believe, upon whether or not the law student took any further steps to have the decree set aside.

I also had to contend with a number of cases involving the election laws that summer, most of which had to be decided prior to the filing deadline in early July. The Supreme Court decision in *Baker v Carr* mandated extensive legislative reapportionment. Some of the legislative districts had not been established for six months prior to the election. This made it difficult for candidates to meet the residence requirement in the district they wanted to represent.

The late Clarence Blount was running for the state Senate. Another involved St. George Crosse, a recent immigrant from the Caribbean who was not a citizen of the United States. He was still in law school and brought his case pro se. Another pro se litigant was a political gadfly named Melvin Perkins, who single handedly was responsible for a decision in the United States Supreme Court upholding the Constitutional language that a representative in Congress did not have to live in the district he or she represented.

Melvin was a brilliant street person who lacked formal education. He was, however, a formidable adversary. The Baltimore City Election Board declined to put him on the ballot because he had not paid the filing fee. He contended that, as a pauper, he should not have to pay a filing fee in order to run. This followed other precedents that permitted *in forma pauperis* proceedings in court without paying filing fees.

I had a three-day trial in the Circuit Court of Baltimore City before Judge James A Perrott in Melvin Perkins's case. The testimony was hilarious. Melvin had numerous explanations as to why he had not shown up at the elections board with the filing fee. He was supposed to meet someone at a nightclub on Baltimore's block, the local version of New Orleans French Quarter, known as the "Pink Pussycat" who was to lend him the money. Because of an altercation to which Melvin was prone, he had been late, his friend had left, and he did not get the money in time to get it to the clerk at the elections board.

At trial, Melvin arrived with his legal documents in a shopping bag. On the second day of trial I returned to the courtroom to find the shopping bag in my chair. I wanted to review my notes, and as I was picking up the bag to put it in Melvin's chair, he entered the courtroom and accused me of rifling his "brief case," grabbed me, twisting my left arm behind my back. At that moment, Judge Perrott entered the courtroom. As I was already standing, I began the proceedings by saying

"Your Honor, will you order the plaintiff to release defendant's counsel?"

Judge Perrott banged his gavel on his desk and said, "Mr.Perkins, you release Mr. Blanton right now or I will call the bailiff."

Melvin, after venting his rage at my lack of professionalism, let go and we continued with the trial. He had subpoenaed a prominent columnist from the Baltimore News Post who had written about his doubts about Melvin's mental status. Over my objection, Melvin asked the columnist whether he could prove that he, the columnist, was sane. The columnist responded by asking Melvin "Can you?"

Melvin produced his discharge from a state mental institution and offered it into evidence as proof of his sanity. I objected because sanity was not an issue. Melvin pointed out to the Court that the reporter, not being able to provide a similar paper, could not prove his competence and asked to have the reporter's testimony stricken. Since the reporter was Melvin's witness, I did not oppose the request.

Another election case I won was immediately appealed by a young lawyer who thereafter expressed his complaint to the presiding judge in chambers. The clerk called me and said the judge wanted to see me in chambers at 1:15. I told the clerk I would attend on one condition: all parties had to be present and a court reporter set up, ready to record every word uttered from the moment I entered the office. As soon as I walked into chambers, I asked the court if my opponent had talked to him without my being present, and the judge said he had. I reminded both of them that ex parte communications are prohibited, but I was not going to make an issue about it because the appeal had already been filed and the lower court no longer had any jurisdiction. So that was the end of it. Chagrined, the plaintiff's lawyer dismissed his appeal.

The other cases were rushed to the Court of Appeals because of the pending election, so I had briefs to prepare. As I had lost three of the six cases, I had to prepare a record extract as well. When I complained, Bob Sweeney was incredulous.

"What are you talking about? It could have been much worse. You could have lost all six cases. You're the only one who ever won a case for those guys."

That made me feel better, although St. George Crosse has never let me forget that when he was a fledgling law student, he won a case against the Attorney General in the Maryland Court of Appeals. In his case, the court decided that you did not need to be a citizen of the United States to be a citizen of Maryland, and that Mr. Crosse could stand for election. My performance endeared me, I believe, to the members of the Baltimore City Election Board because they called me frequently on primary day to fill me in on what was happening.

On Monday night before the primary election the next day my wife and I invited Pat and Harry to be our guests at the Baltimore's Opera's production of Puccini's *La Bohême*. Harry seemed fairly bored during the first act but *Sun* reporters who saw us in the lobby during intermission were incredulous. Harry brightened considerably when Musetta came on stage in the second act. He called me at home on Tuesday night, apologizing for having done so poorly, losing by ten thousand votes. I knew the people on the northern shore could not find anyone better than Harry to represent them, so I knew something had gone terribly wrong. Horrified, I urged Harry not to concede.

"We're going to ask for a recount. I guess I should have let you campaign last night instead of dragging you and Pat to Baltimore."

"Wait a minute. I might have made a mistake. Yeah, I did. I forgot to carry that two over. Looks like I won by ten thousand instead of losing by ten thousand."

"Harry, don't ever do that again. I almost had a heart attack."

The State Law Department office calendar read "Deo Gratias" on primary day in 1966 and nothing else. Herb O'Conor came into my office shortly after noon and asked me what I had heard. I told him there was extremely heavy voting in eastern Baltimore City spilling over into eastern Baltimore County.

"This, my friend, is not good news." He immediately went down the hall to relay this information to the Bobs, and to the Attorney General who had finished his campaigning and, like all the rest of us, was waiting patiently to find out what the electorate decided.

We had failed in our attempts to persuade Bob Karwacki, a former assistant attorney general who was running Clarence Miles' campaign, to withdraw in favor of Tom. This split the conservative, establishment Democrat voters who should have been united behind Tom. As a result, when the votes were counted, there was a dead heat between Congressman Sickles, Attorney General Finan, and George P. Mahoney. Each of them had about 30% of the vote and Mr. Miles had about ten percent.

The results were essentially in by eleven, with the exception of three districts in eastern Baltimore County. The television stations continued to monitor the situation and all we knew was that there was wild jubilation in the headquarters of George P. Mahoney. They apparently knew something the rest of us did not.

At approximately four in the morning, the long awaited results in eastern Baltimore County arrived at the Baltimore County Elections Board, and George P. Mahoney won the democratic primary. I had no authority over the Baltimore

County Elections Board, although the County Solicitors often called me because I represented the Baltimore City Board and they were striving for uniformity across the state. The Republican member of the Baltimore county board delivered the results from those districts to my office.

After examining the results I noted that five thousand people in the Sixth district had voted only for governor and no one else. Another five thousand in the Seventh district had voted only for governor. Three thousand had gone into the polling places in the Eighth District and voted only for governor. Suspecting these votes had been cranked on the voting machines after the polls closed because that is what Mr. Mahoney needed to win, I relayed these facts to Tom and urged him to have the state police seize the machines. He refused, not wanting to look like a sore loser.

When I worked in Nick Shriver's office we were counsel to the Maryland Republican Party. The voting machines were the property of an amusement machine company, rented to Baltimore County, set up and maintained by the employees of the amusement company. The machines were also rented out from time to time to labor organizations, such as the Teamsters and steel workers, for their elections.

While participating in a recount of a Congressional race in 1962, a representative from the voting machine company pulled me aside and briefed me on the mistakes I was making. He told me that it was absolutely essential that the machines be sealed. It was also essential that the seal number on the return and the seal number on the machine be identical. I had run into instances where the seal was broken. I had also run into instances where the numbers varied slightly. He explained that the oldest trick in the book was to set aside seals with similar numbers so that clerical error could be blamed for the mismatch of numbers on machines that had been tampered with.

"You should challenge the vote on the entire machine when that happens. If the seals are broken, or if the seal numbers don't match, you have no assurance that the machine actually reflects the vote of the people. The system requires verification before the vote begins and after the vote is completed. Any departure from the safeguards mandated by law is grounds for suspicion if not outright disqualification of the results on that machine."

He showed me how do disengage the public counter so votes could be added to a candidate, or votes could be taken from one candidate and given to another before the first vote is even cast. What I had learned then, I put into practice when I rewrote the handbook for election judges in 1966. Does it make you feel better to know that we now use computers instead of these machines, and the employees in charge are members of the SEIU, the modern equivalent of the brown shirts who supervised the election of Adolph Hitler as Germany's Chancellor in 1933?

Charlie Flanders took Tom and his wife to Puerto Rico later that morning. When he returned, Governor Tawes appointed Tom to the Court of Appeals, and Bob Murphy served briefly as Attorney General while we waited for December and the swearing in of Bill Burch as his successor.

We had a farewell party for Tom at the Emerson Hotel, and as he bade us goodnight, he urged us not to despair. "Seated somewhere in this room is a future attorney general of Maryland—perhaps a governor—and most certainly several judges of the Court of Appeals."

At least he got the last part right, although I tried three times to make one of the first two predictions come true. Bob Karwacki was there, and he passed my table as he was leaving. I stood up, grabbed his hand and said, "Bob. I just wanted to thank you."

Puzzled, he asked, "For what?"

Suppressing a malevolent grin, I said "Without you this whole evening would not have been possible."

Standing at my side, Bob Sweeney whooped with delight. "Why didn't I think of that? I wish I had said that." He slapped me on the back. I had never been comfortable with Bob until that moment. He later became the Chief Judge of Maryland's district court.

"We are plowing new ground, young man. We have to do this right because we are going to be blazing a trail for other lawyers to follow."

Gene Autry's lawyer,
January, 1967

Governor Spiro Agnew

In the 1966 general election George Mahoney's "Your home is your castle" yielded to "Your kind of man" as Spiro Agnew, the Baltimore County Executive, set out to win the governor's mansion. In early October, to introduce Harry Hughes to my friends and clients, we hosted another party catered by Peerce Lake at our home in Glen Arm. Tom Finan, Bob Murphy and Bob Sweeney from the State Law Department attended, along with many of my friends and clients.

Throughout the house we found combs, matchbooks, fingernail files and political brochures boosting Spiro Agnew. The majority of those present were Democrats, so this augured well for the Republican party in November. When I accused Harry and Tom of being the source, their grins and indirect responses convinced me my suspicion was correct.

My birthday is October 31, Harry's is November 2 and in 1966 I was to be thirty-five and Harry forty. We met for dinner at the Wagon Wheel restaurant near Annapolis on All Saints' Day. When I asked Harry how it felt to be forty, he said, "I look at it this way. If I weren't forty, I'd be dead."

That thought has been a comfort to me as the decades rolled by. We were both attending committee meetings, not only in Annapolis but in Baltimore as well. Whenever we met we had dinner before or a nightcap afterward. I never left Harry without getting a telephone call at home, as he put it, to make sure I got home safely. It was easy to like him and working with him was always fun. With respect to politics, economics and public policy, we never disagreed.

Harry was an occasional overnight visitor at my house. Hearing footsteps in the darkened house and someone whistling, I once found him in the kitchen at four in the morning fixing a snack. He was too tall to go from the guest quarters through my library and down the steps into the dining room without hitting his head on the door jamb. That part of my house was constructed in 1748, and at five feet nine I barely clear the overhead. Harry never remembered to duck, and he had retained his salty-sailor, baseball-pitcher vocabulary, but that was the only time I ever heard him use it.

The first time he came for dinner our frequent houseguest, Frances Motyca Dawson, my wife's roommate at the Peabody, was also there. She had married Dr. Benjamin H. Dawson, who was completing his training as a member of the United States Army at a hospital in Philadelphia. She was completing her masters at Peabody and whenever she had to stay overnight in Baltimore she stayed in our guest room.

It did not occur to me to explain her presence to Harry. When his curiosity got the better of him, he asked me who she was. Because I take my job as a lawyer and a father seriously, I am never serious when I am off duty, so I said, "Harry, you know I'm much too complicated a guy to manage with just one wife. I have to have at least two."

The look on Harry's face was somewhere between envy and disbelief. I did not bother to correct the impression until Frances joined us for dinner, when I asked about Ben. Harry quickly realized I was teasing him, as he so often teased me.

Dr. Dawson is a sailor and I have spent many pleasant hours sailing his Celebrity on Currituck Sound. A member of the Olympic sailing team, he later was professor of hematology at the University of Maryland Medical School and a pioneer in the development of SLA testing, which permitted determinations of paternity through blood tests. He was also director of the Rh Typing Laboratory in Baltimore, a non-profit institution I represented as general counsel, which had contracts with some state governments to provide paternity testing.

One of my corporate clients was starting to grow rapidly and as a director and general counsel, a lot of my private time was devoted to that company. It was formed by Ronald L. Spangler and Larry C. Lewman, television personalities in Baltimore at WBAL TV where my cousin Charlie was still the Atlantic Refining Company weatherman on the eleven o'clock news. They had a children's program known as "Pete the Pirate" which they wanted to syndicate. They acquired the rights to the program from WBAL and set up a company we called Lewron Television, Inc., to video tape the program and market it.

In order to raise the necessary money, a private placement of stock and convertible debentures was marketed by Stein Brothers and Boyce, an investment banking house also located in the One Charles Center building, in which the principal investor was Wallace Lanahan. Assisting him was Buzzy Krongard, later to become CEO of Alex Brown, and still later General Counsel to the CIA before returning to Baltimore to head a second incarnation of Jerry Geckle's PHH.

Buzzy and I did most of the paperwork and I and a family owned private investment company subscribed to units in the private placement. At that time, television was strictly a black and white affair. Color, however, was fast approaching.

After the private placement was completed, Dick Clark introduced Ron Spangler to Gene Autry. I had then joined the Center Club, and Dick was my guest there when he came to Baltimore. Autry owned the California Angels and he was interested in telecasting all of the Angels' road games back to Los Angeles in color. This required a substantial acquisition of equipment by Lewron. Autry's lawyer suggested we meet in St. Louis and prepare the contract.

"We are plowing new ground, young man. We have to do this right because we are going to be blazing a trail for other lawyers to follow."

Lewron had to acquire a forty-foot-long trailer and equip it with four color television cameras, a video tape machine, a switchboard and enough cable to run four cameras from the truck into the stadiums. The video tape machine cost $115,000, the cameras cost $210,000 each, the switchboard cost $85,000, and the truck, cable and installation another $200,000. The cameras were heavy, the video tape machine massive and the coaxial cable so heavy strong men were needed to pull it. So rapid was the electronic revolution that followed, all of that equipment later could be bought for less than $10,000 and carried in a backpack. Now, it's in your hand-held telephone/computer/television set.

Wally Lanahan put us in touch with Irving Blum who ran, with his brother Alvin, a venture capital fund. They made a bridge capital loan to Lewron syndicated among a number of his friends and relatives, including Gerald Hoffberger who then owned the Baltimore Orioles. Harry attended meetings in the conference room in our Charles Center office to help us negotiate the contracts with Mr. Blum.

David Gordon and Gene Fineblatt represented the Blum interests and they taught me a lot. The Blums also had an interest in Pritchard-King which built the first trailer for us. The equipment was installed by RCA in Camden, New Jersey. Somehow Lewron managed to get it all done and the people in California saw the Angels road games in living color in the spring and summer of 1967.

During the 1966 legislative session a bill had been passed to create a Court of Special Appeals with jurisdiction over criminal appeals, and we would all have been better off if it had stayed that way. Bill Burch was bringing Norman Polovoy in as his deputy. As far as I knew, Bob Murphy had little, if any, private law practice. I had helped him prepare a few tax returns for his private clients, and I did not think it right that Bob should go back to being an assistant AG after having served as Attorney General.

As Deputy, Bob had learned a lot about criminal law and argued a lot of cases in the Court of Appeals. When Herb O'Conor stopped by for his morning cup of coffee, which he habitually drank in my office, I urged him to ask Governor Tawes to appoint Bob to that court. Herb smiled and said, "So like you, Ed. Always thinking of someone else. Never yourself. It's a great idea. I'm sorry I didn't think of it. We need to do something about it right away."

He left my office and a few days later came back to tell me that Governor Tawes had decided not only to appoint Bob to the Court, but to make him its chief judge. Bob often mentioned the philosophical musings of a friend who came home from work every day with a cold six-pack of beer, flopped into a hammock in a corner of his living room attached to ropes he used to pull himself above the household fray to the ceiling. He would lie there above the din, consume the six-pack and think elevated thoughts. It was a perfect way to adjust one's attitude as well as one's altitude. I knew I would miss those tales.

As soon as Bill Burch was sworn in he assembled the staff, stared directly at me and forbade any of us to talk to the press. All contact with the press would be through him and him alone. If any of our names appeared in the press, we did not need to come back to the office to find out if we were fired, because we were fired as of the minute our name was printed in the newspaper.

I continued to be busy in the fall of 1966 into the next legislative session working on the massive rewrite of the election laws, as well as the results of the work being done by the "Hughes Commission" which had been appointed by Governor Tawes to get the tax reform bill into an acceptable form for presentation to the general assembly in January, 1967.

I had pushed hard to adopt the adjusted gross income as shown on the federal return as the starting point for determining Maryland taxable income. My idea was opposed by Benjamin Marsh in the comptroller's office, so Louie Goldstein and Harry set up a committee which I chaired consisting of me, Ben Marsh and Louie. I did my best to sell the concept to Ben. Eventually, I won him over and Louie Goldstein signed on to our final bill, including the outlawing of any county or local income tax other than a percentage of the state income tax.

Unfortunately, in those days one-half of all capital gains were excluded from federal income and only the other half was taxed. Later, all capital gains were included but the federal tax on capital gains was computed on a separate form. This was a great windfall for the states and even more so for the counties. I have since paid substantial penalties for not anticipating the extent of legislative tinkering with things they don't understand. The likelihood of ever getting that changed in a state beholden to union bosses is highly unlikely.

Before the 1967 session began, Harry needed to make some changes in the committee lineups. As a result of the Supreme Court's decision in *Baker v. Carr*, old political alliances crumbled. Before attending a Hughes Commission meeting in the state office building on Howard Street, Harry and I met for dinner beforehand with Paul Cooper and William Houck, a western Maryland legislator who was also a member of the Commission. Harry wanted Joe Curran to chair the judicial proceedings committee.

Unfortunately, that committee was chaired by Fred Malkus and Harry did not have the votes to displace him. I knew, however, that Governor Agnew had promised Harry the Republican votes in the Senate if he wanted to be president of that body. After thinking about the possible combinations, I pulled Harry aside and said "I know how to do it."

"Do what?" Harry asked.

"Make Joe chairman of the judiciary committee and put the blame on Billy James."

"I can't do that."

"Yes you can. Add Joe's votes, your votes, and the Republican votes and you have enough to be elected president of the Senate. You can tell Billy James if he doesn't support your effort to replace Fred, you will oppose him for Senate president. Billy can tell Fred that if he doesn't go along, you are going to take his job away from him. That will give you all the votes you need to set up the committee chairs."

I don't know whether Harry took my advice or not, but Joe got the chairmanship. The Eastern Shore lost a lot of power under redistricting, and it was, in my opinion, unlikely the bedroom counties would let Harry keep his job as majority leader and Finance Chairman unless the Judicial Proceeding chairmanship was given to Baltimore City. In 1990, when I ran against Joe for attorney general, I mentioned this episode to a *Sun* reporter who sought verification from Harry, who remembered it differently, but then Fred Malkus was practically his next door neighbor. A former next door neighbor of mine, Tommy Raimondi, was later accused of brokering the votes of Republican senators.

In order to complete the rewrite of the election laws, the Governor made the *Maryland Lady* available to the committee for a weekend cruise on the Chesapeake. Vivian Pierson, Willard and I had presented our proposed drafts at morning, mid-afternoon and early evening sessions. The legislators were having a good time, celebrating the end of a three-year task and the ship's bar was always open. We got the approvals we needed and presented our final work product for review in time to get it printed in the "blue-book," a compilation of approved bills to be presented to the Legislature in January of 1967.

When the implications of what we had written began to sink in, some asked "When did we approve that?" Our standard response was "Don't you remember? We did that on the *Maryland Lady*." This generally quelled the opposition and the bill was passed by the House and Senate with few changes. The night it was considered by the Senate, Senator James asked me to sit with him at the rostrum to answer any questions the members might have. Fortunately, there were none, but the view from the president's chair was a unique experience for someone not a member of the Legislature.

When my friends in the press learned I could not be quoted without being fired, they decided to pull Bill Burch's chain. They did a series of stories on city people who had moved to the country and country people who moved to the city. They picked my family as one of the examples. They quoted us extensively in the paper, and mentioned our names. The story, with pictures, was on the front page of an interior section of the Sunday Sun. Bill Burch said nothing about it because it had nothing to do with my work in his office.

The legislative leaders saw Bill as a possible competitor and he saw me as his nemesis. Bill thought my car loan investigation had political potential. He prepared a bill making permanent the consumer protection division Sergeant Scroggs and Scott Gibson cobbled together in the State Law Department. The legislative leaders did not want to give Bill a horse he could ride to the Governor's office, a position Marvin and Harry both wanted. Marvin asked me to edit the bill, keeping its public relations aspects but removing the enforcement authority vested in the Attorney General. It took about ten minutes to recast the bill and Marvin got it passed with my edits intact.

From my vantage point, the people who had worked with me could continue as a part of the State Law Department which is what they wanted to do. The bill could be, and since has been, strengthened as the need arose and there was support for it. The Division has never accomplished as much or made more of an impact than it did in 1966-1967, doing what the pre-existing law already allowed us to do if anybody had bothered to read it. The Attorney General was less of a political threat to the men running the legislature, and the damage I had done by putting a powerful political weapon in Bill's hands was minimized.

After reapportionment, Harry was no longer representing just Caroline County but all of the upper eastern shore. He was scheduled to explain his tax bill to a group of supporters on the lower shore, but he sent me instead. When Hank Cumberland and I returned to Annapolis, I told Harry that the people down there didn't like us, and there had been initial hostility as I began my talk. When Harry asked Hank what happened, he said "When they started yelling, Ed slipped from his clipped English accent to a slow Southern drawl, and they warmed up to him. It ended well."

I did not enjoy my second year in Annapolis as much as I did the first. I knew more about the individual members of the Legislature, their agenda and their motivation. I did not like what I saw and I did not enjoy being a part of it. I concluded that no lawyer should ever be elected to a legislative body, whether it is the county council, the state legislature or the United States Congress. The temptations are too great and the means too easily veiled.

Lawyers are the judicial branch, frequently a lawyer is the chief magistrate, whether president, governor, mayor or county executive, and lawyers dominate the legislative branch as well. This is too much power in a single profession. The electorate can fix this, but not if they have no idea what is going on. Insist upon term limits, and if an elected official promises to serve for a limited time, hold her to it. Incumbency is the viral cancer of the body politic.

When the 1967 legislative session ended, however, the work we had begun was so impressive that *Time* magazine did a two page spread on the remarkable accomplishments that had been engineered by Governor Agnew in his first term as Republican governor of Maryland. All he had to do was sign the bills. Harry Hughes, Tommy Lowe, Marvin Mandel and Billy James had done all of the work prior to his inauguration. Leaders, competent or not, get the blame or credit for what happens on their watch, whether or not they have anything to do with it.

Time heralded the complete rewrite of the Maryland election law, which included the corrupt practices act; the rewrite of the interest and usury laws, the enactment of the Cooper-Hughes tax reform bill, revisions to the Maryland Industrial Development Financing Authority law; redistribution of state monies to local subdivisions for education and other essential services, the establishment of a consumer protection division in the Attorney General's office, and creation of the State Administrative Board of Election Laws.

My concept of simplifying state and local income taxes by beginning with the adjusted gross income from the federal return is now the national standard. SABEL, just like the coordinated Federal, state and local income tax, was my brainchild, replacing a patchwork of conflicting local interpretations with uniformity and state supervision of the election process.

When the 1967 legislative session ended, John Dallam asked me and my wife to accompany him to San Francisco to attend a meeting of his counterparts in other states who regulated the loan laws and lending activities. John was giving me a crash course in politics, convinced I was a knight on a white horse sent to save Maryland from the political mire.

That meeting was to follow hard on the heels of a meeting of the American Bankers Association Herb O'Conor asked me to attend with him in Dallas. The Bank Commission, however, regulated installment sales contracts, and those contracts were part and parcel of the fraudulent used car investigation I was doing. As counsel to both agencies, I insisted they could also be voided by the Commissioner of Loan Laws, and my political mentor, Bob Gerstung, now held that position in the Agnew Administration.

Bill Burch gave me permission to attend after I assured him I would pay for my wife's airfare, room and board, and that none of her expenses would be charged to the state. We left Friday morning so we could spend the week-end with my wife's cousin in San Jose. Her husband, Clarence Frizzell, was president of an IBM manufacturing subsidiary located there, and they had recently been featured in a *Life* magazine spread as the epitome of the organization couple. Their house was on a high hill overlooking the valley and from the window of our bedroom the Paul Masson champagne vineyards stretched all the way to the Pacific Ocean.

The Frizzells were our guests at the *Blue Fox* restaurant in San Francisco on Saturday night. The food was wonderful and the staff meticulous. The next afternoon we took the train back to Nob Hill. Our room was in the Fairmount Hotel where most of the meetings took place. As soon as we checked in we were invited out to dinner by the general counsel of Commercial Credit Company. He took us to the *Blue Fox,* where we were betrayed by our waiter who remembered us from the night before. My wife said the *Blue Fox* was one of a very few restaurants where the waiters knew how to put a chair under a lady. I have yet to learn how to do that.

During the next few days I attended meetings with Mr. Dallam and met with him at lunch and occasionally at dinner. He was trying to push me into politics, hinting that I should run for Governor. He was giving me a crash course in legislative corruption at the state and national level, identifying the culprits by name, confirming the extent of fealty to corporate America by both legislators and bureaucrats like the two of us.

Bob Gerstung, who was Mr. Dallam's superior, invited my wife and me to the "Top of the Mark" and asked me to represent Dr. Frank M. Ayd, a well-known Baltimore psychiatrist, who pioneered the use of drugs to treat mental illness rather than electric shock treatments in vogue in the 1950's. His pro-life position on abortion cost him the presidency of the American Psychiatric Association. Dr. Ayd had taken his family to Rome in the mid 60's and had left his affairs in trust with his lawyer. When he returned, the lawyer was dying of cancer and told Dr. Ayd that he had "ruined" him.

An investigation revealed that substantial assets had been dissipated by investments his lawyer made. Bob's wife had worked with Dr. Ayd publishing professional journals and papers. When I returned to Baltimore, I met the family and one of the sons, Joseph M. Ayd, who was in his late teens, seemed to have a clear understanding of what had happened and undertook to brief me on the facts. We became friends and his friendship has been helpful to me, both professionally and politically.

We prepared a bill for an accounting naming the lawyer's estate and his partners and his widow as defendants, and they hired Stephen M. Sachs as their counsel and we battled in the courts for several years. Steve was an aggressive litigator and I reciprocated in kind, giving rise to bruised feelings and reduced opinions of one another.

When I checked out of the Fairmont Hotel I discovered my bill had been paid. When I returned to Baltimore I gave Bill Burch a copy of the bill. He fired off a letter to the Fairmont, but I was so naïve I did not know government employees are always guests of the people they "regulate." I gave Bill a check for my wife's share, confident he would get it resolved.

Texas and Oklahoma investors who wanted to start a fourth television network asked Lewron to build a second mobile unit to be stationed in Las Vegas, Nevada, where the network originated. The highlights of the shows in the hotels were taped and shown between guest appearances during the live broadcast. A Midwestern entrepreneur signed the lease for the truck and then assigned it to United Network.

As we were returning from San Francisco we made a stop-over in Las Vegas. Ron Spangler met us at the airport and drove us to a hotel where we could rest before the opening night presentation of "Las Vegas Tonight." The show aired live at eleven on the East coast so we had to be in the studio by eight local time to see the show from the beginning. It was exceptionally well done, better than any late night show since, but the United Network folded a month later. It failed to pay Lewron, so I sued D.H. Overmyer Co, the obligor on the lease, and obtained a summary judgment in the United States District Court in Baltimore, which was appealed to the Fourth Circuit in Richmond.

Overmyer's New York lawyer failed to appear in Richmond for argument and Paul Niemyer, their local counsel, had to argue the case. He had not yet been admitted to practice in Richmond so I took him to the clerk's office, explained our predicament, vouched for him and sponsored his admission by motion when our case was called. Proving that no good deed goes unpunished, the case was sent back to Baltimore for a trial on the merits, which I later won, but only after battling the United Network's delaying tactics in the bankruptcy court in New York for several years. Paul later became a judge on the Fourth Circuit Court of Appeals, sitting on many panels which heard my cases, including the last case I argued there in 1997, at which time he shared with the other judges on the panel our meeting thirty years earlier.

"With Ed's brains and Harry's look's, we've got a team we can drive all the way to 1600 Pennsylvania Avenue."

Conversation overheard on Pealiguor Road,
August 1967

"What did you think might happen to me in the governor's office?"

"There could be an ape hiding behind the draperies. He could hit you in the head and fifteen minutes later you would be at the bottom of the Chesapeake Bay in a fifty-five gallon drum weighted down with concrete."

"Guess it was a good thing you came along."

Conversation with Sergeant Scroggs,
January, 1968

Missing in Action

While we were in San Francisco, John Dallam undertook to share with me his forty years of experience in Maryland politics. I had known from my early days in Washington that stories about corruption in Annapolis I read on the front page of the Washington Post were buried, if they appeared at all, deep inside the Baltimore newspapers. He described, not only in Maryland but nationally, networks of industry retained lawyers who were also members of legislative bodies.

A lawyer can be paid a retainer simply to deprive an opponent of his services. No lawyer can be compelled to say who is, and who is not, a client, nor can a lawyer be compelled to disclose what he has been paid or why it was paid to him. This is known as attorney-client privilege

There is a great deal that can be said about this privilege. Whether it is good or bad depends upon who is asserting it. But this I know for certain. It is essential for corporate control of the political process and control it they do. If you don't like it, never send another lawyer as your representative to a legislative body. From the names, dates and amounts of cash he saw, and the events that unfolded, I believed what he told me.

Companies and industries, just like forest land owners, cotton, corn or soybean farmers, form alliances to help one another. We belong to the groups identified by our interests to protect our interests, and we all participate in it, by joining unions as workers or trade associations as capitalists. It is the essence of political science. Legislative lawyers on retainer by one company or union may be asked to vote for or against a bill that affects an industry different from the one that retained them. These "special interest groups" look after one another because they can never tell when they might need allies themselves. Lobbyist money is the mother's milk of politics, and lobbyists work hand in glove with lawyer-legislators to write laws, which enthrall us and benefit their clientele. They can retain the legislator's law firm clandestinely or publicly contribute to his campaign.

Paid lobbyists work in the open and retain lawyer-legislators to vote as they are paid to vote. When I saw this working against me I wanted to subpoena the 1099 forms reporting retainers paid to determine how many members of the Maryland Legislature were retained by the companies opposing Tommy Lowe's usury reform bill.

During the summer of 1967, Harry and Pat invited Estelle and me to be their guests at their new home on the river in Denton. A number of Harry's close friends came over for cocktails. They were ambitious for Harry, and as I came downstairs I heard one of them say "With Ed's brains and Harry's looks, we've got a team we can drive all the way to 1600 Pennsylvania Avenue."

I froze where I stood, hoping that was not what Harry wanted because it was not something I was ready to do. Harry's constant comment was "up or out." He was tired of the Maryland Senate, mindlessly chanting "so much of the reading of the bill be considered the reading of all of the bill" and the U.S. Senate or the Governor's mansion were both places where I was ready to help him get. There were things I could do, but help run the free world? I retraced my steps to the center hall to wait for Harry, Pat and my wife. We drove over to Oxford for dinner, but my day had been ruined.

In an effort to patch up my relations with Bill Burch, I invited the office staff out for a Labor Day picnic. There were only fourteen AAG's in those days and with wives and staff it was a manageable crowd. We played tennis, basketball and touch football. One end zone was the swimming pool, the other was a grassy area between a lilac and forsythia hedge. My son, Ted, was five and he did not like my referring to Bill Burch as my boss. He confronted Bill on the steps of the swimming pool, angrily declaring "You're not my father's boss. I'm my father's boss."

Bill, an old-fashioned Yalie, was incredulous. The idea of a son being his father's boss was contrary to everything he believed in. Bill said, "You most assuredly are not. I don't know whether anybody is your father's boss, but if he has one, it's me, not you."

This only made Ted angrier, and he turned red, screaming, "You're not my father's boss."

I picked Ted up and carried him inside to his mother, assuring him he was still first in my heart. When I returned Bill had caught the ball in the end zone, ran along the pasture fence and dove into the deep-end of the swimming pool in typical Yalie, Frank Merriwether fashion, scoring the winning touchdown. Tom

Garland, equally competitive, agreed he had, although he thought his route and his methodology were questionable. By that time, we were all too mellow to care who won.

That fall I received a telephone call from Willard Morris, my ally in the rewrite of the election laws in 1966 and the 1967 bill to create the State Administrative Board of Election Laws to supervise the county election boards. This would unify the interpretation of the law throughout the state, an improvement over the crazy-quilt interpretation that existed in Baltimore City and the twenty-three counties, each a separate fiefdom with laws peculiar to it.

Willard said a friend had given him the use of his apartment in Montreal, Canada for a week and he wanted to invite me and Estelle to be his guests. The apartment was located in the Habitat on an island in the St. Lawrence River where Expo 67 was taking place and we were delighted to accept his invitation.

Tony Carey, who had replaced Tom Perkins as Venable's representative in the Attorney General's office, was getting married and he was going to be in Montreal at the same time for his honeymoon. I jokingly asked him his number so that I could look him up. As it turned out, his wife was someone who would cross my path in the years ahead and perhaps it would have been far better for me if I had interrupted his honeymoon to meet her. She became Steve Sachs campaign manager in 1978.

We had a good time in Montreal. It was fun to be on the island where the pavilions were located, although we did get into Montreal from time to time to sample French cuisine and enjoy the local ambience. Unaware of the restrictions on the importation of Russian goods, I purchased a Persian lamb, Cossack-style hat. It attracted a lot of attention, even in Montreal, but even more so when I returned to Baltimore. In a year or two, everybody was wearing them and I was no longer a conspicuous presence on the city streets.

Willard was interested in being appointed by the governor to head the state administrative board, staffed to operate in the 1968 election cycle. He wanted to know if I had any interest in the job, convinced I was the only other person in the state qualified for the position. I told him I would be pleased to support him in any way I could. I wrote a letter to the governor on his behalf, and Willard became SABEL's first administrator.

The apartment belonged to a corporation with which I was not familiar. When I asked Willard about it, he told me it was the parent company of the automatic voting machine company. I learned, again, how rigidly corporate America controls everything that happens, not only in the legislative bodies, but in the every nook and cranny of state government. Business delights in regulation. All they have to do is co-opt the regulators, impose barriers to entry by competitors to insulate the regulated from competition, and they are set for life.

Years later, I received telephone calls from a newspaper reporter wanting to know about that company's influence over Willard Morris. Willard had apparently told them that I was also a guest in the company's apartment in 1967. I confirmed my presence there as Mr. Morris's guest and also confirmed that I learned, after I arrived in Montreal, that the apartment was owned by the voting machine company's parent, the same company whose employee undertook to educate me about the vulnerability of their product in 1962.

I called Willard to see if he were in any trouble. He laughed and told me that this is Maryland, a state blessed with an incompetent press, unable to find a story or verify a fact. There was no story, and the press was trying to create one. That was consistent with my view of the press as well—reporters come with a perceived idea of what the story is. They ask questions to pin down bits and pieces of the story as they conceive it to be. Often there is a much better story—sometimes one worthy of the Pulitzer Prize—which goes unwritten because the reporters don't ask the right questions.

Later that autumn, I was scrambling to try and save the Maryland Industrial Financing Authority. In the 1840's State legislatures encouraged construction of railroads, guaranteeing their bonds in the belief that railroads would improve transportation, the standard of living, and ultimately serve a public purpose. So many railroads were constructed there was not enough freight to make them all profitable. Bankruptcy followed bankruptcy and many states became insolvent and defaulted on their bonds. A provision in the Maryland Constitution adopted in 1859 prohibited the pledge of the State's full faith and credit to payment of a private debt posed a problem for MIDFA.

The lawyers representing banks making loans guaranteed by the State wanted an opinion from the Maryland Court of Appeals assuring them that MIDFA's guarantee meant something. To our surprise, the Court of Appeals ruled that limitations on use of public funds prevented MIDFA from pledging the full faith and credit of the state to the repayment of the bank loans. Although the Maryland Constitution, according to that Court's opinion, does not apply to the Court of Appeals, it does apply to everybody else. Judges, like legislators, exempt themselves from the laws they write.

I resolved this problem with some amendments to the law during the 1967 session of the legislature to make MIDFA an insurance company. We needed to set up a test case to see if our changes had worked. Tom Garland prevailed upon a friend of his to act as plaintiff, and MIDFA approval to pay a $5,000 fee to Richard Case, senior partner at Smith, Somerville and Case, to bring the suit. We put the case on a fast track, got a ruling from the Superior Court of Baltimore City, and moved it quickly to the Court of Appeals. As I finished my argument Dick whispered "Whatever they're paying you is not enough. I want you to work with me."

Dick did a lot of work as bond counsel for the state and that is why I picked him to represent the plaintiff in our test case. Harry, as chairman of the Senate Finance committee, resented paying huge fees to bond counsel for verifying that the steps taken by the legislature to approve a bond bill were proper. This is research work, very similar to that done by title attorneys for real estate transactions. The fees often were a percentage of the total borrowing power authorized by the legislature. Bond counsels argue their fees are justified because the lawyer's opinion puts him, his firm, and his malpractice carrier on the hook if there is trouble. An early version, perhaps, of a credit default swap demanded by Wall Street.

Within a month, Tinka Knopf, the Dean at Peabody in whose apartment Estelle and I became engaged, invited us to dinner at her home. She later married the son of my wife's teacher, Don Julio Esteban. Another guest that evening was Dick Case, President of the Peabody board of trustees. After dinner Dick renewed his invitation and pressed me for a decision. I was flattered by his interest but I knew I could not work for anyone. Partners I could tolerate but I had to be my own boss. How was it my son knew that at age five?

Another test case involved the tax reform bill. The bill passed the legislature in 1967, and George Leibman and I tried a test case in Baltimore City. In just two days, George cobbled together an eighty page brief. We stipulated the facts and argued the case before Judge Meyer Cardin who asked us to prepare a draft opinion, which he edited substantially. Our draft was carefully drawn, framing the constitutional issues for appellate review. Aghast at the changes made by Judge Cardin, we had to rewrite our already prepared briefs to deal with the irrelevant points added by the lower court's opinion.

At the time Judge Cardin's son Ben was chair of the House Ways and Means committee in the Maryland legislature. When appearing before the committee to oppose the state lottery when I was President of the United Christian Citizens, Ben asked me if I thought gambling was a sin. I knew it was a veiled attack on my faith, and I uttered a silent prayer for help, and words not of my thinking said "Yes, I do. You tax everything we have and everything we do, and now you want to tax hope, the only thing we have left. The lottery is a tax on hope, imposed upon the poorest of the poor. To me that is as immoral as you can get."

I had to explain our brief to the Attorney General in the company of two senior employees of the comptroller's office. Bill did not grasp that we had to dispose of the irrelevant paragraphs Judge Cardin added to its opinion. He was in one of his moods, frequently questioning statements I made to him, and when he left the office for a few minutes, the Comptroller's assistant asked, "Is he always like this?"

"No," I replied. "He is often worse. We caught him on a good day."

They asked if it would be better if they left under some pretense and came back another day. I assured them this was our best chance to get the matter resolved and we should stick with it. Bill returned in a more aggressive fashion, and I suddenly remembered it was a dispute with Louie Goldstein over the importance of their positions that got me slammed into the wall at the East Wind two years earlier. It occurred to me there may be some fear on Bill's part that I was not being forthright. When I could take it no longer, I stood up, leaned toward him, slammed my fist on his desk and said "Bill, are you calling me a liar?"

Stunned, Bill pushed his chair back so quickly it turned over, and he fell against the window in his office on the twelfth floor of One Charles Center. For a split second I was terrified he would go through it, and my career would end with my being led away in leg irons and handcuffs. But the glass held and Bill pulled himself up from the floor, straightened up his chair, assured me he was just doing due diligence on a brief he was asked to sign. We persevered and eventually got Bill's signature on the brief. I was mortified.

In early 1967, I went to an American Banker's Association meeting in Dallas with Herb O'Conor. I had used the Chaparral Club where I had reciprocal privileges for business meetings with my private clients whenever I was in Dallas, so I invited Herb there for dinner when he asked my help with a delicate problem. President Johnson wanted Herb to handle his re-election campaign in Maryland, and Herb wanted my help as to what he ought to say when he placed the call. We talked at length, and when we agreed on what was to be said, I went to Herb's room in the hotel to listen in. When the President decided almost a year later to fall on his sword rather than face the possibility of defeat in November, Herb's carefully considered acceptance and work as campaign manager was wasted.

Harry and I were unwinding after a social event at my house. Jack "Shorty" Surrick, former news director at WBAL-TV and his wife, who taught at the Bryn Mawr School with my wife, were also there. Jack sat in on the tail end of a conversation I was having with Harry about legislative networks of retained lawyers. I had forgotten Jack was then Governor Agnew's press secretary.

The following morning I got a call from Shorty in my office at the State Law Department. The governor wanted to see me right away, and wanted to know if I could be there by eleven. I told him I could. Sergeant Scroggs said he was going with me. Bob Murphy thought there were threats on my life, so Sgt. Scroggs was my shadow no matter where I was or what I was doing. We even ate together on occasion. He had taken the three pistols I owned and test fired them at the police range. I kept one in my desk drawer, another in my car, and another in my private office. I never had to use any of them.

When we got to Annapolis, I went up the familiar marble staircase to the governor's office. I told the state trooper I was there to see the governor at his request. Shorty came out to get me, and when I started into the governor's office, the state trooper stopped Sergeant Scroggs, saying, "You can't go in there."

Scroggs pulled me back. "The chief don't go no where I don't go. If I don't go in there, the chief don't go in there."

The state trooper hesitated, "Well, you can go in, but you've got to leave your piece out here."

Without changing his dead-pan expression, Scroggs said, "I don't go nowhere my piece don't go. If I go in there, my piece goes with me."

Amused, I backed him up. "That's the way it's got to be."

So Scroggs, his piece and I went in together. Governor Agnew wanted to know more about my interest in the Comptroller's records. I told him what I knew, what I wanted to do, and told him I had no idea where it was going to go. He thanked me and we left. When we got outside I turned to Scroggs, laughing,

"Did you honestly think I was in danger in the governor's office?"

"Is the Pope a Catholic?"

Scroggs did not like Governor Agnew and he had supported George P. Mahoney in the 1966 Democrat primary. When I asked him why, he had said, "The crooks around Mahoney are small fry. We can handle them. The crooks around Agnew are international. They are beyond our scope."

So I asked, "What did you think might happen to me in the governor's office?

"There could be an ape hiding behind the draperies. He could hit you in the head and fifteen minutes later you would be at the bottom of the Chesapeake Bay in a fifty-five gallon drum weighted down with concrete."

"Guess it was a good thing you came along."

As we were leaving, Frank DeCosta, who had served in the Attorney General's office in 1966, came over to shake my hand. Agnew was not happy having a Democrat Attorney General as his counsel, and he hired Frank as special counsel. We were friends, and I had given him my tickets to see the Orioles whip the Dodgers in four straight games in the 1966 World Series because I had been too busy to use them. Frank took his father, who had been Dean at Tuskegee and was then at Morgan State, to the two games played at Memorial Stadium.

I often had late lunches on Friday afternoon with Frank and David Wright at the Place in the Alley, the only day of the week we had a glass of wine or a beer at lunch. We would return to the office about three and return telephone calls before closing up for the weekend. Frank had an excellent private practice I coveted. He was from an influential African-American family with connections in Charleston, South Carolina and New Orleans, Louisiana from which he had assembled a healthy corporate clientele. As southerners, we had a lot more than politics in common.

David Wright had figured in an early civil rights case in Maryland, later joining Bob Murphy on the Court of Special Appeals. David and Frank sometimes forgot I was not African-American. They would get sheepish looks on their faces and apologize for something they had said.

"Don't worry about it. I don't mind if you forget I'm white. I have just as much trouble remembering you two are black." They were, but it was a category, not a description.

A week after Sergeant Scroggs and I visited Governor Agnew, he dropped me off at the barber shop in the old Mercantile Trust Building at Baltimore and Calvert and went to pick up his pay check. When the barber swung my chair around to cut the back of my head, the man directly in front of me lowered the newspaper that hid his face, brought his index finger in front of his mouth and winked. I glanced around expecting to see a goon with a tommy gun. Grinning, he threw me a kiss and walked out without saying a word. When I told Scroggs what had happened he asked if I knew who the man was.

"My law school room-mate."

"Is he a lawyer?"

"A very good lawyer. Brilliant.

"Who does he represent?"

"He's Sal Traficanti's surrogate son, and Consigliore to the Traficanti family."

"That's the best news I've had so far this year."

"Why is that good news?"

"It's taken care of. You're off the hook. Not in trouble. Somebody else is. We're pulling your protection. But we can still get together for lunch in Little Italy."

That was the last I saw of my sergeant, the next-to-last truly, Damon Runyon character I knew. My experience as a public lawyer was drawing to a close.

In an effort to keep peace with Bill Burch, I had adopted the practice of rarely, if ever, allowing myself to be quoted by the press. If I could get the reporter to let me talk off the record I provided what journalists call "deep background." To some extent, that is what this book is. I am sharing what readers need to navigate the white water rapids that threaten to wash away the American experiment.

"You are a good trial lawyer, and you could be a great trial lawyer. But you have to get your emotions under control. If I can make you angry, I have disarmed you. Law is intellectual combat, and the rational argument always prevails."

William Glendon,
October, 1969

"With the trouble we're in, an aspirin won't cut it. I think we need a lawyer."

Response to employee's question
about 1968 Presidential election

Changing Partners

As the closing days of the 1968 Legislative session approached, my private practice was growing rapidly. Lewron Television, Inc had leased a Consolidated Edison building on West 53rd Street in New York City, constructed like a fortress four stories high with an attractive front. We hired a contractor, who had to make weekly payments to agents of each of the building trade unions just to keep the job moving forward, to convert the building into a modern television studio. The cost was built into our contract, for that is the way business is done in union-dominated towns in New York, New Jersey and Baltimore.

Ron Spangler had a fascination for race cars, owned one, and he had produced a lot of automobile commercials in Baltimore. He installed an elevator in the building large enough to move a car from the street to the fourth floor studio. There were control rooms on the fourth floor and the second floor, where a second, slightly smaller studio was constructed. Offices were on the first and third floors, as well as a reception area and dressing rooms for VIP's, actors, producers, directors and sponsors. The studios were state of the art.

Stein Bros. & Boyce, Inc. was the lead underwriter for a public offering of Lewron's stock in the summer of 1968 and Alex Brown agreed to take a substantial portion of the offering. Piper and Marbury represented the underwriters, and I retained my law school class mate Norman Burke, then at Miles & Stockbridge, to represent my client, the issuer. Norm was scheduled to teach a class in wills at Mt. Vernon Law School, later part of the University of Baltimore. He told me that it would be impossible for him to work on our offering and teach his class at the same time, so I agreed to teach the class for him.

When the legislative session convened in January 1968, I actually dreaded going to Annapolis. Bill Burch became suspicious when newspaper stories had information he knew they could only have gotten from me. In the middle of

February, he told me I was not to go to Annapolis again under any circumstances, and if my clients needed to talk to me, they could do so by telephone or in my Baltimore office. I asked him what territory was included in Annapolis.

"Any place within seven miles of the State House."

The distance from the State House to the Wagon Wheel Restaurant in Anne Arundel County was 7.2 miles. I met my state clients there for lunch or dinner, and I set up shop in a booth to fine-tune legislation. By March, however, what Herb O'Conor called my "fine Machiavellian hand" was painfully obvious, and a reporter who broke the rules actually quoted me in the press.

When I got off the elevator on the twelfth floor of One Charles Center, Bill was in a rage. As soon as he saw me he said, "I told you not to come back to the office if your name appeared in the paper. What are you doing here?"

"Bill, you gave Tom Finan your word that you would not fire me. But I'm going to simplify your life. I quit."

I got back on the elevator and went upstairs to my office and told Bill Manger and Tommy Maxwell I was leaving them as well. Millie Owens packed up my files, arranged for a moving van and moved my office from One Charles Center to a suite of rooms adjacent to those occupied by Lewron Television, Inc. on the 34th floor of 222 St. Paul Street, now known as the Tremont Hotel. Harry was busy with the legislature in Annapolis, so I didn't talk to him first, but Blake McFeely came with me and we practiced briefly as Blanton and McFeely.

Venable represented the underwriters and Charlie Reeves came to Lewron's office to review the minute books and other significant exhibits to be included in the SEC documentation. The board was being expanded and Charlie Fenwick, president of Riggs, Counselman, Michaels and Downs was added to the board along with Allan Hoblitzel, later president of Maryland National Bank. Allan was Jim McHenry's son-in-law and one of my college friends, Cecil Bishop, was the manager of Alex Brown's Towson office. He had persuaded me to become a Republican in 1964. Pat Deering was in charge of Lybrand's Baltimore office, and Lewron had retained him to audit its books.

Freed from my responsibilities in the State Law Department, I enjoyed the practice of law. Ron had a Beechcraft Duke. a small twin engine plane that carried six passengers in addition to pilot and co-pilot. We flew it, either from the Forest Hill Industrial Park or Aldino, both in Harford County, to Teterboro, New Jersey. We kept a car there and commuted directly to the studio on West 53rd Street through the Lincoln Tunnel.

We also had an apartment on East 44th Street and 2nd Avenue, a short walk to the United Nations complex on the East River, for use of company officers remaining in New York overnight. In early March, Jerry Bishop and I, accompanied by our wives, went to New York to see Lefty Drissell's Davidson Wildcats play the St. Johns Redmen at Madison Square Garden in the finals of the NCAA basketball tournament. I had to remain in New York for the first part of the following week and Jerry and Jan agreed to see my wife safely back to Baltimore.

On Saturday night, following the basketball game, we went to the "Purple Onion" in the East 80's to see an entertainer known as Tiny Tim. He wore a straw hat, peppermint jacket and white pants, singing "Tiptoeing through the Tulips" in a high pitched voice. A basket of roasted peanuts was on each table and the shells littered the floor. Estelle and Jan were snickering but they would not tell me why. I turned to Jerry for help. A well-known Baltimorean had entered the bar with a lady not his wife. Not knowing the newcomer, I did not fully appreciate the joke.

We were staying in the Hilton Hotel opposite Madison Square Garden. As we were going back to our rooms from breakfast the next morning, the doors to the elevator opened. The only two people in it were the philandering Baltimorean and his lady friend. We moved as one to the next elevator, and as it began to ascend, Jerry said "If I ever decide to cheat on my wife, I'm not coming to New York City. I'll going to Sioux City, Iowa." After having a marvelous dinner at La Grenoule in a room crowded with large floral arrangements, I saw them off on the Metroliner on Sunday night as a blizzard hit New York. I was supposed to meet the president of a company who was flying in from Atlanta to negotiate acquisition of his company by Lewron. Snow continued to fall heavily during the night and the next morning New York was under two feet of snow. On Monday morning I saw people skiing down 2nd Avenue. The airports were closed and my meeting was rescheduled for Wednesday afternoon. So I had two days off, marooned in a high rise.

The underwriters for Lewron decided that the stock should be split, at least three for one, prior to the public offering in August, 1968, but the shares I owned were restricted under Rule 144. The opening price was approximately $9 a share and the stock reached a high of $20 in the ensuing months. The IPO took place during a boom in electronics, and stock traders may have thought the name "Lewron" had more to do with electronics than television.

In reality, the speed with which electronic components shrunk in size and cost soon turned the huge tractor trailers filled with electronic equipment into dinosaurs. I sold some of my shares when the "lock-up" period ended. Charlie Fenwick, owned Towson Valley Mercedes and I dumped my 1965 Corvair and bought a 1968, 280SE from him.

When I was still at the Shriver firm I did work for Brooks Robinson, the Baltimore Oriole third baseman. Brooks and I planned a visit to hunt quail on my wife's farm in North Carolina, where I had hunted with Martin Kellogg, a lawyer friend from Manteo whose father was a friend of my wife's family. I prepared corporate papers for a sporting goods store which Brooks opened. He had an interest in a restaurant known as the "Gorsuch House" which he owned jointly with Eddie Robinson. There was a key club in the Gorsuch House where the golden gloves won by Brooks and Eddie were displayed above the bar.

Brook's bartender was a former Miami policeman who had soured on law enforcement at age twenty-one and hit the road as a bartender. I met him when he tended bar at the "Place in the Alley" next to the Finan campaign headquarters in 1966. Wherever he went, he gave his employer a scrambled version of his social security number, intending never to file income taxes. But he fell in love with a girl and wanted to marry her, and decided to clean up his life. I had been helping him for at least a year tracking down W-2's from the places he had worked and filing income tax returns for him. In almost every case, he had a refund due.

In early August, John invited me to the Gorsuch House for lunch which he served at the bar. We were watching the Republican convention on the tube. John turned up the sound and I was horrified to learn Governor Agnew had been picked by Richard M. Nixon to be his running mate. I told John what I knew and said,

"We've got to try and stop this. That guy's a crook."

Jerry Bishop had persuaded me to change my registration to vote for Barry Goldwater in the Republican primary in 1964. I had met a number of Republican delegates while at the Shriver firm, some of whom were being interviewed on the convention floor. We tried to get in touch with as many of them as I could, but I had no more luck than I had the first time I tried to stop him in 1966. Maryland is so accustomed to corruption it is routinely ignored. Every now and then a talented United States Attorney tries, but exposes very little of it.

While attending a Practicing Law Institute seminar in New York, I took Estelle to the theater to see Richard Burton in 'Hamlet.' As we were exiting down a narrow stair, the crowd was moving painfully slow. When we reached the street, we shook hands with former Vice-President Richard Nixon and his wife Pat. He was better looking in person than he appeared to be on television, and I was probably one of the few Republicans to shake his hand that night. Lewron was then doing commercials for Hubert Humphrey.

On my recommendation, Lewron adopted a policy for political commercials; one-third paid with the order, one-third when the commercial was taped and the final-third when the dubs were delivered to the networks and stations airing them. Humphrey was a pharmacist and Nixon was a lawyer. When people in New York asked me how I thought they should vote, I replied, "With the trouble we're in, an aspirin won't cut it. We need a lawyer." The following week I was in the control booth reviewing the Humphrey commercials, I was pleased when a Lewron employee told me the country needed a lawyer, not an aspirin.

When Stanley J. Cole, Lewron's chief financial officer, his secretary and I left the office to get his car and drive back to Baltimore, it was not parked where we had left it that morning on company property in a small space between the Lewron building and the public parking garage next door. We asked the attendants if they had seen anyone move the car. They told us a city tow truck had picked it up.

We walked around the block to a NYPD precinct station located in an old brownstone house adorned with a candelabra with three white bowls encasing electric lamps resembling the craft symbol for a pawn shop. The building had sagging floors and walls in need of paint, but it was bustling with activity. We asked the desk sergeant where we might find our car which had apparently been towed by the NYPD. He directed us upstairs to talk to the detectives. A sign—a hand with the index finger pointing up and the word "Detectives" under it—was nailed to the wall by the staircase.

At the top of the steps there were six desks at which three men in civilian clothes with Irish names were sitting. They asked me what I wanted.

"Our car was parked on our property on 53rd Street. We were told that a city truck towed it away. We need to know where we can find it."

"What's the tag number?"

When Stan gave them the number of the Maryland tag, the detective said, "It's going to take sometime to find your car. We put cars we pick up on a pier. This afternoon, the pier started falling into the East river. We had to move all of the cars in a hurry, so they're not organized. Why don't you folks get some dinner and come back in a couple of hours. We might have some news for you then."

"Where can we get dinner?"

Riley thought we should go to a French restaurant on 8th Avenue near 49th Street. Kelly thought we should go to an Italian restaurant on 10th Avenue and 54th Street. Fitzgerald thought we should go to an American restaurant at 55th Street and 8th Avenue. They began arguing as to which was best, the argument became heated and profanities were tossed about. Hoping to avoid fisticuffs, I said "I think the Italian restaurant sounds like the right place for us. Tell me where it is again."

After getting the directions, we walked down the steps, laughing as we made our way to the restaurant. As we ate, people outside pressed their faces to the window, watching us eat. It was an unnerving experience. When we got back to the precinct, Riley said, "I've got some bad news for you. We don't have your car. A ring of car thieves operating in the area are driving trucks just like NYPD tow trucks. We think they got your car."

We rented a car and drove back to Baltimore. The following week when I returned to New York, I met Ron at "The Slate" for lunch, a popular hangout for the people who used our studio. I told him about the detectives and Stan's car the previous week. Two men at the next table started smiling, furiously making notes. When "Barney Miller" later made its appearance on the network, I mentioned the similarity of the show to our visit to the New York precinct station to Ron.

"That's no coincidence. The two guys eavesdropping on our conversation that day were the producer and director of that program. The Barney Miller theme was later repeated, in a more serious vein, in the "Hill Street Blues" and later in "NYPD."

A few weeks before the general election in 1968, Mr. Cole told me the Humphrey-Mondale campaign had not paid for the commercials we did for them in the New York studio. He had only received the initial payment. The campaign needed money to pay for airtime and they could not make the remaining two payments until after the election. My client had, contrary to policy, released the dubs without getting paid.

Stanley Blair had succeeded Hotdog Simpkins as Secretary of State in the Agnew administration. I knew the Humphrey-Mondale campaign would have to file a financial report with him thirty days before the election. I called Stan, later a Federal judge, and asked if he would like to shut down the Humphrey-Mondale ticket in Maryland.

"I sure would." he said. "Tell me how I can?"

"Their committees are required to file financial reports in your office seven days before the election. If you will get those reports, give me the name of each committee, the location of their bank account and the account number, I'll attach all of the accounts on original process. My client did their national television commercials and hasn't been paid."

Stan gleefully got the reports and read the information to me over the telephone. We prepared attachments for each account and filed them along with my complaint, alleging that the Humphrey-Mondale campaign planned to go out of business without having paid its debts. Under Maryland law that is sufficient to justify attachment before judgment. I also had to post a bond, which I arranged through Tongue Brooks and Company, owned by Lewron stockholders who wanted the bill paid.

As soon as the attachments were served by the Sheriff, Democrats called wanting to know what I was up to. Marvin Mandel was chairman of one of the committees, but I had not attached his account because the information filed with the Secretary of State gave his bank balance as zero. He knew I had attached campaign accounts and assumed I had attached his as well. He laughed when I told him his account was safe.

The biggest surprise was that Irving Blum and Wallace-Lanahan, both stockholders of Lewron, were co-chairs of the Humphrey-Mondale ticket in Maryland. They assured me they would personally guarantee repayment of the debt if I would release the attachments. I had to clear it with Lewron's CFO, but I procrastinated until the banks had closed on the day prior to the election. But Senator Humphrey carried Maryland anyway, where government employees and recipients of federal largesse are the majority of the electorate. In fact, they outnumber the private sector two to one. That is why Maryland is an enthralled state in the original meaning of the word. We are not delighted. We are enslaved by the mendicant majority.

When Spiro Agnew was sworn in as Vice-President in January, 1969, Maryland had no lieutenant Governor, and the Maryland Legislature would have to choose one. The candidates were Harry Hughes, my ex-partner and Marvin Mandel. In a scene reminiscent of another in Allen Drury's "Advise and Consent," Bob Murphy told me Harry would not win. Marvin became Governor and appointed Harry his Secretary of Transportation.

When I received a copy of our law firm's tax return for 1968, I was puzzled by the manner in which the return was prepared. Harry had filed suit against two of our former partners and when I looked at the return, I had a pretty good idea why. I retained David Rudow to represent me. I told him I had been treated unfairly in the manner in which the partnership was closed out. David persuaded the firm to close out the partnership's affairs in a more equitable fashion. At the same time, he invited me to become a partner in the firm of Adelberg, Adelberg and Rudow. David's friendship, at a time when I needed it, encouraged me to consider his offer, which also included Blake McFeely, who was still working with me.

One of Blake's clients asked him to reorganize a plastics company he owned and neither Blake nor I knew anything about bankruptcy law. Harry Adelberg, David's father-in-law, knew a great deal about it and he agreed to guide us in our representation of the company. Blake had been playing polo in Maryland and he liked living here, but his wife preferred the West Coast. He was the first of three lawyers from my firm who married west coast girls who insisted on going back to Oregon or California.

Blake had attended Yale with George H. W. Bush and Bill Buckley, and Bill was recording his "Firing Line" programs in the Lewron studio in New York. Blake described Bush as a typical college jock, assuring me no one ever thought of taking him seriously as a thinker.

In May 1969, I moved into the Maryland National Bank Building as a partner in the firm we called Adelberg, Rudow and Blanton. Blake left shortly thereafter for Denver to be General Counsel to Great Western United. Tom Finan had divided his private practice between me and Joseph Kaufman when he joined the Court of Appeals, and when I told him of my move, he asked me to represent Charles Flanders. Unable to offer him a cigar over the telephone, I agreed to meet with Charlie. He was the most insecure man I have ever met.

Charlie had been marketing a product that grew hair on bald heads under the name Volos. His Medical Director, Dr. Harry Robinson, a clinical dermatologist at Johns Hopkins, was vouching for the product. Dr. Robinson's wife gave away stock issued to her husband in exchange for his services to members of her bridge and garden clubs. As a result of her generosity, the corporation had a hundred stockholders who had acquired unregistered securities in a distribution that violated both state and federal securities laws.

Charlie had been represented by Weinberg and Green, had run up a big bill, and he was not happy with the results he was getting. Dickee Howard, the Securities Commissioner, fined Charlie a hundred dollars for each of the hundred violations, even though Charlie had known nothing about them. But, as CEO of the company, he was responsible under the law. Dickee, later wife of Phillip Goodman, former mayor of Baltimore, was part of the State Law Department. She often got letters addressed to "The Honorable Richard Howard." She and Bob Sweeney had been the life of our Wednesday afternoon office party. I once asked her how long she and Bob had known one another. Laughing, she countered, "Socially or carnally?" In those days, Dickee was the only female lawyer in the office, but she was always one of the guys.

When I became general counsel to United Credit Bureau of America, Inc. and Volos, Ltd. other lawyers urged me to avoid Charlie Flanders like a plague. They told me he was a control freak and would want to own me. Their calls were reminiscent of Harvey Firestone's conversations with me when I was a student at Stetson about my roommate, Jack Craparo.

My duty as I saw it was not to choose but to serve whomever God sent me and do it to the best of my ability, so I negotiated a reasonable resolution of the fee dispute. I took a look at the financials of Volos, which operated a plant at 29th and Remington Streets in Baltimore City. They were running an advertising campaign to sell the product as a cosmetic, as well as pursuing a new drug application before the FDA. The company needed a huge capital infusion to pursue just one of its two objectives, and I decided they could not get it.

I recommended that the board shut it down immediately, pay its bills and use the remaining capital for the new drug investigation before the FDA. If the drug were approved, it could be licensed, and licensing fees might rescue the investment of the stockholders. It was quite clear to me, however, that this company could not possibly bring the product to market by itself, even if the product was as sensational as everyone believed.

The product was actually coerqus alba, an extract from the bark of the white birch tree. Charlie's mother-in-law, a Ukranian, had concocted it from an old folk remedy. It did have some hair growing properties, but the drug was in the national formulary from the early twenties and the best Charlie could do is patent a new use for an old product. This was not going to be satisfactory, and Volos eventually ceased to exist. Poor legal representation coupled with poor business judgment at every stage of the company's existence doomed it.

Charlie was concerned that the Securities and Exchange Commission might also take action against him. He had been spending a lot of time in San Juan, where he had met a former OSS operative named Harold Quase, who haunted Paul Young's restaurant in Washington, where he had a table equipped with a gold telephone with his name on it. I don't know what his official position was, but a driver assigned to him once flashed an identity card that caused a state trooper to salute and wave him on when they stopped him for excessive speed on the interstate. "Q" was going to make sure the SEC took no action and Charlie took me to Washington to meet him. For a few months I had lunch at his table as his guest, although I had no idea why he kept inviting me back.

A curious collection of Washington officialdom showed up at that table, including Johnnie Johnson, head of the Civil Service Commission, who had come from Governor Reagan's cabinet in California at President Nixon's request. There were Agency for International Development, or AID, people, as well as Department of the Interior people present when I was there for lunch. As a student of history, I was aware of the Teapot Dome Scandal and I wanted nothing to do with them, but I was curious to know what their gig was.

One young bureaucrat, an "Under" or "Assistant" Secretary from Interior confided that they were the Mafia, confirming a long held belief of mine that the government of the United States was the world's largest criminal conspiracy.

"Great," I replied, "then you must know my law school room-mate." When he asked who my room-mate was, I told him he was the consigliore of the Traficanti family in Tampa.

Harold was raising money for Kenny O'Donnell's campaign, and having also sold me tickets to a fund raiser for Senator Vance Hartke, I stopped by his office at the Underwater Storage Company to pick them up. When I asked about framed pictures of something that looked like an underwater missile silo, he intimated his was one among many CIA companies under contract to Defense. More surprising was a photograph behind his desk of Lyndon Johnson being sworn in as President of the United States on Air Force One on November 22, 1963, with Mrs. Kennedy standing beside him in her blood-stained, pink dress. The handwritten inscription read "Harold. And they said it couldn't be done! Thanks, Lyndon."

Furious, I demanded, "Just what was it that couldn't be done, Harold?"

He ignored my question, stood up, visibly miffed and insisted we go to a nearby delicatessen with a sidewalk café to wait for Kenny, who was going to attend the fund-raiser with us. I still have a set of cocktail glasses I received as a memento of the occasion. Kenny was President Kennedy's Harvard classmate and he was making a second try for the governorship of Massachusetts. We sat for several hours waiting for the party to begin at the Mayflower while Kenny and Harold insisted they were with President Kennedy, in Marilyn Monroe's apartment, on that July night he was nominated for President at the Cow Palace in San Francisco.

Jack was supposed to win on the second ballot, but the West Virginia delegation switched unexpectedly, throwing the nomination to Kennedy. Fearing the press at the entrance to the apartment house, Jack, Harold and Kenny took to the fire escape, only to find a six-foot tall fence with a locked gate when they reached street level. Gripping their hands together, they lifted Jack to their shoulders to get him over the fence. They later encased their white dinner jackets, with Jack's foot print on the shoulders, in air-tight plastic bags. Jack's back was injured, say they, when he jumped to the sidewalk to catch a cab back to his hotel.

Another call from a state court judge who had bought stock in Lewron led to a meeting with his friends who were promoting a new venture in Columbia, Maryland, under the name Dyad Systems, Inc. Carlo Faustini was born in Monte Casino, Italy, during World War II. He came to America and designed an asynchronous circuit called the 'eight gate dyad.' The technology was vetted by Dr. Morris Rubinoff, a professor at the University of Pennsylvania.

Estelle and I had been fascinated by the movie "2001: A Space Odyssey" and its mentally deranged computer, so I asked Dyad's president if a computer like HAL could be constructed with Dyad technology, and when he said that it could, I agreed to represent him.

Patents had been applied for by Howard Rose, a Washington patent attorney who also did the basic patent on fluidics technology. A venture capital company in Philadelphia was interested in Dyad, as was the Singer Company, then the fortieth largest industrial company in the United States. Sewing machines were the least of its products. In a hostile takeover, Singer acquired the American Meter Company. It also owned Friden Calculator and Link Belt, a company that made simulators used to instruct military and commercial pilots in the operation of large aircraft.

Singer was also developing a point-of-sale system. Donald P Kircher, the darling of Wall Street—pictured in a Business Week cartoon sitting in the turret of a tank—was Singer's CEO. Donald Smith, who had been Chairman of the Board and CEO of American Meter Company, was Vice Chairman of Singer's Board.

He also sat on Dyad's board spearheading negotiations for Dyad to redesign the Friden calculator using Dyad's asynchronous circuitry.

The common belief was that asynchronous technology took more, instead of less, circuitry to operate free of the clock that controls computer operations. As Terry Kravitz, Dyad's President, put it, dyads can accelerate and degrade gracefully. Such a computer might predict the weather or control traffic lights. Dyad engineers were 'bread-boarding' the circuitry for the Friden calculator in Dyad's laboratories. At the same time, Carlo had designed a chip to be manufactured to Dyad specifications by Ragan Precision Industries in New Jersey.

A demonstration was to take place on May 15, 1970. At that time, the Singer representatives were to determine whether or not Dyad would qualify for a massive infusion of capital from Singer and others interested in the technology. If the chip was delivered on time, Singer would open the calculator and see one tiny chip operating the entire device, replacing five circuit boards and the mechanical connections to it. As soon as the chips were manufactured by Ragan, they were seized by NSA.

Terry told me I was a fool if I thought I lived in a free country. The government, acting in the interest of national security, could take private property without due process of law, without compensation, and there was nothing anyone could do about it. At no time was I asked to pursue the matter with the government. But Terry was now having lunch with "Q," and perhaps he pursued matters on his own through other channels.

When the May 15 demonstration was conducted at Dyad, Mr. Kravitz satisfied the Singer Company that he had not only operated the calculator successfully using asynchronous technology, but he had actually reduced the electronic circuitry by twenty percent instead of increasing it. Negotiations were moving forward with the Singer Company. There was a vagueness that troubled me, however, as to whether the technology was to be owned by Dyad or Singer.

At a meeting in Dyad's conference room in Columbia, I urged a hurried conclusion to the negotiations because I had to be in New York the following morning for an appearance in the United States Bankruptcy Court, where Lewron, as part of United Network's bankruptcy case, was suing D. H. Overmyer Leasing Co. for money owed under the failed fourth network operation in Las Vegas, Nevada the previous year.

Don offered to fly me to New York in the Singer plane, assuring me his chauffeur would drive me to Lewron's apartment on East 44th Street. As we got on the plane, Don told Terry that when he put the plane in a roll at twelve-thousand feet, he could get me to agree to anything. Terry, having seen a certificate of achievement from the commanding general of the 11th Airborne Division on my office wall, countered.

"The joke's on you, Don. Ed's a paratrooper. You start anything with him up there, he'll just jump out."

Don's attorney, from the Winthrop, Stimson firm flew with us. We were met at the White Plains airport by two chauffeured limousines. Singer's attorney lived in a Westchester estate and he invited me in for dinner and a drink. I declined, for I had some work to do before I appeared in court the following morning. My appearance was before Referee Lowenthal in the southern district of New York at Foley Square. It took a year to try the case because we could get but one day each month on the Referee's schedule.

William Glendon of Royal, Koegel & Wells was my opponent. His office was in the Pan-American building, and he later represented the New York *Times* in the Pentagon Papers case. Samuel Newfield, a friend of Harry Adelberg's, was my local counsel. Referee Lowenthal was a great storyteller with a rich history as a bankruptcy referee. Supreme Court justices drew straws to see who got to sit by him at judicial conferences. As I was examining a witness in his court room, someone bumped my elbow. Referee Lowenthal was standing beside me with a box of licorice candy.

"Have a piece." I thanked him and continued my questions with the licorice in my mouth. On another occasion, he descended from the bench and proffered a box of donuts while I was making an argument. On yet another occasion, he looked down from the bench and said "You are not going to win."

Startled, and offended because I thought he was prematurely deciding my case, I said "Win what?"

"The World Series." he said. The Baltimore Orioles and the New York Mets were about to play in the 1969 World Series.

"I thought you were talking about this case," red-faced and trying to hide my frustration. He replied, "That either."

Near the end of the day, Bill Glendon was waiting for me outside when I left the courtroom. He wanted to buy me a drink. I agreed, thinking he was going to discuss settlement. Instead, he offered me some fatherly advice.

"You are a good trial lawyer, and you could become a great trial lawyer. But you have to get your emotions under control. If I make you angry, I have disarmed you. Law is intellectual combat, and the rational argument always prevails in the court room."

I wish that were always true, but in jury cases, lawyers who scream, shout and cry on cue often get away with it. When our trial ended, Bill led me into an adjoining courtroom where Jacqueline Kennedy's litigation with paparazzi was under way. Front row seats had been held for us by two associates in his firm. We spent the rest of the morning listening to some fascinating testimony, after which he accepted my invitation to lunch at the Marco Polo Club in the Waldorf Astoria.

As one of the best trial attorney's in one of New York's most prestigious firms, Bill took time to mentor an opponent, a younger lawyer from another city he would never see again. I resolved to be as good an example, not only to the young lawyers who worked with me but the lawyers I opposed in the courtroom as well. Mentoring has been part of my life ever since, and it has been far more rewarding than any of my legal victories, when I see Doug Grinnell's success in California or Pat Stringer getting good reviews from young lawyers who appear before him.

"Don't worry about me. I'm surrounded by love so thick it's difficult to see beyond its farthest limits."

Assurance given Natalia Flanders,
August 1973

Governor Marvin Mandel

When Richard Nixon and Spiro Agnew won the election in November, 1968, Marvin Mandel, speaker of the House of Delegates, was elected Governor of Maryland. After he was sworn in he appointed my erstwhile partner Harry Hughes to be his Secretary of Transportation. I reviewed the Maryland Code to determine Harry's duties and wrote him a congratulatory note. The governor had given him half the State of Maryland for his own private domain, including the airport, the interstate highways, the port authority, the bridges, the railroads, state roads, mass transit and countless administrative agencies and licensing functions, all subject to Harry's control. It was a very important post for Harry to have, and his time would come.

Terry Kravitz and I went to New York to negotiate with Singer. Dyad wanted a technology sharing or purchase agreement with an infusion of capital. We arrived at the Singer offices in Rockefeller Center at nine in the morning, and we were ushered into the offices of Joseph Smith, their acquisitions officer. The ashtrays in his office were piled high with cigarette butts. Either the janitors were on strike or we had been the topic of an all night work session.

Before I left for New York, Harry Adelberg warned me to beware of the old 'Sears Roebuck number.' He explained Sears had a reputation for finding a supplier, gradually taking more and more of their product, until Sears became the largest customer. After a few years of that, the supplier's marketing lost its edge and Sears would make them an offer they could not refuse—sell us your business on our terms or we will not buy your product. If the supplier refused, Sears would wait and buy the business from the bankruptcy referee.

When Joseph Smith put his proposals in front of me, I read them with Harry's warning in mind. They seemed to be heading in that direction. On our side of the table, we wanted to make sure that the technology sharing agreement and the infusion of capital agreement were not interrelated. After we proposed changes in the language and the changes had been discussed and negotiated, Mr. Smith suggested we go to lunch, handing the documents to his secretary to retype. We went to the Rainbow Room, high atop Rockefeller Center. Although celebratory drinks were proffered, we declined to participate because we were skeptical of our host's intentions.

We returned to Mr. Smith's office about 3:30 in the afternoon, where we waited for another hour for the agreements, both only three pages long, double-spaced, to be retyped. We continued to talk and we were assured again and again that the capital stock acquisition and the technology sharing agreement were two distinct and not interrelated contracts. When we read drafts of both contracts that was far from clear.

I met with my client privately and called Howard Rose in Washington. I read several sentences of the technology agreement to him. Howard did not want Terry to sign the documents in their present form, suggesting some changes in language. I discussed the changes with Mr. Smith for another hour, and he agreed to have the documents retyped to incorporate our suggestions. He left us alone for about an hour and when he came back he said the documents were not ready. He invited us back to the Rainbow Room for supper.

Thinking our job was done, I accepted a drink and Terry did also. Dinner was longer than lunch, and I refused additional drinks ever so gently, kicking my client under the table to get his attention. At ten in the evening, we went back to the Singer offices to read the latest versions of the contracts. I called Howard Rose, and neither of us had any difficulty with the acquisition of stock in Dyad by Singer. We needed the money and we were eager to have an important stockholder.

The technology agreement, however, was not to our liking. When I went back and confronted Mr. Smith with our decision, he told me what I had suspected all along. There would be no stock investment in Dyad unless Dyad agreed to turn over the technology to the Singer Company. I thanked him for his hospitality and we left without signing either document.

When I returned to Baltimore, I called Jim McHenry at Alex Brown & Sons. Jim arranged a meeting with Frank Bonsal, Bonny White, Jerry Geckle, then a partner and later President of Peterson, Howell and Heather. Jerry Bishop, accompanied me and Mr. Kravitz to the meeting. Terry told Bonny White that within a year people would be using hand-held calculators incorporating technology similar to that covered by Dyad's patents. Bonny pulled me aside later and wanted to know what my client was smoking. At the time, Singer's calculator weighed about fifteen pounds, had five printed circuit boards inside and cost $1,400. Today we have hand-held computers and electronic calculators are the size of credit cards, given away free.

We gained enough credibility for Alex Brown to undertake a private placement of Dyad stock which was to provide the working capital needed to perfect the technology. Jim McHenry, Jerry Bishop and I gathered in the basement of the Alex Brown building at Baltimore and Calvert Streets before a heavy steel fire door, which rolled back to reveal an impressive set of wooden doors with brass handles that opened into a small dining room, with five tables evenly spaced in the room. From behind the walls a waiter appeared and took our lunch order.

Jim explained what he could do and wanted to make sure the terms were acceptable to my client. I agreed to meet with Terry and his board and get back to Jim as soon as Jim's terms were reduced to writing. The next day I met with Jim and Jerry on the balcony of the old building at the corner of Baltimore and Calvert to review the draft of the one page letter outlining Alex Brown's commitment. Jim agreed to some minor changes in the letter and I invited them to have lunch with me at the Merchants Club. When we returned to Alex Brown's office, I was late for another appointment so Jerry promised to deliver the letter to my office on his way back to Towson.

Jerry called to say the letter was going to be slightly different from the one I had seen in Jim's office that morning. While we were at lunch, Jim received a telephone call from Singer's VP Joseph Smith who made statements to Jim which were not only cryptic but difficult to interpret. It appeared that Smith was trying to throw a monkey wrench into our efforts to gain financial support without getting it from Singer by making Jim nervous, so Jim changed the letter from a 'firm commitment' to a 'best efforts' offering.

Dyad was running out of time and we had to settle for something less than I was promised before Smith's interference. I believe, however, that Alex Brown's best efforts would be more than adequate. They had never failed me, and I was booked to leave with my wife and two of our children for a long-postponed automobile trip through Germany, France and England. It was my first vacation in ten years other than our annual August trips to Nags Head, which were often interrupted by a mid-week return to Baltimore or Richmond.

The next day I sat aboard a 747 wondering how they would ever get anything that big off the ground. Somehow they managed. Lufthansa flew us directly to Frankfurt where I rented a new Mercedes with a smoother transmission than the 280SE I was driving in Maryland. We went to Heidelberg, followed the Romantic road through Rothenberg and Dinkelsbühl to Augsburg, places familiar to me from my military service with the army in the mid-fifties.

In Munich we checked into the Kaiserhoff Hotel. My German was still good enough for me to be taken for a native by the hotel staff. The other day I heard someone say we think in English. Maybe we do, but when in Germany or France, I think in their languages however limited my vocabulary may be because what I have to say must be in that languge. Many was the time, when cross-examining German witnesses in my court-martial cases, I was gaveled to order if I forgot the translator and pursued my questions in German.

We visited King Ludwig's Wagnerian Neushwanstein, and spent a few days in Salzburg before turning back toward France. We stopped by the American Airbase near Frankfurt where my sister Faye lived with her three sons and husband, a colonel in the United States Air Force. My sister bought us a case of root beer at the PX for our children to drink. They had been living on Wiener schnitzel and Dover sole, the only things on European menus they would eat. They quickly learned to say "non-gasereuse." They refused bottled water in restaurants, and the root beer slaked their thirst.

When we drove into Paris, we were drenched by a supercharged windshield washer which I engaged when the sun roof of the car was open. My children were delighted to find a McDonald's on the Champs Elyseè. After letting them try some American food, we took a walk down the avenue. It was about ten in the evening and as the lights were coming on, there was still a beautiful blue sky overhead. My son, taking it all in, said, "This isn't Paris, Dad. It's paradise." From his perspective, it may have looked like it was.

The next day we drove to the Chateau du Fere en Tardenois near the Marne where many Americans died in 1918. We planned a visit to the Champagne vineyards the following morning. When we pulled up to the hotel, our Mercedes was the smallest car in the parking lot. The proprietor came out to greet us and we transacted business in French. When I needed help, my six-year old daughter's more extensive vocabulary came to my rescue.

I explained to the proprietress it was my son's birthday. She asked me how old he was, and I told her that he had eight years today. She asked if I wanted a cake after dinner, and I said yes. She showed us to our rooms which were well appointed and charming. When we came down for supper, we were the only people not wearing gowns and tuxedos for dinner. The waiters, also clad in tuxedos, presented each course on silver trays displaying the food surrounded by fresh flowers, each a work of art.

My daughter ordered quail, and when the waiter lifted the lid, she was horrified to see the pitiful bird, complete with head, beak and tiny feet. Ted's fish was served with head and tail intact, lifeless eyes locked on his. We were, as Americans, not in our element. But, to our surprise, when the cake was delivered to our table with eight lit candles after dinner, everyone in the dining room joined in singing 'Happy Birthday' in English. It made us feel better, and very welcome. A few days in Paris had convinced me the French had destroyed their gene pool in 1789 and nothing could be expected from them thereafter. I was won over by the kindness of the country people.

We drove back to Frankfurt, turned in our rental car, and flew to London. There we rented a larger Mercedes with the steering wheel on the right hand side. Having driven on the left in England and Sweden when I was in the army my only problem was going left around traffic circles. We were going to drive around England for a few days, after my appointment with Sandon & Co to be measured for some three piece suits I needed as work clothes.

We drove southeast from London to Canterbury, and from there to Winchester, where we visited the cathedral and Stonehenge. From Gloucester we drove to the Roman bath still in use today. On our way back to London, we were lucky enough to see a fine performance of Henry V. in Stratford. In Warwick, home of my wife's ancestors, we stayed in the Royal Leycester Hotel. The lake country and Lake Windemere was our last stop, and we had tea in a garden which I have been trying to replicate for my wife at our home in Glen Arm ever since. We returned to London for a final fitting on Savile Row before we flew back to America.

While I was away, Jerry Bishop moved to the Green Spring Valley. I met with him and Terry Kravitz at his new home to discuss the Dyad situation and to be updated on what had transpired during my absence. The situation was grim indeed. Terry had put the company on a fast track relying upon the Singer Company's promises of support. When that support was withdrawn, and Alex Brown scared off, the company collapsed like a house of cards.

Terry was desperately looking for what he called a "white knight" company to rescue him from the position in which Singer's interference placed him. His close friends wanted to invest in his company and I planned to participate through a private investment company I controlled, acting as agent for the other investors participating in the loan.

We put together a convertible loan to Dyad secured by a lien on its assets, including its patents. What we hoped to do was to insulate the company's assets from creditors by subordinating any judgment creditors behind the stockholder's claim. Terry was as yet unsuccessful in licensing the technology to other companies, so he closed the company and we filed an anti-trust/tortious interference with contract claim against Singer for its anti-competitive conduct, interlocking directorate and other violations of the Sherman and Clayton acts spelled out in the pleadings.

I decided to enlist the support of the anti-trust division at Justice, and I called Frank DeCosta, who had gone to Washington as counsel to the Vice-President. I asked him to meet me at Paul Young's restaurant on Connecticut Avenue for lunch, half expecting to see "Q" presiding at his table, but he was not there. Frank said Justice would have to do better than that when I told him my appointment was at three.

After lunch, a white station wagon picked us up, drove us through the White House gate and stopped at the old State Department building. Frank used a key to summon an elevator from the car port, and when the elevator stopped, I stepped out into the hall, startling two secret service men posted outside the Vice-President's office.

Frank sat down at Agnew's desk and called the head of the anti-trust division. He insisted they meet with me immediately, and they were kind enough to oblige. Frank sent me over in the white house station wagon, which was still waiting at the elevator. Anti-trust was polite but they thought I could do far more damage to Singer in a private action than they could accomplish, so I left without their support. They were under staffed, had little trial experience and no appetite for a fight. DOJ is a paper tiger, another government façade wasting taxpayer money accomplishing very little in the way of law enforcement.

Although Winthrop Stimson was still representing the Singer Company, they retained Semmes, Bowen & Semmes, located in the same building as my firm, to represent them in court. Jim Garland, whose brother Tom served with me in the Attorney General's office, was lead defense counsel, assisted by Frank Gorman, with whom I dealt on discovery matters. Jim pursued the matter aggressively and I was soon ensnarled in depositions in Baltimore and New York. Interrogatories, document production and the countless motions that constitute modern litigation engulfed us.

At the same time, Ron Spangler wanted to open a television studio on the Metro, Goldwyn, Mayer lot in Hollywood. He was encouraged by Mark Armistead, who had a mobile unit similar to those owned by Lewron and owned the Technicolor process which had been used in the movies since the thirties. He briefed me on the legal difficulties. The union, which represented Lewron employees in Baltimore and New York was the International Brotherhood of Electrical Workers. The movie lots, however, were rigidly controlled by the International Alliance of Theatre and Stage Employees.

IATSE insisted on a new union contract to cover our operations in California. I learned what "golden time" was—overtime on a movie lot on a Saturday, Sunday or holiday. Under those circumstances, the union workers get, not double time, not triple or quadruple time, but quintuple time. Having learned that setting up a table and chairs in our television studio in New York for a stockholders meeting entitled every union worker on our payroll to a full day's pay, I was cautious. When a latter day Gibbon writes the decline and fall of the American Empire, the union bosses will be fingered as the killers of the goose that laid their golden eggs. If you think democracies don't have empires, think NATO and the Delian League.

Jim McHenry was still my friend, and he arranged for Baker, Fentress to invest another million dollars in Lewron. Jim Fentress, a fellow tree farmer, became a member of Lewron's Board. Ron flew the Beechcraft Duke into Meigs field on the lakefront in downtown Chicago to meet with him. The northwest winds blowing through the tall buildings lining Lakeshore Drive make keeping the wings parallel to the ground highly problematical. Fentress was always amazed when we made it in and out alive.

The opening of the Lewron television studio on the movie lot inaugurated a full-scale migration of television shows from New York to Los Angeles, all burdened with the burdensome IATSE contract. The advantage in being there first soon evaporated. No one was sure how long it would last. A television producer with a spacious apartment on Central Park West found himself living in California. Not wanting to give up his New York apartment until he knew whether the television invasion we spearheaded was going to be permanent, he subleased it to Lewron for half of the monthly rent and half the salary of his maid who worked from one in the afternoon until nine at night.

On a typical day, she would come into the apartment, change the linens and wash the dishes from the previous night's dinner. She would call the office to find out how many 'gentlemen' she could expect for dinner, go shopping, plan the menu and prepare the food. When we came home at night, she had set out snacks and ice for cocktails. After serving dinner she would leave, we would work during dinner until we were sleepy, go to bed, get up, fix our breakfast and walk back to the 53rd Street studios.

When I remained over night in New York, that was our daily routine. I also found myself going to California with some frequency, however, and I would never know when I left home in the morning whether I would end the day in New York, San Juan, St. Lucia, Chicago or Los Angeles. It was exhilarating but I missed seeing my children grow up. Like a lot of fathers, I had not yet learned children need love and guidance far more than they need private schools and Ivy League educations.

Adelberg, Rudow and Blanton had the entire 28th floor of the old Baltimore Trust Building at 10 Light Street, now having come full circle as the Bank of America building. Stan Cole was reviewing Pat Deering's notes to the Lewron financials on a very hot, late March day in 1971. It was a Jewish holiday, the office was almost empty and we were working in casual clothes. The air conditioning was not turned on, so I climbed onto the window ledge to raise a heavy iron window. Stan, unaware our floor was the one with the outside balcony, cautioned me to be careful.

It was an off day and I was in a light hearted mood. I said, "Stan, with the information you're giving me, falling might be a blessing."

With that, I jumped out the window and did an airborne roll I learned on the thirty-four foot tower erected next to my BOQ in Gablingen. When I reappeared and climbed back inside, a white-faced friend did not appreciate my theatrics. I apologized and promised not to do it again.

David Rudow and Harry Adelberg were competent and professional lawyers and they were kind and trustworthy, twin attributes Judge Kern thought I would rarely find in the same people.

It was the death of family members that stalked me while I was their partner. In August I was meeting with clients in my office when I was interrupted by a long distance call from Orlando, Florida. The manager of the Cherry Plaza Hotel told me that my mother had been found dead in her apartment that morning of a fatal heart attack. After a visit to Baltimore, I had driven her to the airport so she could visit my sister, Mrs. James J Gallagher, in Atlanta, and then go on to her home in Orlando, where she was the unofficial mother of the Minnesota Twins baseball team sharing the hotel with her during spring training.

As we turned off route 895 to the Baltimore-Washington Parkway, she began giving me some last minute instructions as to family business and her funeral arrangements. There was a finality about her that convinced me that her streak of Irish mysticism let her know life was nearing its end. Her family had come to America in 1828 from County Kerry. When we said good-bye at the Friendship Terminal, I knew I would not see her again.

My friend Iain Wilson returned to Baltimore from Pittsburgh to conduct her funeral, much to the annoyance of another son of Scotland, Dr. Hubert Black, who succeeded Iain at the Franklin Street Presbyterian Church. As eloquent as Hubert Black was, charity was not his strong suit. He made a scene, but Iain was one tough cookie and he stuck by my side.

A few months after my mother's death, my younger sister, Faye returned from Germany with her husband and three sons and visited with us for a few days. Her oldest son, Richard Bradley Curtis, was fifteen. His hair was as long as my sister's; they were the same height and looked so much alike when their backs were toward me I often mistook one for the other, to their mutual disgust. My sister had developed a limp in the two years since I had seen her in Germany, and I noticed involuntary muscle twitches in her cheek from time to time.

When she reached their new home in Wichita Falls, Texas, she was diagnosed with amyotrophic lateral sclerosis. She paid us a final visit in the spring of 1973, and I took her with me, in a wheelchair, to the Maryland House and Garden tour. I took the third degree in Mt. Moriah Lodge while she was here, and I saw tears in her eyes when Charlie Flanders, who was taking us out to dinner, gave her a beautiful ruby encrusted Masonic square and compass to pin on my lapel.

Three months later she was dead, and we buried her in Arlington Cemetery on a hill overlooking the Pentagon. She had insisted she had to keep an eye on the Joint Chiefs, a group she distrusted like no other. Faye's next-door neighbors in Wichita Falls were Senator John Tower—ranking member of the Armed Forces Committee at the time—and his first wife, Lou. They attended the funeral and remained with us, hosting my family for dinner following the service at the Officers Club at Fort Myer.

Charlie Flanders and his wife Natalie called on me in my office to express their sorrow and convey their love. When they hugged me I said, "Don't y'all worry about me. I'm surrounded by love so thick it's difficult to see beyond its farthest limits." I don't think I ever had any clients who left me, and the things they did and said and wrote to me were the things you do and write and say to those you love. I was about to meet a client who would take a bullet for me, at least he always told people he would, as he labored to replace Sergeant Scroggs as a shield between me and the world I did not need.

"Come back to Baltimore. That peanut farmer from Georgia is going to win the nomination, and if you are going to invest your time in anybody's campaign, it should be Carter's."

Advice to Richard Evans,
January, 1976

Quelling a Riot

In the summer of 1971 I met the Black Panthers. A United Airlines ticket agent assumed an Arabic name, organizing a group of young African-American men who wore colorful African clothing to picket Lafayette Market. Our firm represented a grocery store with twenty-one employees, eighteen of whom were African-Americans, including the store's manager. The Legal Aid Society, still being run by my law school classmate and Republican friend, Charles H Dorsey, rented a branch office in the space above our client's grocery store. The Panthers used Legal Aid's copy machines to produce flyers that drew raucous crowds that barred access to our client's store.

Our client belonged to the Pennsylvania Avenue Lafayette Market Authority (PALMA). Most of the members were Jews, and the Panthers solicited contributions for an enrichment program offered to neighborhood children, a cause PALMA supported. But the Black Panthers, like the Chicago School of Economics, re-defined words to suit their politics.

Profit, for example, is theft, and anyone operating a business for profit was, by definition, a thief. The Chicago School insists that monopolies, as the epitome of efficiency, are the consumer's best friend, and that is what newly-appointed Federal judges are taught at Judge's School that monopolies are good for consumers.

Not only were the Black Panthers teaching children that store owners were thieves, they were administering liberal doses of anti-Semitism. This complicated things for our clients. They came to my partner David Rudow for help. We conferred, and while David explored the legal side, I decided to use my friendships with public officials to see what I could do.

I called the Mayor of Baltimore Tommy D'Alesandro, III, Nancy Pelosi's brother, and told him I represented PALMA. The nightly news was featuring three thousand angry, placard-waving, African-Americans marching up and down Pennsylvania Avenue calling our clients thieves. Tommy told me that he did not want the city burned down again and I should give them whatever they wanted.

I then called the State's Attorney, George Russell, who, as an elected African-American, was not eager to pick up a political hot potato.

George Beall, the United States Attorney for Maryland who was yet to gain his fifteen minutes of fame by prosecuting Spiro Agnew for petty thievery and tax evasion, was my last hope. I asked him to read the Racketeer Influence Corrupt Organizations Act, known as RICO, which in my view applied to the extortion the Black Panthers were practicing. When George asked if I had read the annotations, I replied I had read them all and they made it quite clear that what the Black Panthers were doing is prohibited by the statute.

George pointed out that the names in all the cases were Italian. I asked if he expected me to believe that Congress had passed a law that could only be used against people of Italian descent. That was clearly his understanding, and I was on my own. In disgust, I hung up the telephone, and told David we had no choice but to go into state court. With Mike Hendler's help he drew up a complaint seeking temporary injunctive relief, and took it to the Circuit Court with an order limiting the number of pickets with access to our client's business until the case could be heard. The complaint had to be served, but none of them were then known to us by name. Should we sue a thousand John and Jane Does and another thousand Richard and Rachel Roes? David and Mike found a way to bring them forward.

David negotiated an order with Judge Perrot which had to be read to a mob of angry, screaming people. Multiple copies of the court order were certified by the clerk. Two truckloads of deputy sheriffs read the order to the mob using bullhorns, after which the Sheriff ordered the crowd to disperse with the exception of the fifty pickets authorized by the court to remain on the scene. When the mob refused, the deputies arrested a few of them for violating the court order, citing them for contempt, taking them into custody and releasing them on bond.

With the threat of jail time, the number of pickets was reduced from three thousand to fifty. We then got another court order reducing the number of pickets from fifty to ten. We could live with that number until we had a hearing on the merits seeking a permanent injunction and the cessation of all picketing. Attorneys appeared for the people charged with contempt, so we finally had an opponent we could deal with in a civilized way.

The case was scheduled for trial before Judge Perrot and lasted three days. The Panthers defense was that groceries sold in our client's store cost more than those sold in the supermarket. That was theft writ large. Our African-American manager testified he had to deal with more shoplifting than the suburban supermarkets. Accordingly, he had to raise his prices to cover not only the goods that were paid for but those that were not.

The Panthers said the meat sold in our client's store cost more than the meat sold in suburban supermarkets. Our African-American meat manager testified that was also true but he only sold prime and choice meat because that is what his customers insisted on having. They would not buy anything else. Prime and choice grades cost more than the meat sold in supermarket chains. From that moment forward, I always bought my steaks from Graul's or the Gucci Giant, where I can actually talk to the butcher.

As the trial continued, it became obvious that for every allegation made by the Panthers, our employees refuted the allegation with logic and persuasion. We had made a good case on the evidence and awaited the court's decision with some degree of optimism. We thought we had researched the case thoroughly. To our amazement, the judge, or his law clerk, found a case decided in 1934 enjoining picketing at the same street address as that occupied by our client's store.

In those days, law schools still taught law and legal research was done without computers. The pickets in the early case were union workers before the passage of the Wagner Act when state courts still had the power to protect people from criminal conspiracies by labor unions. Today, Congress has bestowed exclusive jurisdiction of labor matters on the Federal courts, which defer to the 'experts' on the National Labor Relations Board, who are selected by the labor unions and their lawyers.

On the basis of that authority, we got a permanent injunction. The Black Panthers left to picket the city jail and the state penitentiary on Madison Street. I received a photo published in a newspaper from a reporter with the caption "Looks like you made believers of them." The photographer had lain on the ground to photograph the pickets at the penitentiary in the background with our client's slogan "Shop at Sam's and Save" on a shopping bag visible in the foreground near the camera lens. It appeared that the Panthers were actually advertising our client's store.

Needless to say, our clients were delighted with the outcome. The city was not burned down and the Panthers had been persuaded that our clients were not thieves and took their cause elsewhere. A few days later, David and I each received gift packages containing ceramic black panthers. Mine had blue eyes, and David's brown. I still treasure it, and David recently told me he still had his.

By the end of 1972, my youngest daughter was ready to go to school. We moved our two older children from St. James Academy in Monkton to Bryn Mawr School and our son to St. Pauls. I had to be a more active participant in my family's life. The antitrust case against the Singer Company was taking more of my office time and it was years away from producing any income for the firm. I thought it unfair for me to continue taking a full partner's draw when my contribution to the firm's income was shrinking because of the contingent fee arrangement we had with Dyad.

We decided to close all the work done through December 31, 1972, and treat it as the income of Adelberg, Rudow and Blanton, which would continue as a non-operating entity until all outstanding invoices were collected. Harry and David would start a new firm on January 1, 1973, and the old firm would be paid $130,000 for the time I devoted to the antitrust case while a partner. I prepared a bill and gave it to Dyad knowing it could not be paid, but I wanted to memorialize the obligation, both with my client and with my partners. I moved my office to Lutherville, bringing to an end the most pleasant four years of my professional life.

I found office space on the first floor of Heaver Plaza on York Road just north of the beltway in Lutherville. Steve Heaver had been a neighbor of mine in Northwood when I was teaching school. He also housed his hobby—antique fire engines—in a museum building located nearby. I shared the first floor of that building with the Maryland National Bank, a travel agency, and the investment firm Salken, Welch and Company.

James Welch was a Baltimore Colt and a neighbor in Glen Arm. He attended Rice University in Texas before joining the Colts. He was bright, had a beautiful wife and children, and our families had spent some time together socially. Jim was the originator of what has become a family staple—charcoal grilled hamburgers with a center of blue cheese. Having offices on the same floor, Jim and I saw more of one another.

Although I continued to spend two days a week in New York as Secretary and General Counsel to Lewron Television, Charlie Flanders was opening a subsidiary in San Juan, Puerto Rico. I added San Juan to my regular travel destinations and worked with John Sauber, a Chicago transplant, who managed the San Juan office. The company developed proprietary software that produced credit reports responsive to the dual last names traditional in the Spanish speaking world.

While working in New York I met a venture capitalist named Mark Witte. When Charlie told me he needed additional capital for his company, I introduced him to Mr. Witte who agreed to lend the Puerto Rican subsidiary $300,000 secured by the computer software and an option to acquire thirty percent of the stock in the United Credit Bureau of Puerto Rico, Inc. Settlement was to take place in the office Mr. Witte's law firm in New York.

I obtained certificates of good standing and prepared corporate resolutions and certifications by the corporate secretary of the currency of corporate action. I also reviewed numerous legal documents prepared by Mr. Witte's counsel, including a loan and security agreement, a note, and an option agreement together with related documents providing for the registration of the stock to be issued upon exercise of the option in the event of a public offering of securities by the issuer. Other assurances were needed such as the absence of liens on the security, the viability of the lease, and the Landlord's recognition of the security interest of the lender, all of which I either prepared, obtained or reviewed prior to the settlement date.

Charlie and I traveled to New York and checked into the Carlyle Hotel. Charlie's family was from New York and he wanted me to meet his uncle who was the doorman at the Commodore Hotel. Charlie said his uncle earned in excess of $100,000 a year in tips. Charlie banked with J.P. Morgan and Company and we had dinner at Latêche, an expensive New York restaurant. The next day, Mr. Witte asked me where we were staying. When I told him, he and his lawyer exchanged glances. When he asked me where I had dinner, I told him Latêche. He laughed and said, "Only borrowers can afford to stay at the Carlyle and eat at Latêche. Lenders have to eat at the corner bistro and sleep at the Y." That is a hard thing for people to do, and that is why there are more borrowers than lenders.

Mark was pleased I had done my homework. He said frequently lawyers arrive with their clients to borrow money from his venture capital company having no experience in corporate transactions and days are wasted getting the paperwork ready and obtaining the necessary documents. Our transaction closed with lightening speed and Mr. Witte was so pleased he took us to Madison Square Garden to watch a track meet. Charlie was bored but Mark and I, having run the 440 and the 220 hurdles as young men, enjoyed the evening.

On one of my visits to New York, I met Hazard Reeves, who reminded me of Buddy Ebsen. He had a beautiful home in Tuxedo Park with an indoor pool. He had a kind spot for squirrels, and he was delighted when I presented him with a huge burlap bag full of peanuts from my wife's farm in North Carolina. He owned a public company known as Reeves Cinetel, and he and Ron Spangler were discussing the merger of their two public companies, something I encouraged.

Ron had tired of the television business and approached me about forming a corporation to be known as Spanair, Inc. to act as a franchise dealer for what Ron called the "Cadillac" of private planes, manufactured by Rockwell. The Commander and the Shrike had the advantage of being able to take off and land on short runways. They looked awkward, however, because the wing was above the body of the plane. Our Beechcraft Duke was such a beautiful thing airline pilots whistled at us as they would, in my youth, at a pretty girl. I though the Rockwells were ungainly and I had my doubts, so Ron decided to fly me out in the Duke to visit the plant where the planes were made.

We took off and flew to Roanoke, Virginia. We landed there, gassed up, and flew to Shreveport, Louisiana. We landed there, gassed up, and took off for Enid, Oklahoma, where the plant was located. The sales manager met us and took us to dinner at what appeared to be a private home converted into a restaurant in a rural setting outside the town.

The next day we took introductory flights in each of the aircraft manufactured by Rockwell. The seats were leather, the airplanes were fantastic, and I was sold on the proposition immediately. They had that elusive 'new car' smell Doug Andrews had enjoyed in my gold and white 1957 Ford. We signed the papers and I found myself a distributor of airplanes in addition to being a lawyer, writer, farmer and community activist. Because of the difference in the air currents, we could fly back from Oklahoma to Forest Hill without landing for gas. I thought Ron's entry into the airplane business was as an investor, unaware he intended it to be his principal occupation.

Scotty McCray, a former navy pilot who flew with the 'Blue Angels,' was a client and he landed his plane at Phil Albrecht's landing strip near my house to fly me and my son Ted to Front Royal, Virginia, where he was planning a destination resort for private airplane owners. We passed over the landing strip on the Mellon estate where the words "Keep Away" were painted in large letters on the tarmac. Although I had worked on some legal matters for the Scaifes when I was with Nick Shriver, I had never been to their farm in Loudon County, and I urged Scotty to land there anyway so I could pay my respect.

Scotty replied there are a lot of old pilots and a lot of bold pilots but there are no old, bold pilots. A year later the wing of Scotty's plane hit the ground when he was performing with the 'Blue Angels' in South America. His death was instantaneous, and I started thinking the best thing I could do for my friends was to keep them as far away from me as possible. My friendship was a death warrant. Far too many people I loved were leaving me here by myself.

In New York I began working on a merger between Reeves Cinetel and Lewron Television, Inc. While touring their studio with the officers of both companies, I received a telephone call from Larry Hogan, Republican Congressman from Prince Georges County who was running for Governor against Louise Gore. As is often the case, no one had filed to run as a Republican for attorney general, and Larry wanted the central committee to name me to fill the vacancy. I owed it to Tom Finan to consider it.

A Spanair pilot flew me to a field near Larry's house where Larry met me and we talked for several hours. He wanted me to run with him in the primary against Louise. Tom Finan had just died of a heart attack on the very day Governor Mandel appointed him chief judge of the Court of Appeals, so Marvin appointed Bob Murphy instead. My Republican friends wanted me to get in a state-wide race, and the post of Attorney General appealed to me. But Louise had enough votes to block my nomination, so I thanked Larry for his interest and flew back to New York to fight a battle I thought I could win.

The employees at Reeves were represented by IATSE as Lewron was in California. Hazard was interested in having Ron serve as the Chief Operating Officer of the merged company, based upon his proven sales abilities and creativity. The merger was attractive to me because I hoped to salvage, for all of the people who had invested in Lewron, an exchange of Lewron stock for stock in Reeves Cinetel. Hardware was not the future of television, creativity was. But that was not to be.

IBEW in New York would not agree, and they preferred to destroy Lewron rather than cede their hegemony. The merger was blocked, Lewron was finished, and Ron Spangler went into the airplane business. I sued both unions in Maryland, a state where a mere vestige of former union strength still controls elections through an alliance with a prominent political law firm. Bob Murphy's Court of Appeals decided we had no cause of action for tortious interference with contract. I regretted even more the part I had played in putting him on the bench.

Terry Kravitz had arranged to license his Dyad patents, all of which had issued, to Advanced Micro Devices in California. They agreed to take over the prosecution of the patents, not only in the United States, but also in a number of foreign countries, including Europe and the Pacific Rim nations as well. Jim Garland had taken my deposition as part of the *Dyad vs. Singer* anti-trust case, and I was going to be called as a witness at trial. I asked Melvin Sykes and Max Israelson to try the case for me before the jury.

Max's son, also a lawyer, came to my office to review documents and gather evidence for a trial set to begin in late 1976. In November, we learned that the Singer Company had written off, as a total loss, its entire point-of-sale system, similar to the scanners now in all supermarkets which read bar codes, operate the cash register and print out a receipt for the customer. At that time, it was the largest write-off in American corporate history. It was the part of Singer, however, that had wanted Dyad's technology.

The case began before Judge Northrup in the United States District Court. As a witness, I could not be in the court room to see what was happening. I understood, however, that the jurors applauded Terry Kravitz on more than one occasion, for the responses he made to Jim Garland's cross examination. Terry was no fool.

When I was called to testify, I had to give up control of my mind while I was on the stand. I could not decide what to think about, for I had to think about the questions being asked. It was far more tiring than I had ever imagined it would be. Until that time, I had yet to try a jury case, but I always asked for a jury trial because I had more trust in juries than I had in judges. I later tried at least seventeen jury cases and the only one I lost was in Chicago in 1988.

The testimony Jim sought related to my conversations with Alex Brown and Jim McHenry. He wanted to know what changes had been made in the firm commitment letter to change it to a best efforts undertaking between the time I reviewed it in Jim's office and read it in my office. I had sketched these changes at my deposition. When testifying, I recalled a two line closing pleasantry at the end of the letter just above Jim's signature. I had not mentioned it in my deposition because it was irrelevant. At trial, I had no memory of the exact words Jim had used. At the end of five full days of testimony, I was happy to be out of the courtroom.

We estimated that the trial would take fourteen months. At the end of the third month of trial, all of the alternate jurors had been taken into the jury to replace those who had dropped out. Judge Northrop feared a mistrial and pressured the lawyers to settle the case. The settlement was sealed and the statement I had rendered to Dyad when I left Adelberg, Rudow and Blanton was paid in full, and Harry sent me a check for my draw. A year later, I was startled to learn that Donald Kirschner's brother had shot and killed him at their beach house in New Jersey. I knew nothing of the details, but the Singer Company had already ceased being a major corporate player.

My practice was growing and in August, 1975 Steve Heaver moved my office to another building he owned at 22 West Road. Jay Strong, Jr. had joined my firm as an associate, and Joseph M. Ayd and June Manzo were also working with us. Mrs. Campion left my employ the year I joined the Adelberg firm and Joan O'Donnell, whose husband was still in medical school, replaced her. Their first child, Bridget, had rheumatoid arthritis, so Joan took her swimming at the indoor pool in the Holiday Inn on York Road before they came to the office. Mr. Heaver built a nursery behind Joan's desk for Bridget, and we may have been the first law firm in America to provide on-site child care for an employee.

We represented companies from Cumberland to Bel Air in Maryland as well as one in Northern Virginia. Our clients had branches in other states and territories. They included an electronic circuit board manufacturer, real estate developer, fuel oil and gasoline distributors, credit reports, medicine, reagents for use in hospital laboratories, fire extinguishers, machine shops, a foundry, landscaping, architect, physicians, dentists, audio and television studios, a resort in St. Lucia and a number of restaurants, including the Flaming Pit in Timonium and the Crease in Towson, which put me in touch with professional athletes like Johhny Unitas, Ordell Braase, and Marty Domres.

Richie Evans, an all-American lacrosse player at Virginia owned the Crease, but spent a lot of time being a point man for Democrat presidential candidates. In January, 1976, he was in Florida with Senator Daniel Patrick Moyniham assembling crowds for Senator Scoop Jackson, who wanted to challenge President Ford. I called Rich and told him to come back to Baltimore because the peanut farmer from Georgia was going to win the nomination, and if he was going to invest his time in anybody's campaign, it should be Carter's.

Richie took my advice, and after Carter was elected President, Richie's restaurant in Georgetown known as Sarsfield's became the unofficial White House as Hamilton Jordan and other Carter White House aides spent their off-duty hours there.

I formed a company known as Flight Three Recordings, Inc. for Louis R. Mills, a talented sound engineer. While at Texas A&M, Lou had been commandant of the corps of cadets. He had less talent as a business man, which explains the fact that Flight Three was his third effort to launch a business of his own. He had trouble with that one as well.

Whenever I needed help with bankruptcy matters, I turned to Jerry Asch, who became a friend of mine when I was working with Nick Shriver. Jerry played tennis at the Orchard Tennis Club on the court next to the one where I played doubles on Sunday afternoons, and Jerry encouraged me to learn that branch of law because he did not like taking money from me for something I could so easily do myself. Jerry died at a young age and I found it necessary to take his advice.

The country was celebrating its 200th anniversary and Villanova University was offering a course on the revisions to the bankruptcy rules and new Bankruptcy Code, then pending in the United States Congress. Until the code was enacted, the rules were promulgated and implemented in the Bankruptcy Courts. Referees were replaced by bankruptcy judges, at least that was the plan until the Supreme Court decided that bankruptcy judges were not judges and could only act, as a result of a delegation of power from federal judges, much as if they were federal magistrates or commissioners.

So I celebrated our country's birthday at Villanova, and formed a quick friendship with a young lawyer from Corpus Christi named Buddy James Levy. His grandfather was a Jew but his parents were Baptist. He was a blue-eyed, blond who had played basketball for the University of Texas and tennis with Roscoe Tanner. His dormitory room at Villanova was next to mine, we were reading the same novel, played tennis and rode aimlessly around Philadelphia talking and discovering the city. He said the minute I walked into the Villanova class room and sat down he knew we were going to become fast friends. That happens to me so often and I have never doubted why. Its called understanding in the Bible.

The Queen and Prince Phillip drove by as Buddy and I were having supper in a downtown restaurant. Our waitress insisted we step outside to watch them pass. We made plans to get together again, difficult to accomplish because of our busy schedules. Buddy had hurt his back playing basketball and worked at a stand-up desk. Long air flights were excruciatingly painful for him.

Once we actually got into the same airport at the same time, but did not find one another because the SEC hearing he traveled to Washington to attend had been inexplicably transferred back to Houston. As soon as he got off the plane at Washington National, he was paged and told to come back to Texas with his witnesses. Another sign of a crack in the wall. Our national government can not do anything without making a mess of it, including keeping appointments. It is ineptitude on parade, and we foolishly keep asking it to do more instead or less, forgetting that burdensome regulations destroyed the western Roman empire.

Three years later, Buddy called me on New Year's Eve and told me he was going to land in Washington within the hour. I jumped in my car and drove to National Airport to pick him up. He wanted to have dinner in a French restaurant. It was after eight o'clock when we arrived in Baltimore, so I stopped by the Café des Artistes, then owned by Steve Levinson, who worked in Tom Finan's campaign in 1966. Steve obliged us with a table, and Buddy spent the night at my house. We talked well past midnight and the next day I drove him back to the airport so he could travel on to New York, where he had a meeting with a Saudi prince who was buying one of his Houston clients.

Years later Buddy asked me to represent the son of the Seminole Chief charged with a minor violation of the law in Alexandria, Virginia. Buddy was then CEO of Transamerica, a private company in Tampa, Florida, which built bingo palaces on the Seminole reservation in Florida. I am not admitted to practice in the Virginia state courts, and other than my military service, I know next to nothing about criminal law and procedure. I asked a lawyer who knew what I did not to take the case, but Buddy wanted me to meet the Chief's son and give him my personal attention.

Criminal law and evidence now constitute a fourth of what the majority of law schools teach, and the majority of judges appointed to state courts are either prosecutors or public defenders. There is abysmal ignorance of the great body of English and American law that is now lost to us by neglect. You do not have to "kill all the lawyers." The crit infested American Bar Association did that without shedding any blood by no longer requiring judges or lawyers to know the law.

The rich history of the common law dating back to 1189 is not found in Google or lexis-nexis searches. Baltimore County closed its bar library in 2005, replacing it with computers. Law students are no longer taught how to do legal research. Instead, their computers print out reams of paper a foot thick and they call it research. The only thing available to them is what the mindless computer sends them from a questionable and incomplete database. The two most recent Supreme Court justices made it through their confirmation hearings asserting that the only thing they needed to know was the Constitution and statutory interpretation. There was but one mention of common law in both hearings, and it was a reference to "federal common law" whatever that is.

The only thing law schools now teach is how to prosecute, defend and litigate. That works for the law school industry as long as the judges are former prosecutors and public defenders. But the common law is lost and knowledge will be lost when we can no longer generate electricity. If a solar flare shuts us down, we will have to start over in a new dark age with no knowledge of our past but that passed down by oral tradition. I wonder how often it has happened, and will again.

Charlie Flanders could not sell investigative mortgage credit reports, those verifying employment, salary and public record disclosures, in Puerto Rico. The banks were only interested in the FHA guarantee, and getting a bad report on a borrower was bad for business. Unable to sell reliable mortgage credit reports, Charlie's company went into the consumer credit reporting business and created proprietary software to generate computerized consumer credit reports, a business with a terrific bottom line because the vendor is selling information that costs nothing. When FHA, FNMA and Freddie Mac began accepting a three-credit bureau merged consumer report instead of requiring employment, income and assets to get a mortgage, the result was the sub prime mortgage crisis that exploded in July, 2007, bankrupting not only American and European banks but America and Western Europe as well.

NINJA mortgages were followed by home-equity loans and reverse mortgages. I was appalled when a widow of a deceased army officer asked me to review documents giving her house to her bank. Banks were not then in the home mortgage business, but state or federal savings and loan associations and savings banks were. Savings banks were being gobbled up by the commercial banks, and I regret that my "how-to" opinion of the Attorney General published in 1967 made that possible.

Banks entered the market when the oil crisis of the 1970's lifted interest rates to unrealistic levels, forcing the government to bail out the failed S&L industry It was then I realized the banks would soon own every house in America. NINJA (**N**o **I**ncome, **N**o **J**ob and no **A**ssets) loans were originated in pizza parlors and Chinese laundries at the urging of mortgage brokers, real estate agents and MAI, i.e.'made as instructed' appraisals. No one in the chain had any incentive to turn down a loan, and no one involved made money unless the sale went through.

George Liebman was at Harry's side as the savings and loan crisis unfolded. As bright as George is, the scope of the problem was nation wide, the genie was out of the bottle, and there was nothing they could do but fight the fire and do their best to contain it. My 1966 hope for Harry going to Washington as a senator was ruined, and we got Barbara Mikulski instead. We still have her, more than a quarter century later. She works hard, without regard to the political affiliation of those who seek her help. In Maryland, that is refreshing, but I would have been far happier if Harry had her job.

"That's Louise Gore all right, and she's not dead. Get her to the emergency room right now."

Asked to identify a body at the morgue,
House Speaker Marvin Mandel,
March 1970

Ambassador Louise Gore

The stagflation of the Carter years exacted a heavy toll on my corporate law practice. Venture capital dried up and the stock market dip in 1974-1975 was severe. Many of my corporate clients were successfully reorganized under Chapter 11. The reorganization provisions of the Bankruptcy Act are a magic wand to be waved over a client's balance sheet, converting debt into equity and restoring financial life to the moribund. If General Motors, Chrysler and AIG had been reorganized under Chapter 11, the 2008-2011 recession would have been much less severe, and the recovery far from anemic. A competitive American automobile business would have arisen from the ruins of Chrysler and General Motors, instead of an Italian company and a failing behemoth jointly owned by union bosses and the taxpayers that gives its product away,

Often an injection of new capital funds the payments, if any, due unsecured creditors at five or ten cents on the dollar, and control of the corporation passes, through the plan of reorganization, to the new ownership funding the plan. Although the Code did not go into effect until 1978, the rules promulgated to implement it were in effect from the latter part of 1976. After initiating reorganization plans for three of my corporate clients, I took an extended break.

As much as I enjoyed driving my 1970 Mercedes 280SE, I could not give it the tender, loving, care for which it was designed. A piece of lint or a speck of dust in the fuel-injection system shut the car down, and my many conversations with the service manager at Towson Valley finally paid off. Mercedes decided to America-proof its cars, making them more tolerant of American maintenance in 1977. I arranged to have a 450 SEL delivered in Frankfurt, Germany.

A burly, cross-country, truck driver named Ed Dzierbicki also owned a travel bureau in Baltimore. He provided the tractor that pulled the twelve-horse van that carried the Boumi Temple Mounted Patrol, of which I was captain, to local parades and Shrine conventions. I asked a young lawyer in my office to do something for him, assuring him the young lawyer was competent. Ed startled the young man when he said, "If you say he's all right, he's all right. If you say he's not, I'll kill him."

Ed saw himself as Scroggs replacement, insisting he would take a bullet for me. His travel agency confirmed most of our travel arrangements. Because our car had to meet American low-speed impact bumper requirements, the factory installed extended bumpers front and rear. Germans stared at us as they passed us on the autobahn. When we passed through customs into Austria, the border guard said "Dass ist ein grossere" amused by the clumsy additions mandated by our Nanny government.

We spent the first night in Heidelberg, and songs from the Mario Lanza movie "The Student Prince" echoed through the car as we drove to our hotel, following the left bank of the Rhine through the wine vineyards from Stuttgart to Heidelberg. My youngest daughter, on her first trip abroad, was transfixed by the ceilings in the Residenz in Würzburg.

We followed the Romantic Road to Rothenburg, where my wife was horrified when our children, having climbed outside the tower on the Town Hall, stood on a ledge overlooking the square with nothing but a fragile rail to prevent their plummeting to the street below. I had never seen her move as fast as she did when she yanked them back safely inside the cupola.

My car needed to have the 'break-in' oil changed, and the hall porter had the car serviced while we slept. We put sixty-four hundred miles on the car before we shipped it back to the Dundalk marine terminal in Baltimore. As we drove into Austria a few days later we passed the magnificent monastery at Melk. The next day we arranged a boat trip back up the Donau (Danube) to explore the monastery, stopping at Dürnstein where King Richard I was ransomed while returning from a Crusade. The troubadour Blondell discovered he was being held there when the King imprisoned inside joined in his singing of a drinking song.

After taking in a light opera and a trip on the Riesenrad in Vienna, we drove south through the mountains to Venice, leaving our car at a suburban parking lot and taking a boat to the Bauer Grünwald Hotel on the Grand Canal. The hotel, as was all Europe, was inundated with Japanese tourists, oblivious to the presence of anyone else. Our hotel served our meals on a balcony overlooking the Grand Canal a block below St. Marks Square, where the gondolas depart on their evening tours through the waterways.

My fatherly concern about my children's table manners did not go unnoticed by our waiter. When he cleared the table to serve the main course, he made an elaborate show of raking the bread crumbs at my place into a dish while my children giggled. They still mimic his showmanship whenever they clear a table. We were the only Americans in the hotel, sharing the balcony with two English and two German families. The Japanese had the rest of the hotel to themselves.

We wanted some glasses to match a decanter we were given as a wedding present, so we took the children, by gondola, to a small island in the lagoon where Venetian glass had been made for centuries. The craftsman made six glasses to our design, which were delivered in a wooden crate to our Glen Arm home several months later. I doubt they have ever been used, but I trust someone will find them in an Alex Cooper auction brochure when we die.

The next day we drove on a route plotted by the Concierge to our hotel to Rome. At a road block in Tuscany we were stopped by two policemen armed with machine guns, but after checking our papers and passports they waved us through. When we arrived at our hotel, the irrepressible Japanese had refused to vacate our rooms, so we were reassigned to a Swiss owned hotel on Palatine Hill.

My fifteen year-old son, who was then a choirboy at Old St. Paul's in Baltimore, was so overcome by the ceilings in the Sistine Chapel he fainted. We enjoyed a performance of Verdi's Aida at the Baths of Carracalla, a site later made familiar by the three-tenor performance at the 1980 World Cup. The grand march featured chariots pulled by teams of white horses with red plumes bobbing above their heads, the sight of which left my eleven year old daughter, still the best horsewoman in our family, breathless.

The roads from Rome to the Riviera, our next destination, were toll roads. Because Italian was not a language any of us knew, when we stopped at the toll booths I peeled off thousand lira notes until the collector seemed satisfied. At our last stop, misreading the collector's body language, I drove off too soon. He ran after me screaming 'dua milla lira." I stopped and gave him two more notes, but to this day any faux pas I commit, whether at home or in public, gives rise to my children chanting 'dua milla lira' in unison.

We stayed in a hotel in Rapallo perched precariously on a cliff overlooking the sea. The swimming pool had under water portholes offering a view from the dressing rooms into the pool, which led to a lot of bubbles rising to the surface when my children were swimming. Between Rapallo and Monte Carlo, we marveled at Italian engineering which bridged every valley, no matter how deep, and tunneled through every mountain, no matter how thick, to provide a level road all the way to France.

After tiring of the stones on the overrated-beach in Monte Carlo, we tarried too long at Arles and the Pont-du-Gard. We had a six o'clock deadline for our hotel in Carcassone, so we struck out on the autoroute needing to cover almost six hundred miles in five hours. I set the automatic speed at one hundred twenty miles per hour, and we made the hotel safely with minutes to spare. After dinner we walked across a meadow to the walled city, surprised to hear hard-rock music from within. Restaurants and sidewalk cafes inside were crowded with young people singing and playing music, mostly American.

The next day we had a more relaxed drive to the Loire Valley, the traffic being so heavy we could not reach, much less exceed, the speed limit. We stayed in a chateaux et relais hotel for three days that had a tennis court and pool, and our children exercised every afternoon before supper. During the day we toured Valençay, Loches and Amboise, watched the Son et Lumiere at Chenonceau, climbed the spiral staircases at Chambord, possibly the inspiration for modern parking garages, drank the wine of Rabelais beneath the walls of Chinon and paid our respects to long dead ancestors at Fontevrault.

While completing my obligatory, six-year military obligation as a member of Maryland's Dandy Fifth Infantry Regiment, I met Stafford Klotz, portrait painting son of a famous father whose works grace the walls of Maryland homes. After his death his wife received guests in her Chateau de Rochefort en Terre in Brittany, located above a charming town of gray stucco houses covered with flowers, thanks to the encouragement of the American family living in their midst for more than a century. Known as the flower village of France, it boasts two highly rated Michelin restaurants. We were astonished at the massive platter of shell fish placed before us as an appetizer in one, and delighted with the simple goodness of the food in the other.

We did not see the Cardinal's ghost in the wing assigned to us. Madame Klotz invited us into her quarters one evening for cocktails to meet her nephew, who was on his way to deliver a manuscript of Agathie Christie's biography to a New York publisher, a previous copy having gone astray in the mails. We saw a picture of Madame Klotz and our neighbor, Anne Deford, on an end-table. They were friends, and Anne's twin children, Sallie Buck and Rob Deford, had often occupied the rooms we were using when they visited Brittany.

When we drove into Normandy, we stopped in St. Lô where so many Maryland and Virginia men died making a breakout from the beaches in 1944. After locating the place where the 29th Division came ashore, we walked through the American cemetery, overlooking the sea that was later in the opening and closing scenes of the movie 'Saving Private Ryan'.

When we returned home I sketched our French itinerary on a napkin for Rich Evans. President Carter was going to Paris, and Hamilton Jordan sought Rich's help in suggesting places for him to visit in France. Pilgrimages to the cemetery and D-Day beaches by every American President since have become almost obligatory, although President Obama has yet to go. Richie shared with me a thank you letter he received from Mrs. Carter for his help in planning their trip.

After a few days in Paris we drove to the battlefields of Crecy and Agincourt. Crossing the channel by ferry, we stopped in Canterbury to pay our respects to St. Thomas a Becket, whose martyrdom gave birth to equity jurisprudence. We had visited three sites linked to Richard the Lionheart: Dürnstein where he was ransomed, Chinon where he died, and Chateaux Gaillard, his most famous fortification. The common law of England and America dates from Richard's death in 1189, which is why a silver statuette of Richard mounted on his charger graced the conference room in Nick Shriver's office where I began to treasure his legacy.

The litigious playwright Shakespeare previewed his plays for London's lawyers at the Inns of Court prior to performances in the public theater, but the practice of tolling the bell for each year of a prominent barrister's life when he dies is associated with Hemingway and John Donne. We visited Grays and the Middle Inn while we were in London, before driving out to Stratford to see Henry V, beginning with actors wearing black dungarees and turtle-neck sweaters on a dark stage. Only their disembodied faces were visible at first, but as the play progressed, the costumes and scenery appeared so gradually the beauty of the language was never lost.

We visited York, where we found York Minster, known locally as St. Peter's, marvelously restored. No one fainted while looking at the ornate ceilings. We walked the walls of York, and later those of Hadrian, before going to our hotel in Peebles, Scotland, a prelude to Edinburgh for the Tattoo at the castle. Returning late at night to our hotel, we were stopped on the road by police, suspicious of an expensive car bearing international plates. Shining their flashlight into the rear seat, they awakened three young Americans thankful they live in a country where such things do not happen. It was the second such occurrence within a month.

Before leaving England, I needed to pay another visit to Bosworth for research on a novel I was writing. Upon leaving the battlefield, I found the nail—for want of which the shoe was lost for want of which the horse was lost for want of which the crown was lost—in my tire. By God's grace, I managed to locate the spare and the jack and effect a change in a driving rainstorm.

We were due to load onto a ferry for a return to the continent from Harwich to the Hook of Holland, a trip I had made many times before and since. We had sleeping accommodations on the boat, and breakfast before our car was rolled off in the morning. It reminded me of the night boat trips from Baltimore to Norfolk I took as a child visiting the outer banks of North Carolina, another pleasure no longer possible.

After arranging to have the car shipped home, we rented another without an automatic clutch. I had driven a jeep with a clutch in the army and the transportation officer revoked my military driver's license after I hit a rut in a dirt road, tossing me out of the jeep into a ditch, where the jeep fell on top of me. My children were amused by the pathetic screams of the car as I drove them through Brussels traffic. The car and I battled one another for three days before we dropped it at the airport in Brussels and flew back to Baltimore.

Joe Ayd's extended family helped me reorganize Flite Three Recordings for Lou Mills under Chapter 11. They eventually expanded the operation into a facility they built on Cold Spring Lane containing two large and several smaller television studios, attracting commercial advertising as well as editing and post-production work for many of the movies and television programs filmed in Baltimore. Joe and his family came up with the capital to save Flite 3, agreeing to continue Lou Mills as the chief sound engineer in his original studios on Cold Spring Lane.

Joe decided to take a more active role in his family business, and to replace him I sought help from resumes I had saved from among the many I receive. I was intrigued with a letter from a student at Pepperdine in Newport Beach, California, who was only 20 years old. Pepperdine benefited from Mellon-Scaife money, and I was curious to know how a John Carroll student found his way there.

I learned he was leaving the next morning for California, so we decided to meet at Peerce's Plantation for dinner, where I met Doug Grinnell waiting by the fireplace, looking even younger than he was. He quickly agreed to spend the following summer in my office as a law clerk.

In April of 1978, Marvin Mandel had been indicted while serving as Governor of Maryland by the United States Attorney Jervis Finney. When he was convicted, of exactly what I have never been sure, Blair Lee became Acting Governor. My former partner, Harry Hughes was running for governor against Blair in the Democrat Primary, and Louise Gore, the Republican nominee in 1974, was planning to run again. She was the person responsible for having me removed from the House chamber in 1966 when Governor Tawes sent me out to round up votes for the Cooper-Hughes tax reform bill.

Louise was credited with rebuilding the Republican Party after Barry Goldwater's defeat in 1964. She had read a letter I wrote to the editor of the Baltimore *Sun*, and I agreed to meet her at the Center Club if Joe Ayd would go with me to make the introduction. She knew I had battled Steve Sachs in the courts on behalf of the Ayd family, and there was no love lost between Steve and me.

Steve was running to succeed Bill Burch, who was seeking the Democrat gubernatorial nomination. Louise wanted me as her running mate. She had already lined up Sam Culotta, a close associate of former Governor Theodore R. McKeldin. Sam was the last Republican from Baltimore City to serve in the Maryland legislature, and he agreed to run with Louise for lieutenant-governor, a post created to avoid repetition of the need for the Legislature to elect a replacement in the event of elevation, disability or death of the incumbent.

Louise owned the Fairfax Hotel in Washington, where the Jockey Club lounge attracted the famous and infamous. Steve had ignited her ire by referring to her as a "bar maid" at some point, and she was not amused. She wanted me to take his measure. My being a resident of Baltimore County added value to her ticket. We discussed Maryland politics over lunch.

She said the press had never understood how familial Maryland politicians were. In the company of other legislators from Montgomery County, she attended a Montgomery County Lincoln Day dinner. Driving back to Annapolis that evening, their car was involved in a crash and she was adjudged DOA at the hospital and her body sent to the morgue.

Marvin Mandel was called to identify her body, and when the coroner rolled out the slab, Marvin noticed a muscle in her ankle twitching. As the story was related to her, and by her to me, Marvin said, "That's Louise Gore all right, and she's not dead. Get her to the emergency room right now."

Her injuries were severe, and I do not believe ever healed. During the ensuing campaign, she had trouble sleeping, and often called me late in the evening or the early morning hours. Although they had been opponents in 1974, Louise and Marvin were friends, just as Joe Curran and I are, and Louise later sought my help persuading French Smith and Ed Meese to have Marvin pardoned. Since I don't know why he needed a pardon, I refer you to Brad Jacobs book "Thimbleriggers."

At lunch, Louise mentioned a young Republican Senator had paid her a visit and asked her to do for him what she had done for Barry Goldwater. My interest quickened because in my view Senator Goldwater was the most qualified man to run for President in the twentieth century, with the possible exceptions of Theodore Roosevelt and Ronald Reagan. I became a Republican in 1964 to vote for him in the primary, so I asked her what she did for Barry. This is what she told me.

After Richard Nixon lost the presidency to Jack Kennedy in 1960, the Republican National Committee was faced with the task of rebuilding the party from the ground up. The party faithful were asked to form new Republican Women's Clubs. Louise was in charge of that effort, and she promised each club with fifty charter members a speaker from Washington to present their charter. Each club with a hundred charter members would get a speaker of their choice. Otherwise, they got Louise and the junior senator from Arizona, who had a plane of his own and knew how to fly it.

Between 1961 and 1964, Barry and Louise flew all over the country, Barry talking and Louise bestowing charters. One night, in a town in the heart land, they had to stay over night due to a snow storm. After checking into her room, Louise received a call from the club organizer who could not drive home due to the weather. She asked if Louise had an extra bed in her room, and Louise graciously invited her in. A convention in that city had made hotel rooms scarce.

The next morning, when Louise was checking out, the clerk apologized because the hotel did not have a room for her pilot. They had allowed him to sleep on a sofa in the lobby as a courtesy to her. Appalled, Louise grabbed her key, found Senator Goldwater asleep under a blanket, woke him up, handed him her room key and sent him to shower and shave while she had breakfast. A few minutes later Senator Goldwater returned, red-faced and unshaven.

"Louise," he said, "why didn't you warn me there was a woman in your room?"

Louise had forgotten she had been awakened in the middle of the night to take in another member of the Republican army. But by 1964, Barry was the best known of all the Republican candidates for President among the people who matter and made up the majority of the convention delegates.

I accepted her offer, provided my wife did not object. I knew she would never approve. Brent Kansler, who was Louise's campaign manager, had successfully managed Citizens Against Tydings, or CAT, in 1970. My wife and I met with Brent, and he briefed us fully as to what we could expect if I got involved. Getting into politics in Maryland is more dangerous than the uninitiated know. Its hard ball, and they aim for your jugular. Taking someone out means disposing of them, literally or figuratively.

Harry Hughes was one of five Democrat candidates, the others being Wally Orlinsky of Baltimore City; Ted Venetoulis, the Baltimore County Executive; Bill Burch from Baltimore City; and Blair Lee, the Acting Governor, from Montgomery County.

Blair and Louise had been friends since childhood, their fathers having been active in Maryland politics. As I would soon learn, between the Bealls and Gores, there was a half-century old Hatfield- McCoy style feud. Sanford Donald was our campaign Treasurer, and his name would authorize actions on our behalf.

There was also unusual interest in the Attorney General's office in 1978. Jon Oster, Bill Burch's Duputy Attorney General, was challenging Steve Sachs, as well as two other lawyers, a Mr. Byrd whom I did not know, and Walter Finch, who attended the church where I had been a ruling Elder since 1968. The day before the filing deadline, Louise, Sam and I had lunch in Annapolis with the chairman of the Maryland Republican party, Dr. Aris Allen, at the Treaty of Paris Restaurant. Dr. Allen did not know anyone else who was going to run. He was so pleased the party was going to have a full ticket that he picked up our lunch check.

The very next day, however, such being the ferocity of the Beall-Gore feud, the brothers Beall had put together a ticket of their own, headed by former Senator Glenn Beall for Governor, Dr. Allen for Lieutenant-Governor, a lawyer named Warren Rich for Attorney General, and our candidate for Comptroller, who jumped ship overnight to ally himself with Glenn, who had, after all, actually won a state-wide election. So I not only was in the middle of it, I had a primary opponent. We opened our campaign headquarters on the second floor of the Belvedere Hotel in Baltimore.

After making obligatory calls on the press in outlying counties, Louise invited me to Marwood to meet her parents. We had met the day before with Phillip Merrill, an opinionated magazine and newspaper publisher in Annapolis. During an exchange of deep-seated political beliefs with the restrained anger attending such discussions, I blurted out "Phil, we are really not as far apart as you seem to think."

His concern for the poor and downtrodden of the world matched mine. Our differences concerned the means of accomplishing our aims. He wanted to keep the poor dependent on his party; I wanted to help them become self-sufficient and independent. In any event, Louise thought my remark was hilarious, and repeated it to her parents, who shared her mirth. If there is something about it I am missing, let me know.

Marwood is a replica of the Chateau de Malmaison, which Napoleon built for the Empress Josephine. It sits high on a ridge near the Great Falls of the Potomac, at the end of a long and winding road through a wood after passing a stone gatehouse as large as most upper-middle-class, American houses. As you emerge from the wood, there is a large open lawn in front of the house. It was, with the exception of the Vanderbilt residence at Biltmore, the most impressive private home I have visited in America.

Colonel Gore told me that Ambassador Kennedy tried to buy it in 1960 when his son became president. Being originally from Tennessee, the Gores were delighted to learn I rode a Tennessee walking horse born in Murfreesboro. Mrs. Gore said that was just what she needed. Colonel Gore joshed, "What would you do with a horse? You have trouble walking; you can't possibly ride at your age?"

"If I had a horse, I wouldn't have to walk. I could ride him wherever I wanted to go."

Their house was so big, she could have ridden him around inside, but I would not recommend it. We settled in to some serious political talk as to how we should conduct our campaign. The colonel recommended we call on former Congressman Thomas Johnson when we campaigned on the Eastern Shore, to get his advice as well. Tom Johnson had a loose affiliation with Harry Adelberg, whose friend and confidant he was. I had seen Johnson's name on Harry's office door when I met with him to form our partnership in 1969.

After being successfully vetted by the Gores, the Colonel had this piece of advice: "Stand at the front door of the Court House and accuse your opponent of doing the very things you will have to do to win. Tell the press he's taking money from this or that special interest and he's tainted by it. Then you run out the back door and get all the special interest money you can get your hands on from those very same people. The press will never suspect you of doing the thing you are accusing your opponents of doing. The first one to make the accusation wins."

I remembered this advice as I watched the contested 2000 Presidential election dispute. Al Gore is Louise's first cousin, and that campaign tactic is apparently a Gore family staple regardless of party affiliation. Louise and I left with their support, confident we had the money we needed to run our campaign.

"Harry. You are going to win. When the public looks at Blair, Wally, Teddy and you, they are going to pick you."

Advice to Harry Hughes,
Crisfield Crab Festival,
July, 1978

The 1978 Primary Election

After participating in a 'debate' with the other five candidates for attorney general in College Park, I joined Louise in Worcester County. Brent had leased three identical cars, matching our campaign colors, and we were on our way to meet with Blan Harcum, an important Republican leader whose support we needed. Brent wanted to see how the watermelon farmers on the shore would react to Dr. Allen's presence on the Beall ticket.

After meeting Colonel Gore, I knew the history which fired his animosity of the Bealls. I expected trouble, but I knew I would get along with Mr. Harcum when he said, "Dr. Allen is not just a black man. There's a great deal more to him than that."

I respected Dr. Allen, and I wanted to earn his respect despite his decision to run with Glenn. Glenn and I were both Masons and Shriners and if I had not signed on with Louise, I would have had no difficulty supporting him. On the way to Congressman Johnson's house, I told Brent any disrespect shown Dr. Allen was political suicide. We had to concentrate on issues, not personalities, and most certainly not race.

When we joined Ambassador Gore at the Johnson's home, as all present referred to Louise, she introduced me to Maureen O'Hara, a movie actress who was a friend of Mrs. Johnson. Tom talked about issues urging a single issue campaign, believing the right issue with the broadest possible appeal simplified things for the press and the public. Like most Democrats, he had no respect for the intellect of either.

He mentioned Harry Nice's campaign in 1934, when he was elected Republican Governor of Maryland in the midst of the depression on a single issue—rolling back the price of an automobile license tag which Governor Ritchie had just increased. Because I agreed with his thesis, I related a similar story by my political mentor, Judge Robert Gerstung, about a mayor who declined a gift of a baby elephant to the zoo because the city could not afford to feed it. His defeat was assured when his opponent blamed the incumbent's mismanagement for the city's poor financial condition, so poor, in fact, they could not even feed a baby elephant a generous citizen offered them for free.

The next day we called on central committee members and attended sporting events, church picnics, and community events. It was hot and humid. We had yellow baseball style cloth caps for each candidate, with our names embroidered in brown thread. I was a shy campaigner, so Louise teamed me up with Sandy Donald and a tall blonde woman who worked in our headquarters. She was concerned about how well I was tolerating the heat. When the bartender asked me what I wanted. I said your vote would be appreciated.

"You've already got that." he said. "That willowy blonde is mighty fond of you. A man who inspires that kind of devotion from a woman like that is a man I'll vote for."

Bolstered by his encouragement and more at ease, I became more outgoing for the rest of the campaign. That day was such a blur of faces and conversations and handshakes I do not remember where we spent the night, although I vaguely recall sitting at a table with Brent Kansler and Sandy Donald overlooking the sound in Ocean City talking over our schedule. The next day we attended a mandatory seafood event in Crisfield honoring former Governor Millard Tawes. As our caravan pulled into the parking lot, Louise saw Harry Hughes park his car, get out and walk toward the gate. Horrified, she said, "There's goes your buddy, Ed. Don't let him walk in there alone. Catch up quick and go in with him."

I sprinted across the parking lot, yelling for Harry to wait. He turned, slightly smiled and put out his hand. Out of breath, I hit him with a torrent of words.

"We don't have a lot of time. Bill Burch is going to withdraw tomorrow. You've got to stay in. I know things aren't going well for you. I've read the stories in the paper that you are low on funds and go to events that are poorly attended or canceled altogether. I also know you're going to win. When the public looks at Blair, Wally, Teddy and you, they're going to pick you."

"What makes you think Bill Burch is going to withdraw tomorrow?"

"Tomorrow's the filing deadline. Monday night in College Park, Bill was sitting in the front row at the AG debate making inane and incoherent remarks. He wouldn't be doing that if he were going to stay in the race."

Harry smiled, broader this time, "Don't worry. I've got to stay in. I've no place else to go."

"Thanks, Governor. See you at your inauguration."

When we parted to go our separate ways, Jon Oster, the deputy attorney general, was waiting to talk with me. He had come to the Attorney General's office as I was leaving in 1968 from Hinckley and Singley, a firm which had a huge trust practice which I knew well. Jon said he was tired of counting other peoples money. He had been a guest at the Labor Day picnic my wife and I hosted in 1967. I complained to him about the tactics of my Republican opponent, Mr. Rich.

"I have never heard of this guy before, and he's attacking everything about me, including my masculinity. Who is he and where did he come from?"

Jon said, "If you think he's treating you badly, you should see the things he's doing to Steve Sachs. He threatened Steve physically and took a microphone away from him."

At least, I thought, that should please Louise. Jon told me Warren was an assistant attorney general assigned to the Department of Health, handling environmental law matters. He had no idea Warren was a Republican until he filed with the Beall ticket. He was glad he was my problem and not his.

When the seafood had been eaten and the beer barrels emptied, our caravan pulled into the parking lot of the Salisbury Sheraton, expecting to spend the night there. The desk clerk was a Republican, but he shook his head when I told him I needed five rooms. He didn't have them.

"Why not?" I asked, incredulous that a hotel this far from Ocean City would be filled.

"We have set aside the top floor for the Governor and his staff, and we can't put anybody else up there."

"Is he using the entire floor?"

"Just three rooms."

"Is he up there now?"

"Yes."

"Call him, and tell him I need to talk to him." Blair and I were vaguely acquainted, because he had been vice-chairman of the Senate Finance Committee Harry chaired when Harry and I were working together in the mid-sixties.

Blair's cheery voice came over the phone. "Hey, Ed, what can I do for you?"

"Take us in. We need shelter. The inn keep says he has no room for us because you have the whole top floor."

"What've you got?"

"I need five, one for me, one for Louise and three doubles for our staff. We are so tired I promise you won't hear a peep out of us after dinner."

I put the clerk back on, and Blair graciously gave up the other end of the hall. At dinner that evening, we had a round table in the middle of the dining room, laughing and re-living the events of the day. Blair was sitting in the corner with three men I did not know. Louise nudged me and whispered, "Blair wishes he was with us."

"What makes you think so?"

"He hates being stuck with those muldoons. He keeps looking over here and rolling his eyes to the ceiling."

Sure enough, a few minutes later somebody nudged me. Blair was standing behind my chair, plate, silverware, napkin and drink in his hand.

"Please, Ed, make room for me?"

"Sure," I said, pushing my chair in the opposite direction from Louise. Blair put his plate and drink on the table between us, pulled up a chair from the next table, sat down, dropped his napkin in his lap, leaned over his plate with knife in one hand and fork in the other, and said, "All right, guys, what's our plan."

We had nothing to hide from him, so we talked freely. The United States Court of Appeals for the Fourth Circuit was expected to rule momentarily on Marvin Mandel's appeal of his conviction. I asked Blair what he would do if the conviction was reversed. Blair grinned and said, "Every night they bring a file box full of papers I'm supposed to read or sign. They put it in the corner of my room and make me feel guilty for not doing my homework. Nothing would please me more than turning that box over to Marvin so I could go out, happy as a kid on spring break, and campaign my heart out."

Knowing just how he felt, I reminded myself winning was not all it was cracked up to be. When we campaigned in Southern Maryland, I was as comfortable as I was on the Shore. I had been counsel to the Tri-County Council and approved the move of the State tobacco warehouse from the inner harbor to Charles County back in the mid-sixties. We called on Bud Wade, who had been Louise's running mate in 1974. Later, Louise confessed that she had used Bud shamefully in 1968. Sensing another piece of political history, I urged her to tell me about it.

"Bud did not like Spiro Agnew. Nixon had promised Senator Thurmond if he delivered the South's votes for Nixon on the first ballot in the convention, Strom could pick his running mate. So I told Bud that Agnew was being considered and it was up to him to stop it.

Bud agreed to meet Strom for dinner, and he droned on and on why Agnew would be a disaster for the party. He was too conservative, he was an opportunistic politician, and he had antagonized black politicians in Maryland by blaming their lack of leadership for the riots following the assassination of Dr. Martin Luther King in 1968. When dinner was over, Bud excused himself, confident he had done the party and the country great service. Thurmond was impressed by the negative report, and he said 'By God, Louise, I think we've found our man.'"

Thurmond and Louise were friends, and he was at every political event I attended at Marwood, often with his very young and very beautiful wife.

For the next six weeks, I was a good trooper, going where I needed to go. At a firehouse in Baltimore County former students in my mathematics classes at Mergenthaler were tending bar and cooking pit beef. Most had gone on to college, one had been my jeep driver in the National Guard, and another was an undercover detective in the BCPD. I gave my standard stump speech, adhering to my basic belief. It was a fight between those who care about others and those who care only about themselves.

The press would say that the latter were Republicans and the former Democrats. My thesis was the opposite, same ends, different means. I was startled by how quietly a packed hall of supporters would listen and how loudly they would cheer and applaud when I finished. As I was leaving, a man I didn't know followed me to the parking lot and said, "You are an anomaly. A lawyer everybody likes. I can't find anybody who doesn't like you. How do you do that?"

"I don't invite my enemies. It's not good for the party."

I was beginning to fear I might win, a thought I did not want to contemplate. Louise and I stopped by my house in Glen Arm because I wanted Louise to meet my wife and children. Although my wife's family was active politically in North Carolina, she was not happy about my being involved in politics. I thought Louise might change her mind. She didn't.

One of Louise's brothers lived in Georgetown and he hosted a fundraiser for us. He had learned I had an interest in the classics and I was also a Knight Templar in the York Rite Masonic Order. He had invited someone I had never heard of named Lyndon LaRouche, an intense, dark browed man with a withering tongue.

As I moved from the garden into the salon, shaking hands and introducing myself, I came face to face with a Neanderthal standing in the corner facing the center of the room. My effort at 'polite cocktail-shake-your-hand-hope to never-see-you-again- talk' brought incoherent guttural responses. I saw a counterpart in the opposite corner, and I realized the two men were body guards.

After speechmaking time was over, Louise's brother introduced me to Mr. LaRouche, who questioned my Masonic connections, and a half-hour of lively discussion followed. He was convinced that Queen Elizabeth and Prince Philip, through their alleged control of a bank in Hong Kong, were the principal profiteers from the worldwide drug trade. The world, he said, picking up on my trademark campaign stump speech, had been divided into the good and the bad since Alexander the Great. Half of us were spiritual followers of Plato, the other half, including Alexander, of Aristotle. The German poet Schiller figured in one group, and the Freemasons and Mozart in the other. Whichever group to which he assigned me, I thought I was in good company.

According to him, Athens lost the Peloponnesian War because Alcibiades disclosed Masonic mysteries to the uninitiated. And Alcibiades, I knew, had Socrates for a mentor and Plato for a playmate. Poor Alexander, on the other hand, was mentored by Aristotle, who had been ostracized from Athens. I suspect it was from Aristotle that Alexander got his contempt for Athens. I never found out why the Gores wanted me to confront Mr. LaRouche, but I enjoy debate when my opponent is well armed. It was a satisfying but mystifying day.

In early August, Sam, Louise and I were interviewed by the editors of the newspapers in Baltimore and Washington. Brad Jacobs asked me why I thought we could win. I was doing well, and Louise had been the party nominee four years ago, so I jumped right to the general election.

"Simple, really. If Blair wins the Democrat primary, Ted Venetoulis would prefer Louise for four years to Blair for eight, so the liberals will support us in November. If Ted wins, Blair would prefer Louise for four years to Teddy for eight."

Knowing how badly Harry was doing in the press, and a powerful Democrat Senator "soft shoe" Harry McGuirk having called Harry "a lost ball in high grass", I discounted Wally Orlinsky and violated the first of the two rules imposed by my wife. The first was "Never say anything that's not necessary" and the second

"If you can't say something good about somebody, don't say anything." I volunteered the only guy we could not beat was Harry Hughes.

Brad looked up in his annoying and probing way and asked, "Why can't you beat Harry?"

"Because nobody knows what Harry is. The conservatives think he's a conservative. The liberals think he's a liberal. Harry doesn't know what he is. There's no reason for any of them to oppose him. Like him they may not, but he doesn't threaten anybody's core values."

Within forty-eight hours, and more than three weeks before the September primary, the *Sun* endorsed Harry for Governor. He went from nowhere to the top like a rocket. Sorry, Harry, but trust me, it worked. Even Dr.Paul Cooper, who loved you like a brother, told me you never had an idea of your own. He argued that was your strength, because you could more easily assess the ideas of those around you.

On August 13, 1978, for the first time during the campaign my wife agreed to join me, Louise and Sam campaigning in Little Italy and along the Baltimore Waterfront. The promenade was there, but not Harbor Place. In fact, there was no place to eat, drink or visit a wash room. In late afternoon, a sudden thunderstorm came upon us. A large white ship was docked at the quay on Light Street, and as the clouds darkened, thunder roared and lightening lit the sky, the Captain invited us on board. He found us a table large enough for our group in the dining room where we waited out the storm.

Because it was our eighteenth wedding anniversary, I ordered champagne. Two chilled bottles arrived with our supper. When the bill was delivered, the captain whispered that the champagne was his anniversary gift to my wife. Too bad we did not have her with us in the campaign from the beginning. But by mid August, it was time to go to the outer banks for our annual end-of-summer vacation. I had never been so ready to get away.

Our campaign was heading to Western Maryland, traditional Republican country and Glenn Beall's home territory. My quarrel was with his brother. My wife had family in Hagerstown. I thought I had western Maryland sewn up, so I took off for the beach.

The press was incredulous. One angry reporter asked my assistant Joan O'Donnell what kind of a politician goes on vacation in the middle of a campaign. She told him I was not a politician but a competent corporate lawyer seeking to be retained as the state's general counsel.

When I returned to Baltimore in September, I saw Harry at a candidate forum in northwest Baltimore County. We talked for a few minutes. The press, as usual, were oblivious and knew nothing of our past association and friendship. "Harry, it looks good for you. We were in northern Baltimore County last night, and in the straw polls being taken in the Democrat clubs, you came in a close second behind Ted in two and actually lead in three others. If you are doing that well in Ted's home county, you are a shoo-in to win state-wide."

"I hear you are pretty popular yourself. I've heard some good things about you."

"My Masonic friends have been encouraging. Do you think we can work together if I win?"

"I don't know why not. We were a pretty good team before."

"I've got to go say my piece. See you at the Governor's Mansion when you are sworn in."

Joe Ayd, who was helping John Shoup, a lawyer running against Ellen Sauerbrey for an open seat in what was then the 10th Legislative District, grabbed my arm and asked me why I was talking to a Democrat. I said I just wanted to make sure I had a friend in the State House for the next eight years.

Warren Rich's attacks on my character were increasing in intensity, and Senator Jack Bishop of Baltimore County, a friend of Joe Ayd's, threatened to withhold support for the entire Beall ticket unless Warren produced evidence to support his slander. My cousin Charlie Herndon had practiced law with Jack at O'Connor & Preston for several years, and Jack was planning to sublet space from me in the Bosley Building where I was relocating my law office as of the first of the year.

Just before we went to the outer banks, my former partner, Harry Adelberg called me to report one of the partners brought in to take my place when I left in 1972 had been a law school classmate of George Beall at, I believe, the University of Virginia. George had heard there was some scandal connected with my leaving the firm, and he wanted the evidence to give to Senator Bishop. Harry cautioned, "These guys are really after you. You frighten them, and they want to hurt you. When we told him we didn't know what they were talking about, we got the impression they were offering us something to say your departure had been on less than honorable terms. We would never do anything like that, but I wanted to warn you so you can protect yourself. If you need me, just call, and we will jump in with both feet on your behalf."

I was equally puzzled. I told him about our pleasant stay at Tom Johnson's house the previous month. Harry said,

"Politics is hardball. You do what I couldn't get Tom to do. He was so convinced he was innocent; he talked too much trying to clear himself. I told him to clam up and they couldn't prove a thing. If he had taken my advice he would still be in Congress. You can't fight slander with the truth."

I thanked Harry for his friendship, wondering to myself what George Beall was up to. I had left Nick Shriver in 1965 on the best of terms. There was litigation between Harry Hughes and my former partners when I left that firm in 1968, but, as far as I knew, none of it had anything to do with me. Warren Rich told my partner, Standish McCleary, that I liked business deals, but his words to Sam Culotta were that I was not as straight as I looked.

During the final week before the primary, there were live televised sessions for the candidates for attorney general. Steve Sachs and I, united in our distaste for my opponent, got together whenever we met to trade information and swap war stories. Steve said Warren was from south Philadelphia, and he had been recruited by Robert Baumann, a Republican Congressman from the Eastern Shore, to run with Glenn Beall.

If the Bealls subscribed to the same political tactic as the Gores, ascribing to their opponents the actions they themselves were guilty of, counting on the naiveté of the press never to suspect the accuser was actually the accused, Warren's connection to Bob Baumann and his attacks on my character made sense. Friendship developed between Steve and me from opposition to our common foe, replacing the animosity that had marked our relationship as courtroom adversaries.

Warren avoided me, and he was not present in the green room where Steve and I were exchanging information. Stan Stovall signaled for me to come in for my time before the cameras, and while I responded to Stan's questions, I saw Warren enter the anteroom and take a seat, studying some papers in his hands. This was the first time I had seen him since the College Park debate. As I left the studio, I stopped beside Warren's chair, startling him. Looking as menacing as possible, I said, "I know what you're doing. When this campaign is over, you're going to get a bill from me you can't pay."

I did not see Warren's performance on camera, but Joe Ayd did, and he asked what I had said to him just before he went on the air.

"Why do you ask?"

"Whatever you said rattled him so bad he was incoherent on the air."

I told Joe what I said, and he asked me what I meant. I told him I didn't know what it meant. It was just something that popped into my head when I walked through the studio door. Before my interview, I had sent up a silent prayer for help in saying the right thing at the right time. I guess what it meant to Warren was what was important about it.

On primary day, my bag was packed for a trip to San Juan to meet with the lawyer I hired to defend the United Credit Bureau of Puerto Rico from suits filed under the Fair Credit Reporting Act. I had breakfast at home with volunteers who were going to man all of the polling places within miles of Avondell. My wife and children were going to supply the workers with meals and refreshments throughout the day. I wished them well, thanked them and drove to the Long Green firehouse to vote.

One of my corporate clients was embroiled in a union organizing effort that summer, so after voting I met with Sam Cook, a labor lawyer at Venable. After spending the morning in his office, we had a quick lunch. As captain of the Boumi Temple Mounted Patrol, I had to be at the McDonough School for equestrian drill practice that afternoon. Our drills were intricate, choreographed to musical accompaniment and requiring some skill at managing a horse in an environment stressful for both man and beast.

We were to leave for Wildwood on Friday following the primary for our annual Mid-Atlantic competition. I drilled in muck boots, dungarees and denim jacket. Being fair, I am sun-sensitive, so I also wore a white, ten-gallon cowboy hat. Afterward, I drove to the Belvedere Hotel, tired, dusty and thirsty. Louise had voted in Montgomery County, and she had not yet arrived at our headquarters on the second floor.

I stopped in the Owl Bar to get a beer and a crab cake on crackers. Vic Frenkil, who had been on Tom Finan's finance committee in 1966, owned the hotel. He greeted me and handed me a roast beef sandwich. Louise had asked him to give me a key to her apartment so I could shower and change clothes. I stopped by the headquarters on the way up and the tall blonde campaign assistant was absolutely frantic. My old adversary, Melvin Perkins, an unopposed Republican candidate for a seat in Congress recently held by the late Goodloe Byron, wanted to meet the press in our headquarters. She had told him he could not, but he had sent out notices of his intentions which he could not recall.

"I'll deal with him later. I've got to shave, shower and change."

"I'm going with you," she said, locking the door and following me to the elevator. She was afraid of Melvin, and she did not want to be alone in the headquarters when he returned. As I was coming out of the shower, she called, "Ed, he's at the door."

Wrapping a towel around my bare body, I opened the door and glared at him. "Melvin, if you don't leave this hotel right now, I'm going to rearrange your face. The press won't know you any more."

"Just wait till I tell the press you are naked in a hotel room with a blonde."

"Promise me you will go do that. With the kind of stuff thrown at me during this campaign, I can't think of anything I would like better than your spreading that tale around town. But you better not do it anywhere near the Belvedere, or you are going to feel some serious pain."

In any event, when the polls closed in Baltimore County on primary night my vote was four times that of Mr. Rich, but the Beall-Allen ticket won handily statewide. It turned out that a well-done campaign newspaper, contributed by the Gore family and mailed prepaid to every Republican voter in Maryland, lay dormant in the Carroll County post-office until after the election was over. No one in any County west of Baltimore had received it before they voted. Another bit of political hardball by Maryland's governmental oligarchy.

I had done well in Baltimore County, but I did not know how my race had turned out. But my vote was twice that of Louise in the polling places where we had workers. Many of them stayed at my house late into the night, hoping for a miracle. Some took my loss worse than I did, but knowing I had let them down was far worse than losing.

It did not matter, for Steve would win the general. Before the "I am an American Day" parade in Patterson Park in mid September, Steve was sitting in an open car. Dressed in my ridiculous Boumi Temple parade uniform on my Tennessee Walker Choco, I rode over to chat. Steve told me I was the lucky one because I had lost, but now he would have to do the job for four years, a heavy price to pay just for the fun of the campaign and the excitement of winning. He put his hand on Choco's nose and said, "Thank God I don't have to run against you. You look magnificent on that beast."

Charlie Flanders, the client I had taken on as a favor to Tom Finan, and who had taken Tom and Isabel to Puerto Rico the day after the primary in 1966, arranged an elaborate diversion, producing an urgent teletype message from our local counsel in San Juan requesting my presence the day after the election, so Charlie and I hopped aboard an Eastern Airlines flight early Wednesday morning.

When we landed in Puerto Rico I kept asking when and where we were to meet with the lawyer. Charlie said we were going to the race track. Knowing that no self-respecting, aristocratic Castilian lawyer would be caught dead in a casino or racetrack, I called Charlie's bluff.

"You brought me here to play, didn't you?"

When he admitted that he had. I asked him if the Baltimore office had the final results of the election. At dinner that night Jack Sauber handed me a teletype message from the Baltimore office. I had 40,000 votes and Mr. Rich had 45,000. My life was still my own. When I returned home to the bucolic beauty of Long Green Valley, I vowed never again to risk another foray into politics as a candidate.

The Republican Party was sponsoring a kickoff for the general election at a hotel in downtown Baltimore. Louise, Sam and I had to appear to have our pictures taken with Glenn. I had become genuinely fond of Dr. Allen during the campaign. Sitting beside him at political event, he had consoled me by saying, "Don't fear, Mr. Blanton. Out of adversity, comes growth."

But shake hands with Warren Rich? Louise told me that I had to do it for her whether I wanted to or not. Faking a smile, I made trite and congratulatory remarks for the camera. As soon as the photographer had finished with us, I hurried into the men's room and threw up. It wasn't something I ate. Years later, a Chicago lawyer testifying falsely in the only jury trial I ever lost, got s surprised look from me, the only person in the room who knew he was lying, and fled from the court-room to throw up. There must be a medical explanation that words so repugnant to one's basic belief evoke physical consequences.

"It's the Court of Appeals. Those guys are making mincemeat out of the law, chopping it to shreds. Only two of them ever practiced law. They don't know what they are doing."

"Two? Which two are you talking about?"

I identified two men, one of whom I did not know and had given him the benefit of the doubt. Harry, however, knew his history far better than I.

"You're wrong about him. He never practiced law a day in his life."

Conversation in the Governor's Office,
May, 1979

Governor Harry R. Hughes

I returned from San Juan on Friday morning and drove directly from BWI to Wildwood, New Jersey where the Mid Atlantic Horse Patrol competition, for which I practiced on primary day, was being held. The competitive drills were Friday afternoon, and Choco and I managed as best he could, for the traditional walk, trot, and canter which are the mainstay of synchronized equestrian routines are not natural gaits for a Tennessee Walker. But he was a gamester, convinced he was the herd master, so he faked it.

A dinner at which the results of the equestrian drill competition would be announced was scheduled at six. I began to don my tuxedo, but in my rush to get away from Baltimore, I had forgotten to pack my tux pants. In an era when cell phones were unknown, I frantically grabbed the yellow pages, called a taxi and a men's clothing store. Explaining my predicament, I persuaded the proprietor who was closing at six to pull out all the black pants in my size and hang them in a dressing room.

Telling the cabbie to wait outside, I began taking off my uniform pants as I ran into the store. The third pair I pulled on fit and I kept them on, grabbed my red jodhpurs and paid for the pants as I hurried back to the waiting cab.

I was the reluctant captain of the Boumi Temple Mounted Patrol, but I did not want to be late. Thomas Evans, who was Potentate that year, had been a fraternity brother in law school. He appointed me Counsel to Boumi Temple as well as Captain of the Mounted Patrol. But I was also Captain-General of Beauseant

Commandery of Knights Templar, and both groups met on the same night, thirty miles apart, creating an impossible scheduling problem for me. I alienated my fellow Knights when I tried to alternate attendance at monthly meetings of both organizations.

Having already published an article in the Mid-Atlantic Shrine Horse Patrol magazine entitled "Miracle at Wildwood" detailing the events of that night and the day following, I will say only that my patrol took first place in the street parade, thanks in large part to some forgetfulness, or prank, or charity about which me and mine knew nothing. Zembo, as the Harrisburg, Pennsylvania temple was known, won the competitive drill but they were disqualified in the street parade. As the second place finisher, we got the first place trophy, which brought tears to the eyes of some of our troopers and got me thrown into the swimming pool.

My wife sent Pat Hughes a dozen roses on inauguration day, when Harry was sworn in as Maryland's governor, and we were invited to the Governor's Mansion for a reception. I was surprised to see so many Republican friends there, and I thanked Harry for inviting them to make me feel at home. Harry is a serious guy and my best efforts at humor often went missing. He said, "I didn't invite them to make you feel at home. I invited them to make me feel at home. These are the people who got me elected."

I could not quarrel with that, although I have never told Harry about my meeting with Brad Jacobs and the *Sun* editorial board that summer. I never doubted he would win the Democrat primary. I knew he was a winner long before we met.

Louise took note of my affinity for horses, remembering that my walker had clinched her parent's acceptance of me as an all-right guy. She was appointed to the Civic Center Commission by Mayor Schaefer and solicited my help in promoting horse events in Baltimore. I called upon an equestrian journalist who managed the Boumi Temple Horse Show for his assistance. Louise acted upon his recommendation, and our first event was the Gold Cup Competition, in the spring, featuring world class riders and horses that compete in the Olympics.

The event coincided with the running of the Maryland Hunt Cup on the last Saturday in April. I hosted the male riders on a chartered bus, fed them gourmet picnic lunches and took them on a walking tour of the course before the race. The height and solidity of the fences awed the Olympians. I heard one say that the difference between the Hunt Cup fences and the ones in the Civic Center is that 'ours fall down when we hit them, but out here, the horse and rider fall and the fence stands firm.'

I knew what he meant. Benjamin H. Murray, or Laddie as we called him, was a fierce competitor. Six months before he succumbed to brain cancer his wife had been killed when her horse hit a fence at Middleburg, Virginia and rolled, crushing her to death. The professionals, riding through a beautifully decorated course in the Baltimore Civic Center, cleared fences made of balsa wood, which collapsed in a heap if hit, just like the ones we used at the Boumi Temple horse show in Owings Mills.

That August, I received an invitation to a "Scarlet" reception at the Washington Hilton from Lorne Green, president of the American Horse Protective Association. Black tie and white tie I could handle, but scarlet? I called my former polo playing Yalie partner, Blake McFeely. If I were the master of a particular foxhunting club, I could wear a scarlet coat with what is otherwise a white tie and tails outfit. Since the event in Washington was being supported by the combined Maryland and Virginia foxhunting clubs, quite a few attendees wore scarlet coats. The rest of us wore black with white ties.

Estelle, Louise and I sat with a young Senator from Iowa named Charles Grassley, with whom I discussed my contempt for the Internal Revenue Code, calling it an instrument of social policy instead of a tax law, convinced the future of the Republic required its repeal. But he was then addicted to it and its political goodies grab bag features, so I considered the evening a waste.

Grassley is now ranking member of the Senate finance committee, and it appears his views have changed over the years for the Code becomes more outrageous each time Congress meets. Sometimes it takes several pages of complex codeese, my term for the ridiculous language employed by the legislative staffers to disguise the fact that a section had been added just to reward a single taxpayer, usually one represented by a lobbyist who has unlimited access to campaign contributors. To put the same provision in a private bill would reveal the subterfuge and expose the member and the recipient of her generosity to public scrutiny. But a complex provision, sprinkled with cross references to other code sections which only one taxpayer in the entire United States can satisfy is perfect camouflage. The only lawyer in America who understand that page, or pages, is the one who drafted it.

Doug Grinnell reported to work when he graduated from Pepperdine in Malibu, California in January, 1979. He passed the bar and was admitted by the Court of Appeals the day before his twenty-third birthday in May. Doug was a marathon runner and rode his bike to work from the Colony apartments in Towson, arriving at nine sharp. There was nothing on his desk when he arrived and nothing on it when he left at five and not a minute after. In between, he quietly worked away. It was not until after he joined the navy and I tried the cases he had been working on in the federal courts in Newark and Philadelphia that I discovered just how good a lawyer he was.

My client, Richard Evans, had opened another of his successful "Crease" pubs in the Atrium in Alexandria, Virginia. From the outset, there were disputes with his landlord, who had failed to provide a waterproof covering for the atrium. Richie invested heavily in improvements, seeking to replicate his success in Towson, Baltimore, and Georgetown. As the dispute degenerated into litigation, I asked Doug to prepare amemorandum in support of a motion for summary judgment.

The case was pending in the U.S. District Court in Alexandria known as the "rocket docket." Rarely did three months elapse between the date a case was filed and the date it was tried. He presented his work to me about a week before the case was set for argument. I did not like his view of the case, and I suggested it be argued differently. Doug flatly refused. That had never happened to me before. I was not sure what to say next. So I explained as kindly as I could that it was my client, my responsibility and I was the guy who paid his salary.

Doug was not impressed. Becoming angry, I slammed the flat of my hand upon the offending Memorandum, and said "Damn it, Doug. If you won't change it get your butt down to Alexandria and argue it yourself." He did, and after arguing the motion, he came into my office, ecstatic.

"Ed," he said " when I got up to argue with the judge, I had an epiphany. This is what I was born to do. Something came over me, and I felt like I had been doing it all my life. I loved it."

Doug had lived as a child with an alcoholic father, an officer in the military. As the oldest boy it was his job to stay with his father and hide the car keys. So arguing with judges and lesser authority figures like me came to him quite naturally. Doug suffered with me through the jury trial in December. We were staying with our client and witnesses in the Telegraph Road Holiday Inn, made necessary because in that court cases began early and end late. The judge, being the prime mover of the rocket docket, constantly pushed us to get it over with. In three days, the jury trial on our claim and the defendant's counter-claim, concluded. I felt as if I had just run a marathon.

The last night we spent in Alexandria, I dreamed I was standing in a flower garden in a town that looked like Williamsburg, Virginia. The street was dirt and picket fences surrounded the houses. In the distance, I could hear a train coming ever closer. I was not concerned, because trains stay on their tracks, and although noisy, it would soon pass and the noise would go away. But not this train. It had no tracks and was plowing up the dirt street, destroying fences, flowers and houses, heading right at me when I awoke. What a relief.

When the jury returned that afternoon, we won our claim, and the defendant won his counterclaim for rent, which we did not dispute. When I returned to my office in Towson that night, the dream became clear. Norman Burke came into my office as I was putting down my briefcases and said, "You better sit down, Ed. I have some bad news for you."

I sat down and he said "Bill LaBanz is dead."

I was glad I was sitting, because the blood drained from my head. Bill was my age. He had flown jets in the Korean war with my childhood friends Johhnie and David Connor. He had launched a company that sold fuel oil, gasoline and synthetic lubricants for industrual machinery and engines, and we were working on a contract to buy a competitor. I liked working with him, we had become friends, and he was in excellent health.

"Auto accident or plane crash?" My voice broke and what I heard did not sound like me.

"Murdered."

Six months earlier, Bill's wife Barbara had flown to an island in the Carribbean. Bill had consented to the jurisdiction of the local court, which granted them a divorce. She was developing, with my assistance, a subdivision in Harford County called Plumtree Estates. Because I was representing both of them, I arranged independent counsel for each as I always did when a married couple, both owning and participating in the operation of a business we represented, insisted on a divorce.

Several years before, Bill and Barbara had flown to Spain for a vacation, signing a quickly drawn, stop gap wills that set up a trust for their children and named one another as Personal Representatives and me as alternate in case there was a simultaneous death. The wills were signed in the airport as they got on the plane, with the promise that they would, when they returned, give the matter more thought and do a more thorough job.

Bill had purchased several lots in the Plumtree project from his former wife, and built a house for him and a second wife he married shortly after the divorce. I had prepared a new Will for Bill about two weeks before his death, mailing it to him with instructions for its execution.

Bill's death was investigated by Sergeant Van Horn and Detective James Harkins of the Harford County Sheriff's Department. When they came to my office they told me a man wearing a ski mask and gloves entered Bill's house about supper time. Bill's wife of six months was fixing supper, and Bill's son, Joey, was visiting them. Joey thought the man was his uncle playing a practical joke on them.

When he asked Audrey when Bill would be home, she said he was expected shortly. Audrey and Joey were led to the guest bedroom where they were gagged and bound. When Bill came home, the intruder strangled him with his necktie. Joey, in the next room, heard his father's dying gasp while struggling to get free, climbed out a window and ran to a neighbor's house for help.

The Sheriff's deputies placed the envelope I used to mail Bill's will in front of me. Bill had never opened it. They asked if they could see the Will signed before Bill flew to Spain. They were pleased I was the Alternate Personal Representative and had to probate Bill's estate. Barbara had renounced her right to act as such or participate in Bill's estate in the divorce decree entered in the Caribbean. That night at the funeral home, she asked me if Bill had made a new Will. I told her he had but it had not been executed. She asked me to help her administer Bill's estate.

When I reminded her she had surrendered her right to participate in Bill's estate, she denied having done so. I told her I would review the documents and let her know if my memory was not accurate. I had spent hours reviewing the papers with the sheriff's deputies, and I feared she might have been the one who hired the hit man.

The sheriff hired a psychic to help with the investigation, after Bill's abandoned car was found at a remote city location. Building on names and telephone numbers given them by the psychic, some wire taps were authorized which yielded helpful information, but the evidence was circumstantial. There were several indictments years later but no convictions, although the Sheriff's wire taps proved a hit man was hired to murder my client in order to turn control of the company over to a less demanding boss who was a party to a stock buy-out agreement.

The employee was represented by Dominic Iamele, who spent almost five hours with me reviewing documents and asking me questions. He did not have to prove anything. The prosecutor, who had the burden of proving the case beyond a reasonable doubt, never talked to me. When I realized the extent of his incompetence, I filed a motion with the Court in Harford County for authority to hire a private prosecutor, English style, to prosecute the case. The Court would not act, however, unless I got the Governor's approval. Harry said he needed Steve Sachs, who took office as Attorney General in 1978, to approve my request before he could act on it. The trial went forward on schedule and the employee was acquitted.

A year later, the trial of the alleged hit man was removed to Snow Hill, Maryland. The same inept prosecutor was trying the case and Van Horn called me and told me that snow was expected on the Eastern Shore the day I was to testify, and at his urging I went down to Snow Hill the night before. Harford County had booked rooms in a small hotel next to the court house for use by its employees and state witnesses. When I awoke the next morning, a foot of snow had already fallen.

After breakfast, I went next door to the Court House. The Court room was empty, but evidence connected to the trial was in the court room. The bailiff told the judge I was there. A friendly voice from chambers invited me to join him before his fireplace for a cup of coffee. The judge was former Secretary of State Lloyd Simpkins. "Hot Dog," told me that Richard Karceski, who represented the defendant, had a four-wheel drive vehicle, and he was bringing the prosecutor with him from the motel where they were staying. The jury was waiting, and as soon as they got there, the trial would start. So for several hours the judge and I talked politics and caught up on one another's lives.

This trial also resulted in an acquittal. I got a call from a reporter who told me he had talked to the jurors after the verdict was announced. A juror said "Oh, we knew the guy was guilty, but the prosecutor was so obnoxious we didn't think he deserved to win."

Think about that for a minute. It speaks volumes about the adversary system. The defendant was guilty, but his lawyer was so mild, gentle and believable he deserved to win the case. The prosecutor deserved to lose. The evidence and the guilt of the accused were meaningless. But then, truth is the first casualty in a court of law. Only the rules of evidence matter.

From time to time, I would discuss judicial appointments with Harry. Louise Keelty handled Harry's appointments, and I called her to get a spot on Harry's calendar. He was walking between four desks, each staffed by a typist, editing, correcting and signing letters on my first visit. Before we sat down in his office to talk, I asked, "What are you doing?"

"Doing my mail." he responded.

"Harry, this isn't our law office. You're the Governor. Somebody else should do your mail. How can you run the state if you're writing letters all day."

That's my problem when I really like somebody. When you think he or she is perfect, you are too quick to jump on the slightest hint that some small thing they do is less than perfect. Not a good way to keep friends. I regretted my harsh words. Harry asked what else was on my mind, looking hurt that I had come to Annapolis just to yell at him.

"It's the Court of Appeals. Those guys are making mincemeat out of the law, chopping it to shreds. Only two of them ever practiced law. They don't know what they're doing."

"Two? Which two?"

I identified two men, one of whom I did not know and had given him the benefit of the doubt. Harry, however, knew his history far better than I.

"You're wrong about him. He never practiced law a day in his life." Harry related the judge's history from the time he graduated from law school. He had been an administrator and a bureaucrat until kicked upstairs to the Court of Appeals. The situation was even worse than I suspected. The Chief Judge, my old boss Bob Murphy, spent his entire career in the Attorney General's office, and only one of the other eight judges had actually practiced law. He was the one Harry put on the Court, and it was his desk in Denton Harry searched one day looking for an order the judge had promised to sign before he went to lunch. Small towns are so different, but we need more men from small towns running things.

Bob Murphy and I were no longer on good terms. He had urged me to argue his case for higher judicial salaries with Harry and I had refused. I thought the intermediate court was a mistake, and I didn't think the judges were worth what they were being paid as it was. Bob had changed the rules to deny direct Appeals, vesting appellate jurisdiction in the Court of Special Appeals, which decided almost all of its cases in unpublished memorandum opinions which never saw the light of public scrutiny, can not be cited as precedent and can not be reviewed unless one of the second-year law students assigned to do the work of the Court of Appeals judges sees something she thinks is important in a petition for certiorari and interests other second-year law students working for other judges in it.

Law clerks working for panels of three judges who hear cases in the Court of Special Appeals write opinions which ignore or restate the issues raised by lawyers who have passed the bar examination, had their character assessed by a committee of veteran lawyers and have been responsible for ordering the lives of their clients for decades. The court substitutes made up facts for those established by sworn testimony tested by rigorous cross-examination and supported by documentary evidence which satisfies the rules for admissibility. And the indolent judges take years to decide simple cases, ignoring the provisions of the Maryland Constitution which mandates they *shall* render a written opinion within ninety days of argument.

This is not a system designed by lawyers who have given their lives to the law. It is a system designed by bureaucrats to manage the docket and prevent private disputes from intruding upon or interfering with what they consider their well-earned retirement. They demand dignity, respect, and comfort while half-educated law students do their work. A century and a half ago Charles Dickens wrote that the law is an ass. If it were not then, it is now.

As long as Harry was Governor, and for the next eight years when my friend Don Schaefer succeeded him, I made every effort to redirect the judiciary by recommending good lawyers and honorable men and women to them. I did not ever recommend anyone that Harry or Don failed to appoint. But their numbers were too few to do much good, and when the bar started voting on eligibility for appointments, I gave up, because not doing criminal law or personal injury law, I did not know the lawyers who corralled the most votes in the popularity contest, and I feared making another catastrophic mistake.

Harry appointed me to an advisory board for the Maryland Training School, which is located near the Long Green Valley where I live. I was President of the Long Green Valley Association and Historic Long Green Valley, Inc, and public-spirited citizens joined me on the board. After working with the Department of Juvenile Justice officials who ran the school I had became convinced the state was engaged in institutional child abuse. I wrote a letter to the other members outlining how I thought the school should be run.

Recognizing that we only had custody of the youthful offenders for a short period of time, we should construct an artificial environment offering immediate reward for positive behavior and immediate loss of privileges for negative behavior. The system had to be administered, however, within a community which offered both love and respect to boys who had never known either. Sister Pat Hangis, a retired Baltimore Police major who had become a Franciscan nun; Elizabeth Brownell, a tireless child advocate; Buzzy Krongard's wife, now deceased, and Tommy Bromwell, the Democrat Senator representing the Eighth Legislative District where I lived, were my allies.

Sister Pat took me to the Glen Mills School in Pennsylvania which, it turned out, was run on the principles I outlined in my letter. No razor ribbon fence around this beautiful open campus that looked like a New England prep school. It was privately run, based on Biblical principals. Youthful offenders from Wilmington, Philadelphia and New Jersey urban centers were sent there to complete their GED or to learn a trade. Positive peer pressure, a well-trained and dedicated staff, four meals a day and a competitive sports program combined to bring tears to the eyes of boys who were being sent home when their sentence expired. They loved being there and wanted to stay.

The recidivism rate at Glen Mills was thirty-three percent versus eighty-three percent at Hickey. It was costing the State of Maryland about $60,000 a year to keep an offender at Hickey. We could send them to Glen Mills for $28,600 annually. At one point, we had over two hundred Maryland boys there, but we could only keep them there for six months.

I accepted an invitation to attend the Maryland Republican party December convention. Joe Ayd was running for the Chairman's position but he lost to Allan

Levy from Montgomery County. Mike Eagan, the Baltimore County Chairman, insisted I attend the central committee meetings on Allegheny Avenue in Towson, two blocks from my office. Marjorie Newman, a member of the Central Committee in my district, had run unsuccessfully for the Baltimore County Council. Marge was a client and we undertook to do in our county what Louise Gore had done nationally.

We incorporated the Eastside Republican Club, which attracted a surprisingly enthusiastic following from Dundalk, Essex and Middle River. We had formed the club for the Eighth District, but it was quickly taken over by newly minted Republicans. So we formed the Eighth District Republican Club and incorporated it. Soon two of the three delegates from our district were Republicans, and some fine balancing was required on Election Day to make sure that Tommy Bromwell and Joe Bartenfelder, two Democrats I trusted, were not defeated as well. Note well, however; no good deed goes unpunished.

At state party conventions, Mike Eagan substituted me for absent members of his delegation, and we worked together on the issues that came before that body. We formed an alliance with the remnant of the party in Baltimore City, and reached out to the delegates from western Maryland, who had been voting with the over weighted delegation from Montgomery County. Mike and I had some mutual clients, and we trusted one another. Mike taught me a lot about politics and investing. It was he who first referred to me as consigliore of the Maryland Republican party. I was not elected to the State Central Committee until 1982.

In 2009 the adult population of Maryland was 4,160,620, and the Department of Labor, Licensing and Regulation reported that 3,030,064 of them were employed. But 954,064 were employed by Federal, state or local governments; another 695,336 were over age 65 and potentially recipients of Federal social security checks; 854,345 were receiving disability payments and 7.1% are unemployed. Do the math: 2,718,940 adults in Maryland are beholden in one way or another to government largesse for all or part of their income provided by the 1,441,660 adults working in the private sector.

The private sector in Maryland is the enthralled minority enslaved by the mendicant majority. Voting results in the 2010 general election prove that the four Federal District bed-room counties and Baltimore City and County –where the majority of the mendicants live—are heavily Democrat; the remaining eighteen counties are heavily Republican. Is it any surprise that Maryland taxpayers, taxed enough already, are facing even more burdensome tax increases from a legislature controlled by the Democrat party?

"You don't need to know any tax law to be the head of the Tax Division at Justice. All you need to know is how to sign your name."

Conversation with Blake McFeely,
December, 1980

President Ronald W. Reagan

In 1980, the Baltimore County Republican State Central Committee invited the candidates seeking the party's nomination for President to speak at a series of fund raising events at the Hunt Valley Marriott. I was asked to co-host the VIP reception for Governor Reagan with Congresswoman Marjorie Holt. It was a popularity contest and I hoped to get more people to the Reagan dinner than were mustered a few weeks earlier for George H. W. Bush. His supporters boasted a headcount of six hundred attendees.

As a moderate Republican from the Northeast, Bush had the support of the Montgomery County leadership in the Maryland Republican party. He annoyed me by referring to Governor Reagan's economic plan as "voodoo" economics. My undergraduate major, and a lifetime of postgraduate reading, was economics, and I knew the Laffer curve was sound economic policy. Sound economic policy is rarely if ever sound political policy.

Determined to get a bigger turnout for Reagan, I made telephone calls to people I knew. My old sailing buddy, Bernie Treuschler, then Chairman of the Baltimore Gas and Electric Company and later Constellation Energy, was interested, as a regulated-industry CEO, in public policy. His chief lobbyist was George Gephardt, whose mother attended my church, covered his office walls with framed bills enacted at his urging by the Legislature, with the pen used by the Governor to sign the bill into law neatly attached to the frame. I thought antlered stag heads would have been less offensive.

George and Bernie had managed a Houdini maneuver to extricate Baltimore Gas and Electric Company from regulation of Public Service Commission by transferring power generating plants to an unregulated affiliate, which sold the power back to the regulated utility at market price, determined solely by the vendor, thereby dodging regulation and guaranteeing a profit for both the unregulated, power-producing parent and the regulated subsidiary selling it to end users. Bernie had bought three tables for the Bush event, so I asked him what he could do for me.

"I can't do anything," he said, "I spent my entire primary budget on the Bush dinner."

I pleaded to no avail. I could not get Bernie to buy even two tickets for himself. This was fairly typical of what I encountered at other companies which were politically active. As a fundraiser for the Republican Party, company contributions were permitted, which would not have been the case if the money was to be used by the candidate running for President. With hard work, Joe succeeded in surpassing the attendance at the Bush dinner.

The "VIP" reception at the Marriott provided participants a chance to meet, talk and be photographed with Governor Reagan in exchange for an extra thousand dollars. At the appointed time, Congresswoman Holt was held up in traffic, and I was on my own. Governor Reagan was not a small-talk artist and I struggled to make introductions less painful by telling him something about the person being introduced hoping to get something more said between them than 'hello-glad-to-meet-you-good-bye and good-luck.'

I began to fret, wondering when Marjorie would get there and take the Governor off my hands. I hated campaigning, and sensing tightness in my chest, I decided that this must be as difficult for the Governor as it was for me. So I took a deep breath, relaxed, picked up two glasses of red wine, handed him one, and asked,

"So what's the most important thing you want to do when you are President."

He flashed a smile. "End the cold war."

"Have you read President Nixon's new book 'The Real War'"?

"No, I haven't. What's his thesis?"

"Pretty straight forward. World War III began in the day World War II ended and has continued ever since. It pits our government and our institutions against theirs. If we challenge them to an all out arms race, our economy and our institutions, being stronger than theirs, will survive and theirs won't."

Governor Reagan grinned, tossed his head and said, "Sounds right to me."

We had a great time from that point on, laughing, talking and drawing other people in. I don't remember whether Marjorie ever got there, because we both relaxed and enjoyed the evening. At the dinner afterward he gave his famous stump speech, which was enthusiastically received. Many years later I talked with Lyn Nofziger in that same room, thanking him for making Reagan President. Lyn demurred. "I didn't make Ronald Reagan President. He made himself President."

After winning the Republican nomination, Governor Reagan came to Maryland for a presidential debate in Baltimore, and I was asked to drive Mrs. Reagan's car in the motorcade. She was a small, delicate lady, who seemed to be more comfortable socially than her husband. Years later, at a dinner meeting of the Baltimore Opera's lawyers committee, I asked Justice Anthony Kennedy about Reagan's aloofness. The Justice, who had been Reagan's lawyer, said he never interacted with the President socially, for they had always met in Kennedy's office.

Estelle and I were asked to host the VIP floor of one of the five inaugural balls in January, 1981. The secret service wanted us in the Museum of National History no later than six as they intended to seal the building at that hour. I was instructed to park my car opposite the building in a garage across the Mall. No matter how often I tried, I could not get to either building. Twice I was directed across the 14th Street Bridge and up the George Washington Parkway, and twice I fought my way back. Finally, in desperation, I stopped the car, removed the barriers blocking my path across Pennsylvania Avenue and drove to the Museum door to drop my wife off.

I had to remove more barriers to get my car to the garage. As I walked across the darkened Mall to the Museum, in white tie and tails, fireworks shot up all around me, sending colored fire high in the sky. Acrid smoke and sparks were falling on me like snow flakes, trapped as I was in a bad scene from a James Bond movie. My wife persuaded the Secret Service to let me in, and we sat down to dinner in the staff dining room to await the arrival of the President and Mrs. Reagan.

The guests in the Museum of Natural History were from Maryland, Missouri, Massachusetts, West Virginia and Kentucky, five states where Republicans are usually a minority. The band was setting up in the well, where a huge stuffed elephant, with trunk raised in triumph, dominated the space. My wife, watching the Secret Service perform a security check, located the door through which the President would enter later that evening.

We stood at the top of the marble staircase on the second floor, where we were to welcome the VIP's. Tables for four, with a chilled bottle of California method champagne and four glasses, lined the balustrade overlooking the well. As we stood at the top of the stairs welcoming our guests and directing them to their assigned tables, Bernie Trueschler and his wife were coming up the steps.

As I shook his hand I said "Bernie, I'm really surprised to see *you* here."

"Come on, Ed," he said, looking pained, "you aren't going to remember that, are you?"

"Bernie, I have a memory like an elephant, but not like that one," nodding toward the stuffed one in the well below. As the evening wore on, Bernie asked me what, if anything, there was to eat. There was nothing. I reminded him he was much better off than the guests on the first floor, who did not have anything to drink either. It was one of those just being there things you could say you did. It was not a thing to enjoy.

Shortly before eleven my wife nudged me and said the Secret Service had just come through the door with a dog trained to sniff for explosives. Looking down to the floor below, we saw the President and Mrs. Reagan, accompanied by fanfares, walk through the door Estelle had pointed out earlier that evening. They danced a single dance and left almost as quickly as they had come.

There were four other Inaugural Balls in progress, and security concerns being what they were, it is not surprising that their stay was so brief. The purpose of such balls is to pay the cost of the Inaugural and the transition. I resolved never to go to another even if my best friend were to be the honoree, and I would advise you not to go either.

I was disappointed in the President's cabinet. I had taken Donald Regan's deposition in New York when he was President of Merrill Lynch. I did not like or trust him.

Joe Ayd asked my help in getting Bob Gerstung appointed to the federal bench. Bob had languished in the Maryland district court system far too long, not at all a good use of his genius. He was opposed by the large Baltimore law firms accustomed to having no longer needed partners appointed to the federal bench, as convenient in getting rid of unwanted partners as the State Law Department had been in training up and coming partners.

I engaged in heated letter exchanges with Rudolph Giuliani, a young lawyer working in the White House whose job it was to vet all appointments to the federal bench. I threatened to go over his head to the President, but he effectively blunted my efforts.

Blake McFeely attended Yale with the Vice President. As General Counsel to an aerospace company in California, he had retained French Smith's law firm to assist him in a number of legal matters, and French offered Blake the Tax Division at Justice. When Blake and I worked in Washington in the 1960's Blake was writing Byzantine regulations for the IRS. By 1981, he thought he had forgotten all the tax law he ever knew.

When he came to Baltimore to talk to me about it, I said "Blake, you don't need to know any tax law to be the head of the Tax Division. All you need to know is how to sign your name." He either did not believe me or refused to be an ignorant boss. He wanted the Civil Division, and it was promised to someone else, so Blake remained in San Diego.

At the time I was representing a company in Alexandria which manufactured, tested and distributed reagents for use in stat analyzers patented, manufactured and sold by Beckman Instruments in Fullerton, California. My client had been asked to develop a second source for the reagents by Howard University Hospital. The staff was not comfortable relying on a single source product for performing stat tests where immediate results were vital to adopting a course of treatment with life or death consequences.

My client's reagents were manufactured for use on Beckman's Astra® Analyzer for testing Glucose, BUN, Creatine, and the four electrolytes. The reagents were not patentable and could be made cheaply. They were being sold by Beckman at a price twenty-five times the cost of manufacture, a gross profit margin of ninety-six percent. Beckman's profit on the reagents was greater than its profit on all the other services and products it sold put together.

Beckman set out to retain it at all costs, and its anti-competitive acts were ethically offensive to my client. I filed suit in the U.S. District Court in Baltimore alleging violations of the Sherman and Clayton Acts. Two other plaintiffs which manufactured similar reagents followed our lead, one in California and another in Minnesota. Beckman was represented by a lawyer from Miami, Florida practicing with a firm in the Sears Tower in Chicago. My clients products were distributed by American Hospital Supply Co, a Chicago based company represented by another law firm also in the Sears Tower.

For the next four years, I spent a lot of my life in that building. The Merchant's Club in Baltimore had reciprocal privileges with a private club there, which made life easier for us. Once, when we adjourned our deposition for lunch, we worked our way through the maze of escalators and elevators. Our opponent, Richard Horne and his assistants seemed to be on the same path as we. As he entered the revolving door to the Club, he turned to block me, insisting it was a members-only facility. His office was in the Sears Tower, and we had been eating in the club all week, but this was the first time we had seen him there. The maitre de recognized me, and bypassing my opponent, addressed me by name and escorted us to our table, leaving Mr. Horn waiting in line.

Beckman's first line of defense was to seek a protective order sealing all documents and depositions to be taken in the case, which was assigned to Judge Walter Black, who had been Fred Singley's partner before his appointment to the bench. It took two years for Beckman's essentially unopposed motion to be decided, and Beckman used the time to destroy the most incriminating documents.

Discovery in depth did not begin until the summer of 1983, when I took another lawyer and two law clerks to Newport Beach, California to review a warehouse full of documents in English, German, Italian and Spanish. By pooling our skills, we could decipher everything we found. In the next three years, I took more than a hundred depositions in Fullerton, Newport Beach, Salt Lake City, Atlanta, Chicago, Baltimore, St. Petersburg and Miami, Florida.

As I was walking to my seat on an airplane bound for Chicago, Jervis Langdon pulled my sleeve and I sat down beside him. He had been appointed trustee of the Penn Central railroad by the bankruptcy judge, and he handed me a copy of the prospectus containing the plan of reorganization the creditors were being asked to approve.

"It's a lawyer's dream," he said, "I always wondered why, when I was president of the B&O, why those two railroads always reported a profit and we couldn't. Now I know they never did any maintenance on their tracks. The ties under their rails were the same ones they put down a hundred and fifty years ago."

The Pennsylvania Railroad and the New York Central were both publicly held companies, and their accountants certified their annual financial statements were prepared in accord with generally accepted accounting principals. That something as important as routine maintenance was neglected made me very uncomfortable taking the Metroliner to New York. It also added to my skepticism about the competence of the Securities and Exchange Commission's role as a watchdog over Wall Street.

In December, 1986, I was returning to Baltimore on the Metroliner after attending a week-long review of the Internal Revenue Code of 1986 at New York University. My seat was in the middle of the club car, and there were other lawyers from Baltimore who also attended the New York Tax Institute seated in the same car. When the train stopped in Philadelphia, two ladies carrying large bags of gaily wrapped gifts boarded and stopped beside my seat just as the train lurched forward. Elizabeth Taylor fell into my lap and her violet eyes, in a face immersed in black fur, were mesmerizing. She said, "I'm so sorry."

I steadied her packages, set her back on her feet and helped her into her seat opposite mine across the aisle, I said, "Don't be. I'm not."

She was then married to Republican Senator Warner of Virginia, and she and her companion were returning to Washington after having done their Christmas shopping in Philadelphia.

Lawyers I hardly knew made it a point to wander down the aisle to talk to me about my career as Republican consigliore, hoping, I suspect, to draw the famous actress into a conversation in which they were participants. I was embarrassed, and so was she, for it was obvious to her what they were doing. I quickly let it be known I was getting off the train in Wilmington, which is where I park my car when I take a train to New York.

I also made trips to Somerset, New Jersey, Columbia, Maryland and Atlanta, Georgia to branch offices, where Beckman insisted the documents we requested, and which were not produced, were located. A two-year document retention policy had remained in effect while the protective order request lingered, but the documents we asked them to produce were destroyed while we waited for Judge Black to address the motion.

Fred Smalkin, then a United States Magistrate, decided all discovery motions. When we proved Beckman's guilt, the only penalty he imposed was to make the defendant pay the legal fees and expenses incurred chasing the no longer extant evidence. The litigators —I no longer call them lawyers because very few of them are —have learned it is far better to pay tens of thousands of dollars in sanctions rather than hundreds of millions in damages. But destroy the evidence at all costs, and corporate America is highly skilled in doing that.

Although Judge Black found there was ample evidence of anti-competitive activity by Beckman, he did not believe there was a separate relevant product market for the seven stat tests performed in hospital emergency rooms. He disposed of the case by granting summary judgment in favor of Beckman. A few years later, my client died, I suspect, of terminal disgust. As we left the court room, however, he said "Now I know why they check people for guns before they let them in here."

"Mr. Blanton, you are through with this witness."

"But I am not, your honor, most respectfully, I must complete my examination of this witness. If nothing more, I have a record I must protect with his testimony."

"You ask this witness one more question, and I will hold you in contempt."

———————

"Oh, no, you don't, we have been all through this before with another witness. That has already been explained."

"It may have been explained to your satisfaction, your Honor, but that does not mean it has been explained to the jury's satisfaction. They do not have to believe a word said by any of the witnesses, and they, and they alone, can decide who they believe and who they do not believe."

Colloquy between Court and my co-counsel
BWX, Inc v Control Data

Wished I Had Said That

While trying to solve the murder of my client, Bill LaBanz, Sergeant Van Horne asked me to notify an insurance company that I, as personal representative of his estate, would sue them if they paid the proceeds to anyone later found to be guilty of, or an accessory to, Bill's murder. The sheriff hoped to deprive the suspects of the money needed to pay the hit man who committed the murder.

The insurer predictably filed an interpleader in the District Court and paid the money to the clerk. The beneficiary suspected of complicity in the murder filed his claim, and I filed mine, represented by Richard Bennett and Michael Marr, a young lawyer who assisted me in the trial of some of my cases. I had taken him through a Bible study program offered by the Christian Businessman's Committee, finding him to be a receptive student and a committed Christian, and I was delighted to learn he was instrumental in bringing some young law school graduates I was trying to educate to their senses.

The case was called to trial before Judge Norman Ramsey. While I was on the stand, there was conflict between Mike and the judge. Mike had to prove that a person who had not been indicted for murder was guilty of murder, not beyond a reasonable doubt but by a preponderance of the evidence. That was an easier burden to meet, and the sheriff hoped we would stumble across something that would help him gain a conviction in state court on the murder charge.

The sheriff made his evidence, except the wire taps, available to us, and I thought we had an excellent chance of winning. But Judge Ramsay continued to differ with Mike over the questions he was asking, which seemed innocuous to me, particularly since I was the one answering them. I began to suspect that Mike was pushing the edge of testimony prohibited by a motion *in limine*, a tactic often employed to keep the truth from jurors, on the flimsy ground jurors can't handle the full truth the witnesses are sworn to tell.

Exasperated by Mike's persistence, Norm declared a recess and invited me into chambers for a cup of coffee. Since I could not talk to anyone during the recess anyway, I accepted his offer. The week-end before, I was riding Choco through the Soldiers Delight wilderness with my friend Richard Jenkins, the oldest member of the Boumi Temple Mounted Patrol. Dick's son was a U.S. Attorney in Sacramento. Dick was a member of the Virginia Society of Maryland, and Estelle and I were often his guests at the Maryland Club for their meetings.

Dick was a retired Exxon executive, and as we made our way through the scrub pines Dick was describing the schools for federal judges supported by Exxon and other major corporations. Scheduled throughout the year at posh resorts, the schools make sure every judge appointed to the federal bench is wined, dined and indoctrinated with pro-business propaganda by the biggest names at America's leading law schools.

One of my associates, Laurens MacLure and I had spent two weeks at Harvard Law School in 1984 studying anti-trust law with Professor Philip Areeda and Securities law with Professor Louis Loss. They wrote the text books used to teach their courses. I tried to interest Professor Areeda in my suit against Beckman, but he declined because he was retained to teach the judges everything they needed to know to get rid of troublesome and time consuming anti-trust cases, a cause corporate America was eager to subsidize at the indoctrination schools Dick was describing.

While Judge Ramsay and I were chatting in chambers, I asked him if he had been to judges school yet. He said that he had. I asked if I could see the instructional material. He pulled a few pamphlets off the shelf and handed them to me, promising to call me when it was time to go back in the courtroom. To my disgust, the lawyers settled the case during the recess, the Sheriff learned little, and the Harford County prosecutor did not even try to convict my client's partner of his murder.

But while I was waiting in chambers, I read the judge's school pamphlet on antitrust law, and just as I suspected, the error proof, appeal proof way to avoid a lengthy antitrust trial was for the judge to grant defendant's motion for summary judgment on the ground there was no relevant product market or relevant geographic market for the product. That is a question of fact, and yet the judge can not be reversed on appeal if he finds, without benefit of any testimony or evidence before the trial begins, that no such market exists.

In February 1988, I tried my last jury case in Chicago, and the only one I ever lost, in the United States District Court for the Northern District of Illinois, representing Charles Flanders in a suit against Transunion Information Systems, one of the three major repositories for credit information in the United States. The Pritzger family owned it, along with Continental Airlines, Hyatt Hotels and the Union Tank Car Company, and only God and their accountants know what else.

My client's chief financial officer, who hoped to remain a part of the Pritzger empire, negotiated the contract. On one occasion, when the negotiations had bogged down, I was in Chicago taking depositions in the Beckman case. Charlie called me and asked me to have lunch with the Transunion people and get things back on track. They were kind enough to take me, a diehard Southerner, to lunch at the Union League Club. As I looked around at pictures of Lincoln, Grant and Sherman, countless Lees and Blantons in Virginia were probably spinning in their graves.

When the contract was finished, I was asked to review it. I wrote my clients a five page letter, urging them not to sign the contract unless a full page of warranties was removed. A warranty has to be absolutely true, and any creative lawyer can argue that a warranty had been breached. Any damages sustained, or potentially to be sustained, were deductible from the next installment payment due under the contract. I advised my clients that unless the warranties were removed, the money they got at settlement might be the only money they ever saw. But my clients were just divorced, wanted no more of one another and they were determined to proceed.

The two corporations being sold had twice as much cash in the bank as the initial payment Transunion was obligated to make to the sellers. It's easy to build an empire when you are clever enough to negotiate such contracts.

As I predicted, various alleged breaches of warranty preceded the due date of the first and second installments, and large amounts of money were withheld by Transunion. The contract bestowed jurisdiction on the Illinois courts, where the Pritzgers were major philanthropists. As the trial drew to a close, Natalia testified before the jury completely opposite to her deposition testimony and the facts related to me when I agreed to file suit on their behalf. The six jury members, all of whom held post-graduate degrees, were required, instead of bringing in a general verdict, to answer a series of questions, and it was apparent to me early on that I had just lost my first jury case.

The judge, however, was not so sure. He ran his courtroom with the assistance of the Court Reporter, who doubled as a clerk. He told me his clerk, his law clerk and the bailiff were too busy working on other cases to waste their time in Court. On several occasions during the trial, responding to an agreed upon signal from me, the judge quietly rose from his chair, tip-toed behind the jury and violently shook the chair of a dozing juror. Two-week breach of contract cases also put me to sleep unless I'm trying them.

All during pretrial meetings and during the trial, I suspected that the judge liked me and wanted to talk to me about something, but the need for impartiality prevented his doing so. Once the jury retired, however, he became quiet friendly. He was fascinated by my accent, which he could not place. He had recently watched a public television series about American accents. After listening to me for two weeks, he wanted to know how and where I grew up. He told me I did not sound like I was from Maryland.

At judge's school, he had roomed with Judge Walter Black, so he knew how people from Maryland talked. He was delighted to find that Judge Black and I were friends and foot soldiers in the Republican Party. When the jury returned, the judge threaded his way through the jury's responses to the questions he had asked them to answer, seeking a trail that would give me the victory I had not won. I had to explain to him how I had lost a case he thought I had won.

Despite the fact Judge Black always called me to the bench whenever I appeared in his court room for a private conversation, he was the judge who let Beckman off the hook in my anti-trust case because that was what he had been schooled to do. He found, as Phil Areeda had taught him to do, that there was no relevant product market. And another Federal judge in California threw out People Soft's claim against Oracle on the same grounds —lack of a relevant product market.

A year previously, a tall, dignified black man made an appointment to talk about two lawsuits he wanted to file. He wanted me to take both of them on a contingent fee basis. I told him I would consider one but not both. The first case involved the cable franchise for Baltimore City through a minority-owned company which he had formed and of which he was the dominant shareholder, officer and director.

After the minority dominated government of Baltimore awarded the franchise to my client, the telecom company, having got what it wanted, pulled a double-cross and cut my client's company out of the deal. The documents shown to me clearly supported the story I was told. It was a slam-dunk but it would have to be tried in the state courts in Baltimore City, a jurisdiction I avoid like the plague.

The second case involved the Minneapolis company Control Data. My client, along with a former Control Data employee and a friend of mine from the Baltimore Christian Businessmen's Committee, had formed a company to acquire what must have been the only manufacturing plant in the District of Columbia. At least, if there were another, I do not know where it is or what it makes. The plant, located on North Capitol Street within sight of the Capitol itself, was a showcase plant built by Control Data to prove that District residents could be gainfully employed in high tech work.

My client had a letter of intent signed by Control Data to sell to his minority-owned corporation, BWX, Inc., the assets of the plant as well as the building in which it was located. My client had designed a compensation scheme for the work force which he called value sharing. From what I understood about it, a modified form of piece work best describes it, but does not do it justice.

BWX made a deposit of $15,000 and spent about $8,000 flying to Minneapolis to negotiate terms. Shortly before the closing, Control Data scheduled a meeting in the cafeteria to explain to the hundred or so employees that the plant was about to be sold, and they would soon be employed by a new company. A revolt ensued, and the employees marched out of the cafeteria en masse loudly singing "We Shall Overcome." Control Data panicked —allegedly—and called off the deal.

But before the employee meeting was even scheduled, Control Data had signed a contract to sell the building at a higher price to another buyer before BWX's option expired. My client thought BWX had lost between three and four million dollars on the building and half that much again on the loss of the business. This case would have to be filed in the District's equivalent of a state court, but Control Data would surely exercise its right to remove the case to the Federal system, which is where I, as a corporate lawyer, preferred to practice. It was a more efficient use of my time, and the lawyers I opposed were more competent. It was vanity, preferring to play in the majors instead of the minor leagues. It cost me dearly, as vanity always does.

I opted for the case against Control Data, and the other case went to another lawyer in Baltimore, who settled it, a few years later, for stock in a publicly owned cable company with a fair market value of $108,000,000. I would be on a perpetual beach somewhere had I taken both cases, but since I didn't, I am spending my retirement trying to make sure that others do not repeat my mistakes and my country is still here for my grandchildren.

Predictably, as soon as we filed our suit, alleging fraud and breach of contract in the D.C. Court, Control Data's attorneys promptly removed it to the federal courts, which we could not prevent. Just as predictable was their next step, seeking to remove the suit to the federal court in Minneapolis under the doctrine of *forum non conveniens*, which we could and did prevent by pointing out the economic discrepancy between the parties and the proximity of the plaintiffs and most of the witnesses to Washington, D.C.

Discovery ensued, which necessitated my traveling to Minneapolis in the dead of winter to take depositions of a number of witnesses. Snow there was but most of it was just blowing east parallel to the ground rather than falling and piling up. Buildings in downtown Minneapolis were linked by glassed-in skywalks, and the locals were walking around inside their glassed-in city in shorts and tee shirts while outside the snow was Chicago bound.

The depositions went well, and on my last night there I put on my L.L. Bean fur-lined, down-stuffed coat, boots and gloves given me by my coastal Carolina wife who thought I was going to the North Pole. I had to tell her I had ventured out into the Artic and survived. As I was leaving the restaurant I encountered one of the Chicago lawyers who defended Beckman in my anti-trust case. My associates had referred to him as "Les Nessman", a television character he greatly resembled from "WKRP Cincinnati". He was startled to see me, quickly assumed I was consulting with the Minneapolis law firm that hired me to assist them in the anti-trust case they were pursuing against Beckman.

"I know why you're here" he said, putting out his hand and inviting me to join him in the bar. I laughed.

"I bet you do. Wish I could stay, but I have a lot to do tonight. Thank you, anyway."

Slogging through the snow, I fought my way back to the Epcot-like, glassed-in, city-center. When I reached the door, I asked a young man standing inside how to get to the Marriott. He said he was going there and he would show me. As we walked, he introduced himself, and I was startled that his name was identical to that of Control data executive whose deposition I was going to take the next morning. I asked him if he knew my witness.

"Sure do", he said, grinning, "he's my father, but we aren't on the best of terms right now."

"We aren't either," I responded, and invited him to join me in the bar for a nightcap. He was but twenty-one years old, with the usual complaints boys that age have about concerned parents. The next morning, I was strangely sympathetic to the witness, knowing more about his personal life than I should. He must have sensed something, because we got along well and his responses to my questions were helpful to my case. I did not believe the encounter was chance.

A pretrial conference was scheduled in the judge's chambers in Washington which I could not attend. My clients were offended by the judges attitude toward them, believing that he was so biased they could not get a fair trial in his court room. They related their version of what had transpired, and when I talked to my local counsel he essentially confirmed that the judge, a highly respected Harvard Law grad, had made remarks which might well have betrayed racial prejudice.

My clients insisted that I seek the judge's recusal. I obtained affidavits from my clients and local counsel, and filed a motion which the judge summarily denied. I appealed immediately to the Court of Appeals for the District of Columbia Circuit, not to be confused with the United States Court of Appeals for the Federal Circuit. The former is a kangaroo court where future justices of the United States Supreme Court incubate and prove their political dependability; the latter is a star chamber which validates actions of the federal government no matter how outrageous they may be.

As I knew it would, the denial of the motion to recuse was affirmed, and I was required to try my case before a judge I liked and respected, but nevertheless a judge I had just accused of bigotry. When I explained my predicament to my client, he smiled and said, "At least the judge knows, and I know, that you are courageous. I will get you some help."

Shortly before the trial began, Control Data's lawyers sought and obtained a motion in limine. The truth precluded by the now certified, unbiased judge was any mention of the employee unrest, and particularly the fact that the employees had marched out of the cafeteria singing "We Shall Overcome." Our argument, however, was that Control Data, having agreed to sell the real estate for twice what they were obligated to sell it to my client for, intentionally antagonized and alienated the employees in order to create an excuse to get out of their agreement with the District of Columbia government to sell the business and the building to a minority buyer.

Moreover, it appeared that the newly found buyer had approached Control Data before the letter of intent was given to my client. To win our case, we had to prove that Control Data never intended to actually sell the business or the property to my clients, and when it discovered my clients had not only the means but the ability to run the business, they intentionally created employee unrest as an excuse to cancel the contract.

We had to prove fraud in the inception by clear and convincing evidence, and we had to do it by keeping the most compelling evidence from the jury. But then, winning David versus Goliath cases is not supposed to be easy and that is why I like it.

On the Friday before the trial began on Monday my help arrived in the person of Willie Ray, a graduate of Oral Roberts University and the University of Notre Dame Law School. In fact, he was then on the board of trustees of the Law School. He sat in my conference room all week-end, reading my files. We talked, but not a lot. As I always do, I prepare my questions and the anticipated response of each witness in advance, based on their deposition testimony, documents, interrogatory answers, and whatever personal information I want the jury to know about them.

I needed the Court's permission to have Willie with me at the trial table. I wanted him to look as harmless as possible, saying nothing until I obtained his admission to assist me at trial. He sat with his back against the wall in chambers while I sat before the judge's desk, attending to the usual pre-trial impedimenta. The judge granted my motion to admit him with a nod and a perfunctory "good morning." Big mistake.

On the second day of trial, I had avoided, thus far, being imprisoned for contempt. The judge was icy-cold, glaring at me and threatening. In mid-morning, I was in the middle of my examination of a key witness. Willie had said and done nothing other than stand up when the judge entered and left the room. The judge summoned counsel to the bench, locked his eyes on mine and said "Mr. Blanton, you are finished with this witness."

"Oh, no, your honor, I have at least thirty or forty more questions to ask him."

"Mr. Blanton, you are through with this witness."

"But I am not, your honor, most respectfully, I must complete my examination of this witness. If nothing more, I have a record I must protect with his testimony."

"You ask this witness one more question, and I will hold you in contempt."

I have enormous contempt for many judges before whom I have practiced. To be put in jail for expressing that contempt while zealously representing my client was a badge of honor I coveted but had yet to earn. But I was not eager to go to jail in the District of Columbia, even for a few hours. So I returned to counsel table and whispered to Willie.

"The judge is going to lock me up if I ask this witness another question. I have gotten this far on my examination." drawing a line under the question I had asked just before the judge summoned me forward to get even with me for exposing his obvious dislike and contempt for my clients. "You have to take over."

Addressing the court, I said, "Your honor, obedient to the Court's instruction at sidebar, my associate will complete our examination of this witness."

You could have heard a pin drop in that court room. The jury looked at me, then the judge, then at Willie. Given the judge's clear dislike of me and his disdain for my clients, the jury was baffled, trying to figure out why the white judge wanted the white lawyer to turn the case over to the black lawyer. The judge glared at me, then at Willie, and said "VeryWell."

Willie stood up, took off his glasses, which we had put on him just to make him look like Clark Kent stepping out of the telephone booth by hiding the intensity of his intelligent face and bird-of-prey eyes, and asked the next question. Before the witness could respond, the judge thundered.

"Oh, no, you don't, we have been all through this before with another witness. That has already been explained."

Willie thundered back. "It may have been explained to your satisfaction, your Honor, but that does not mean it has been explained to the jury's satisfaction. They do not have to believe a word said by any of the witnesses thus far, and they, and they alone, can decide who they believe and who they do not believe."

I fought hard to keep from laughing. The jury, all black, were nodding in unison, clearly on our side and happy to finally have someone put the bully in his place. The judge glared at us, defeated momentarily, and in a quiet voice, mumbled,

"You may continue."

The next obstacle was jury instruction, and that is where the judge got even. Maryland law, Minnesota law, and the non-federal law of the District of Columbia differ with respect to the damages recoverable when fraud is proved. In most states, a finding of fraud triggers punitive damages. But not in D.C.. Had we been able to establish breach of contract, the damages would have been approximately $5,000,000. In Maryland or Minnesota, the damages the jury could have found would have been the same if fraud in the inception of the contract were shown. But the judge had granted partial summary judgment for the defendant with respect to our contract claim against the real estate.

Thanks to Ralph Nader's work some years before, in one of the few fraud cases ever decided in the District involving, if memory serves, airline tickets, the rule was laid down that the only allowable recovery was a refund of the expenses incurred in the transaction shown to be fraudulent. There were to be no punitive damages, because the fraud took place in the District, even although the contract fraudulently procured and the deposit paid were subject to the law of Maryland. As the District was Maryland's gift to the nation, District judges often adopt Maryland law as a binding precedent, particularly if there is no precedent in the District.

We fought long and hard for a change in the law of the District, where more fraud takes place daily than in all the other fifty states combined. Does the fraud take place there because of the law, or the law is what it is because of the fraud? Whichever, it is a symbiotic relationship which provides a comfortable environment in which the parasites infesting our national government prosper. It is little wonder, and not without substantial truth, that the government of the United States is called the world's largest criminal conspiracy.

When the court instructed our jury that the only damages they could return was a refund of my client's $15,000 deposit and reimbursement of the expenses incurred in flying to Minneapolis to negotiate the contracts, the jury's anger at the judge was visible. My jury wanted to storm the bench, and I think the day is rapidly approaching when their children will. What was it Thomas Jefferson said about the tree of liberty being watered by the blood of patriots?

Labor unions fund the Democrat Party and corporate America funds the Republican Party. The media, with dueling sound-bites, encourage us to believe what the politicians want us to believe—that the parties compete for power. They don't. They share it, and behind the scenes collude with one another to put on a good show for those not in the know that someone is speaking for them and looking out for their interest. A life time of close association has convinced me that most politicians look out for their own interest and for one another. It's 'you scratch my back and I'll scratch yours' and we can keep a good thing going for both of us. America does not need a third party, it needs a second party. The Democratic Republican Party of the founders has endured. It just pretends to be separate for primary election purposes.

"Ed, what do you think about Sunday racing?

"We don't have enough horses to run the dates we now have. If we go to Sunday racing, you'll have to repeal the ban on lasix and butuzahline. That's the only way we can add a day."

"I like the way you think."

"That's why they call me consigliore."

With Delegate Thomas Chamberlain
March, 1985

Fighting Back

My effort to reduce the stranglehold the Democrats hold on Maryland did not stop Democrats calling on me for advice, including St.George I.V. Crosse, who challenged a member of the powerful Mitchell family for a congressional seat in 1988. My association with United Christian Citizens had taught me that more important than party is character, and just as I helped Harry Hughes and Don Schaefer I help other Democrats when their views are like mine.

Malcolm McKnight was my neighbor, and he had made several attempts to unseat Clarence Long in Maryland's Second Congressional District getting closer each time he ran. I advised him to keep trying. The Army taught me that if you want to break down a door, you have to hit it successively, harder each time before it eventually gives way.

Before Malcolm could break through, however, he was defeated in the Republican primary by Helen Delich Bentley, formerly maritime reporter for the Baltimore *Sun* and hostess of a popular television program, the "Port that Built a City and State." After winning the primary, Helen sat in my office for four hours, discussing issues. Adhering to Tom Johnson's advice I told her too many issues are difficult for the mass of voters to grasp. Go with something simple.

There had been some political skullduggery in the Towson courthouse, and towing licenses were taken from long-standing holders with employees and friends and passed out as political favors. Here was an opening we could exploit. We attended a meeting with hundreds of angry Democrats, looking for the police chief's scalp, a fire we fanned for all it was worth.

I challenged the police chief's action in the Circuit Court of Baltimore County, lost, appealed and won in the Court of Special Appeals. Helen was, on her third try, elected to the United States Congress. Shortly thereafter, Senator Mac Matthias published a politically suicidal article in *Foreign Affairs* and lost his seat, after which appointments to the federal courts in Maryland were routed through Helen's office. After I lost my bid to put Bob Gerstung on the federal bench, I was determined not to let that happen again. One evening after a meeting of the central committee I urged Helen to appoint a committee to screen and review future appointments to the federal bench so the party could speak with one voice at the White House in Washington.

Helen took my advice, but appointed George Beall to chair it. More interested in the concept I had ignored the composition of the committee. When I told Helen what she had done to me, she was aghast. She offered to remove him at once, but doing so would open old wounds that were better left healed. The important thing was to get good appointments and avoid party infighting.

Jay V. Strong, Jr, a young lawyer in my office had invited me to the Hunt Valley Marriott for lunch. Guest speakers talked about the change in their lives after they became Christians. Having been a Christian, or so I thought, all my life, I was not impressed with the talks, wondering what it would be like not to be a Christian. My father was a lifetime member of the First Presbyterian Church in Fayetteville, North Carolina and going to church on Sunday was as much a duty as military service.

In May, 1981, Hank McGrew, a former test pilot, spoke, entertaining us with funny stories about his near misses with death in the cockpit. Hank repeated Scotty McCray's comment about old pilots, bold pilots, but there are no old, bold pilots. His commercial airline pilot son had been more than bold when he persuaded a man pointing a gun at his head in the cockpit of his plane to hand it over, perhaps saving the lives of hundreds of people.

When the laughter subsided, Hank talked about the one man in the Bible whose heart God knew, the man to whom God compared all other kings of Israel and found them wanting. My ears perked up when he said that man was David. I knew David was no saint. He lusted after Uriah's wife and sent him to his grave so he could have her. Bathsheba was Solomon's mother. With all my many faults, I had not knowingly done anything that bad.

Hank said that it was not so much what we do but why we do it that determines how God sees us. David, when confronted, was genuinely grieved and expressed his grief profoundly and poetically. This was just what I wanted to hear, and when Hank closed with a prayer I silently prayed with him. A few days later, Dr. David Field and Gene Neff, Baltimore County licensing director, stopped by my office to make sure I knew what I had done.

Tom Ramsay, the CFO at Sweetheart Cup in Owings Mills mentored me through a two-year study to help me understand the difference between being a Christian and living a committed life. The following summer I broke my collarbone while loading balsa wood jumps into a pick-up truck following the Boumi Temple horseshow. While I was mending, Estelle and I spent a week at Sandy Cove, at the head of the Chesapeake Bay, with Bill Nickerson and his wife. At my urging, Harry had appointed Bill to a Circuit Court judgeship. Our children had met at meetings of FOCUS, the Fellowship of Christians at Universities and Schools.

Bill had not been happy with his daughter's involvement in FOCUS and set out to prove what she had been taught was nonsense. He began reading the Gospel of John, and got as far as Nicodemus, a man so highly placed in Jerusalem his position was equivalent to that of a Supreme Court Justice in America. Bill immediately became a Christian, one of the most faithful I know. When Bill wanted to move to the federal bench, he asked for and got our committee's support. Recently, when a county judge I knew was in trouble, I called Bill and asked him to counsel him. He didn't hesitate a minute.

While attending a meeting of the Republican State Central Committee one night in 1983, a dark haired young man was taking notes. Not having seen him at any of our meetings before, I spoke to him as the meeting was breaking up.

"What paper are you writing for?" I asked, assuming he was a reporter. He was wearing lime green, polyester pants with slash pockets, and a short-sleeved, dark-blue, knit tee shirt over a well muscled upper body.

"I'm not a reporter," he said, looking offended.

"Then what brings you to our meetings?" I asked, somewhat defensive myself, suspecting he was a spy.

"I'm interested in running for office"

"As a Republican, I hope."

"Probably" he replied, "It depends on the situation."

Although I'm impatient with situational ethics, I asked him where he lived.

"Arbutus," he answered. Now I was interested, because I wanted to replicate the success Marge Newman and I had on the eastern edge of Baltimore County in the southwest. It is not that I have a dislike for Democrats, because I don't. I think government is more responsive when power is divided.

When I asked him what he did he responded that he had just graduated from Wake Forest law school and was waiting for his bar results. He was working for Ober, Grimes and Shriver, the same firm a merger or two later I had left in 1965. I put out my hand and introduced myself.

"Glad to meet you," he said, "I'm Bobby Ehrlich."

Over the next few months we met frequently for lunch or dinner at the Crease, around the corner from headquarters. I introduced Bob to my client William Ford Peck and my associate Laurens MacLure, both squash players Bob's age who were members of the Towson Exchange Club. They recruited Bob, who moved from Arbutus to the old Tenth Legislative District, a decision which disappointed me because we already had three Republican incumbent legislators there. Bob had a stubborn streak and he could neither be managed nor taught.

In our conversations, I learned Bob was convinced that Tom Chamberlain could be defeated in the primary by a good campaigner. Tom was the only Republican officeholder in Baltimore County who did not support me in the 1978 primary, later telling me he had given his word to Warren Rich that he would support him.

"You wouldn't want me to go back on my word, would you, Ed?"

"Of course not Tom, you can't do that."

Tom relied on me for advice on legislative matters. Knowing my love of horses, he once asked me what I thought about Sunday racing, a hot issue in the Legislature at the time.

"We don't have enough horses to run the dates we now have. If we go to Sunday racing, you'll have to repeal the ban on lasix and butuzahline. That's the only way we can add a day."

These drugs, essentially horse aspirin and a drug to help bleeders, or horses who have breathing complications when they race, were banned in Maryland. Tom said, "I like the way you think."

I laughed. "That's why they call me consigliore."

I was backing Tom's wife, Helen, for the post of National Committeewoman, against my friend Louise Gore, who held the post at that time. It was not something I wanted to do, but something I had to do. Louise had asked for and received my support and that of Baltimore County to make Richard Taylor, a Washington lawyer at Steptoe & Johnson who lived in Montgomery County the National Committeeman from Maryland two years earlier.

We backed him on the strength of a firm commitment that the post of Committeewoman would be ours two years later. When the final vote was taken, Helen looked at me and smiled. Votes in the State party convention are calculated to five decimal places. The final vote was, to the last decimal place, equal to the vote that had been pledged to us the night before which Helen had written down on a yellow pad and handed to me.

Bob went to the spring convention in Ocean City with me and we shared a room at the Sheraton. There was a reception around the pool cabanas prior to the evening session, and I wanted to introduce Bob to people I thought might help him. I wanted to test his marketability among a few pros in the party. Barbara Chinn was a classic Republican woman, and without Republican women there would be no Republican party. I told her I wanted her to meet a young man who wanted to run for office in Baltimore County.

"Is that the young man who came down here with you?" she asked. When I said yes, she said, "Don't you dare bring me another good-looking young man who wants to run for office. I get all worked up getting them elected, and they turn out to be gay."

She was still smarting from the embarrassing events surrounding Bob Baumann's political career. I replied that she did not need to concern herself with this one, he went to Gilman on a football scholarship, was captain of the Princeton football team, and coached the backfield at Wake Forest to earn his way through law school.

"That's just what I'm afraid of," she said "there is way too much needless body contact in football, running after one another, grabbing each other around the waist and falling down together in a heap, with all the others piling on. It's got to be a game invented by gay men."

So that is how women see football, I thought, it's no wonder they hate it so, reminding myself never to mention I was a scat back who consorted with Johnny

Unitas, Marty Domres, Al Neville and Jimmy Welsh, all famous Baltimore backs, to name just a few of my tennis buddies. I introduced Bob to her anyway and counted on him to win her over. We made the rounds of the hospitality suites, which almost every county had, featuring things like stuffed ham from St. Mary's County and muskrat and beaten biscuits from the shore counties. Yuck.

I was busy making sure I was holding my pledged vote while explaining to Louise why I had to turn on her. When I went to bed, Bob was still out plying his charms on the young ladies, who had been signing up to work for him in droves. One pulled me aside to ask if he was married or going steady with anyone. I was intentionally vague in my answers, in part because Bob had agreed to escort my daughter to her post-debutante presentation at the Washington Cotillion in November.

I was pleased with Bob's performance and told him so Sunday afternoon as we were driving back to Baltimore. He was sitting in the passenger seat, wearing nothing but the pair of white shorts he had worn on Friday. The sun roof of my 450SEL was open, he had no shirt on, and his bare feet were resting on the dashboard. Drivers of other cars, mostly women but not all, were driving erratically as they passed, stretching their necks to see if Bob were completely nude.

"Bob" I finally said, "you are going to get me arrested for creating a traffic hazard. Everybody passing us is trying to see if you are buck naked."

He looked hurt, dropped his feet on the floor and put his shirt back on. I began to wonder if it were possible that he knew nothing of the birds and the bees. As we approached Baltimore, he warned me that he was an only child and his parents doted on him.

"When you go in my house, be prepared for a shock. My parents have made it a shrine to me. Pictures everywhere, wall to wall, floor to ceiling. Every football picture published or program I was on are blown-up, framed, and hung. If you know about it before hand, you won't hurt their feelings by saying something about it."

I told him not to worry, for if he were my son, I would probably do the same. Bob's father had served in Korea with Laddie Murray, who was his father's platoon leader. The fact that Bob, Laddie and I had all worked in the same law firm pleased his father. Bob's mother organized the Arbutus Fourth of July parade, and Bob prevailed on me to bring the Boumi Temple Mounted Patrol to Arbutus on July 4, 1984 to participate.

We were scheduled to be in the Dundalk parade at ten, the Towson parade at noon, Catonsville at two and Arbutus at four. Dundalk was longer than expected, Towson is always long, so I did not even un-tack the horses, putting them in their stalls in our trailer fully tacked with loose girths. It was a hot day. When we pulled up in Arbutus, Bob met the van and helped us unload.

My younger daughter was hosting a Sewanee classmate from Colorado who had come along to help me with the horses. One of my troopers had broken his bridle, and the Colorado cowboy repaired it. I did not want to leave a horse behind in an unfamiliar locale, for he would have been hard to manage. Like voters, horses are herd animals, and he would have insisted on coming along with us.

In November, Bob and I went to New Haven, by train, for the Princeton-Yale game. As we checked into our hotel, Ray Charles, who was going to perform in New Haven that evening was sitting in a chair while someone was checking him in. We were expected at dinner at Mory's with my daughter and Chris Edgar, who had worked in my office with Tommy DiBiagio in the summer of 1983, when we spent three weeks in Newport Beach reviewing thousands of boxes of documents in the Beckman case. The Ray Charles's event was sold out, so we attended a Wiffenpoof concert instead.

After breakfast the next morning we walked to the Yale Bowl. At halftime, Bob excused himself to meet with former Princeton players who wanted the Princeton coach replaced. Bob had been asked to be their spokesman. After Yale won, we walked around the outside of the stadium through clouds of marihuana smoke so thick you could get high just breathing. It gave me a severe headache and made me hungry.

My daughter's college was Davenport, a schizophrenic architectural horror, Gothic on the outside and Georgian facing the courtyard, the perfect college for Maryland mug rumps. The dining hall was crowded and the lines in the cafeteria were long. A student pushed a double-tiered cart, filled with ice and imported beer, courtesy of the college president who wanted to apologize for the wait for service. Yale, like American state and local government, is staffed by unionized workers on strike more often than not.

Bob was ready to make his bid for the Legislature in 1986. Gary Brewster, son of Harry's friend Danny Brewster, was also a member of the Towson Exchange Club. Sitting between them at dinner one night, I put a change of party affiliation in front of Gary and urged him to sign it.

"Gary, you and Danny are better Republicans than I. Make it official."

Gary demurred, contending that he had to remain a Democrat.

Many of the Exchange Club members were serving on Bob's finance committee. Mac MacLure, Bill Peck, Steve Kreseski and I met with Jon Tower, Bob's campaign manager. The first event was at the Holiday Inn in Timonium, and Bob made his first speech at the end of the evening announcing his candidacy. It was not a great speech, but it was straight forward, simple and direct, better than I expected. In a parting in the curtain of time, I saw Bob running for Governor of Maryland making a mature and impassioned speech in the house of a friend. It actually happened, at Trevor Lewis's house in 2002, and I told Bob that night I had foreseen it at the Holiday Inn in Timonium in 1986. How does God do that? Perhaps that might be a future dissertation for an Einstein-like physicist?

There were difficulties. Wade Kach, Tom Chamberlain and Ellen Sauerbrey held together in the primary. I wrote letters on Bob's behalf setting the record straight and threatening repercussions. The breach was healed by some careful political sidestepping by Ellen and Wade, both of whom maintained that Tom Chamberlain had prepared the offending diatribe, they had approved the concept and authorized their signatures, but they had not approved the text.

The 10th Legislative was not the only Republican primary in Baltimore County that year. I was supporting Jim Ports, Al Redmer and Gary Snyder in the Eighth

Legislative District. Michael Kosmas, a precocious teen-age supporter of Helen Bentley, distributed, on primary day, an "official" pink Baltimore County ballot, "signed" by Helen, supporting a ticket not of my choosing. The party symbol, a star-spangled elephant, trumpeted from the masthead.

Gary was convinced the ballot, which was distributed at some, but not all of the polling places, had cost him the election. Suit was filed in the Circuit Court of Baltimore County. Judge Leonard Jacobson, himself formerly a member of the Legislature, heard evidence and decided against us. An emergency appeal to the Court of Appeals won a reversal by a four to three vote. The case went back to Judge Jacobson for a new trial.

I called Tommy Bromwell, still the Senator from the Eighth 'and as far as I was concerned the person most knowledgeable of the voting habits of the various precincts. I asked him to testify as an expert witness and he was looking forward to it. But someone prevailed upon him not to. We lost again, and again I filed an emergency appeal, which we lost by a three to four vote.

I called Helen Bentley, who had referred the issue to a Washington law firm. She told me she authorized Michael to support the ticket, and although she had not seen the ballot she authorized him to sign her name. She had violated Federal Election law, which prohibits primary ballots masquerading as official party documents. I urged her to stick to her story—she had approved the ticket but not the ballot. That way Mike, who was a juvenile, could take the blame. Just to scare him, I urged Sandra O'Connor, the Baltimore County State's Attorney—a Republican in name only—to charge him under the penal statutes. She refused.

After the election, Bob invited Estelle and me to his apartment in Timonium for dinner. There were some nonsensical election law violations which needed to be addressed. The State Prosecutor, a legislative invention to address the problem that exists where State's Attorneys are elected to prosecute crime in their county, but no one is authorized to prosecute a crime that is statewide in scope. The real reason is that Anne Arundel County is predominately Republican, and Democrat legislative leaders are not about to subject their crimes to review by a Republican states attorney. To assure that convictions are the exception and not the rule, the office is understaffed and under funded.

I did not do criminal defense work nor am I competent to represent defendants charged with the most mundane of offenses. But I had no qualms about representing Bob because I drafted the law his campaign allegedly violated, and I knew I could win the case on preliminary motion. We had a pleasant time that evening, and Bob and I both knew that he had taken the first step toward fulfilling his dream.

Bob became a favorite of the eastern Baltimore County delegation in the Legislature, men I liked but avoided— Norman Stone, Joe Bartenfelder, Joe Minnick and John Arnick. I think of them as "Republicrats" because they are as conservative on some issues as they are middle of the road on others. My biggest problem for the next few years was keeping Bob in the Republican Party, because his newfound friends tried as hard to get Bob to switch as I had tried to take Gary Brewster away from them.

Bob was interested in the U.S. Congress, and I hoped to get Helen Bentley to run for the Senate. I urged Bob to have a ready-made campaign for Congress, set up and ready to go—a schedule of what would be done the first twenty-four hours, the first week and the first month after Helen filed for another office, or died, whichever occurred first— banners, bumper stickers, handouts and planned fundraisers—all geared to the federal requirements for raising money. These were the things I learned in classes taught by Newt Gingrich when I was a member if the State Central committee.

When I lost my battle to get Helen in the Senate race in 1994, she filed for Governor and the very next day there were blue and white banners on the courthouse steps below my window on the fifth floor of the Alex Brown Building in Towson, proclaiming "Ehrlich for U.S. Congress."

It was painful for me, because Bob's opponent was Gary Brewster, whose father was an avid supporter of FOCUS, the Christian outreach at private schools founded by the Von Trapp family, which Estelle and I supported. Gary and his sister were still riding horses in the My Lady's Manor races. I sat that one out, and encouraged Bill Frank by contributing to his campaign, not because I thought he could win, but because I wanted to keep him interested in Republican politics.

Bob waged a good campaign and won. He took Steve Kreseski with him to Washington as his administrative assistant. Another Exchange Club member, Carl Aumann, ran his district office, and Carl's wife, Susan, was elected to the state legislature.

Al Gore, Louise's first cousin, was running for President in 1988. To celebrate his fortieth birthday, Louise invited us to a fund raiser at Marwood. Estelle and I took my client Richie Evans with us, hoping to persuade him to work in Al's campaign instead of that of Governor Michael Dukakis, but an unfortunate accident near Memorial Stadium put Al's son to the hospital, and he dropped out of the running.

Although I shrank from the challenge at Harry's house in Denton in 1967, many unfit men have occupied the White House since 1989 oblivious to the way the world works. Their ignorance jeopardizes our future. In retrospect, I should have jumped on the Pealiquor Road express and never looked back. Harry and I might not have done any better, but it would have been impossible for us to have done any worse.

Savings and loans were in deep trouble when they started offering interest rates higher than five percent in the late 1970's. When banks offered home equity loans in the 1980's, I knew the day would come when the banks would own the majority of houses in America. When Fannie Mae and Freddie Mac accepted a three-dollar, computer-merged credit report in the 1990's in lieu of an investigative mortgage credit report, the business of creating mortgages became a "win-for-all" game, in which real estate broker, mortgage broker, mortgage originator, appraiser and money lender all had a monetary reward only if the sale went through and a mortgage lender was found, I knew a financial collapse was near. "Bank Owned" has replaced "For Sale" signs. NINJA loans (No Income, No Job, No Assets) are now in the dictionary.

“That’s the trouble with you, Ed. You are never satisfied. Every time I give you what you want, you keep coming back, always being critical of me.”

William Donald Schaefer,
December,1984

Governor William D. Schaefer

Baltimore’s Mayor for fifteen years was Don Schaefer, a protégé of the United Christian Citizens. The UCC’s annual dinner meeting was held on the same day the Mayor’s term in office began. When Dr. Monsman and her husband Gerald, both members of the Franklin Street Presbyterian Church who founded the organization, retired and moved back to the mid-west, they asked me to nurture it. I became its President and attended its monthly luncheon meeting at the Hopkins Club.

While Mayor, Don habitually showed up at our annual dinner meeting without notice, over which I presided as master of ceremonies even after I passed the gavel to others. Don was unpredictable, and some of our officers were fearful of annoying him. Room would be made for him at the head table, at my side, so I could entertain him during dinner. I used these occasions, depending on my sensing of his mood, to make headway on projects that interested me.

Tourism is as necessary to Baltimore as it is to Vienna, Austria. At one annual meeting, I reminded Don Baltimore was not as organized streetwise as New York and Washington. Visitors would have difficulty finding their way around. As a frequent traveler in foreign countries, I described the pull-overs on the major auto routes, autobahns or motorways just outside major European cities displaying a map of the city with clearly-marked locations of the hotels and tourist sites. Because foreign travelers are used to this in Europe, I wanted Baltimore be the first American city to follow the practice on the interstates leading into the city. I also wanted each school in Baltimore to learn the language, literature and cuisine of different foreign countries, so their graduates could excel in hosting visitors, but we never got to that before Don died.

Don liked my idea, pulled out a little notebook, and wrote down “signs to guide tourists”. Within the next few months, green and blue signs with white arrows pointing right, left, or straight ahead appeared all over town. It was not at all what I had in mind. The next year, sensing Don was in a receptive mood, I brought up my idea again, implying in Don’s mind my unhappiness with “signs to guide tourists.” Don exploded.

“That's the trouble with you, Ed. You are never satisfied. Every time I give you what you want, you keep coming back, always being critical of me.”

It was not the time to make any progress, so I let it drop. I do not have my pullovers, and the little green and blue signposts have survived and multiplied.

After eight years in the Attorney General's office, Steve Sachs decided to run for Governor in 1986. Harry's second term as Governor was running out, his Lieutenant Governor Joe Curran was going to run for Steve's slot as Attorney General. Don challenged Steve in the Democrat primary and won. Steve joined an influential law firm in Washington, probably thankful that Don would have to do the thankless job of governing Maryland.

Bob Ehrlich was making his first run for elective office as a candidate for the Republican nomination for the House of Delegates in the old Tenth Legislative District. A meltdown of state insured savings and loan associations coinciding with wrongdoing at federally insured institutions nationally fell unevenly, and Harry got the blame. His hope of being a U.S. Senator vanished, so I devoted my time to Bob's campaign and my law practice. Why don't people know that high interest rates mean high risks? Why is it that when greed breeds losses, the taxpayers are called upon to make the greedy whole?

Bob won the primary, and faced Gary Brewster in the general in November. Don Schaefer re-appointed me to the Citizen's Advisory Committee of the Charles H. Hickey School, and I worked hard to persuade him to privatize it. It was time, I decided, to make permanent changes in the operation of the Hickey School. I wanted a private company that ran Glen Mills to replicate its success in Pennsylvania in Maryland. Sam Farranola, who ran Glen Mills, was so disgusted with the RFP put together by Juvenile Services, he declined to get involved.

The problem was that Glen Mills was faith-based, and political correctness make that impossible in Maryland, supposedly the most Catholic of states run by Catholic politicians, all of whom should be excommunicated if the Pope had the courage of his convictions. The consequences were tragic, and we continue to pay more for less while ruining the lives of thousands of young people left on life's doorstep.

The Maryland Training School, now “Hickey,” was originally set up as a privately endowed facility to civilize angry young men whose deprivation of love and necessities drove them to crime. The State took it over in 1912, and the situation went, gradually at first and more rapidly later, from good to bad to worse, which is where I found it. We knew what to do, but our efforts were hampered by entrenched interests in the Department of Juvenile Services and the Department of Social Services. While we fought to free the school from their grasp, we continued sending as many young men as we could to Glen Mills.

While sitting out a hurricane at our Nags Head cottage one September afternoon, I watched a C-Span program with a long interview with Governor Schaefer. I learned more about him in those hours than I had in the past thirty years. I wrote him a letter, telling him his place in Maryland's history was fixed forever, and if he never did another thing for the state, he had already done more than enough.

A few days later, as I was leaving a meeting of the over-sight committee for the Hickey School Tommy Bromwell engineered to make it more accountable, Nancy Grasmick was coming in. She had been a trustee of St. James Academy, as had I. She stopped me, planted a kiss on my cheek, hugged me and said Don had shown her my letter. With tears in her eyes, she thanked me for it. The Committee members, who knew us well, looked on in surprise, wondering just what we knew they didn't.

When the Department of Juvenile Justice realized the threat Glen Mills posed to their fiefdom, they interfered with our sending boys there. It was saving money, but more importantly, the recidivism rate at Glen Mills was thirty-three percent while the rate at Hickey was eighty-three percent. Cutting the number of young criminals coming online each year in half was a goal worth pursuing. Here was a chance to do something important. The savings to the state, long term, were inestimable. The cost of prosecutors, public defenders, judges, clerks, prison guards, housing, feeding and clothing the inmates would reduce state spending dramatically, to say nothing of the medical costs of the victims killed, maimed and raped and the loss of property burnt, stolen or wrecked.

Elizabeth Brownell and Sister Pat Hangis were as determined as I was to get the state out of the business of running the Hickey School. We argued that the state can not fire itself when it should be fired for doing a poor job. Rather, the state should be in the role of supervisor, with the ability to hire, or fire, the private contractor running the school whenever change was required.

At an annual banquet of the United Christian Citizens, when Charlie Benton was Maryland's Treasurer and third member of the Board of Public Works, he was honored as Christian Citizen of the year and the framed proclamation from Governor Schaefer was given to him. Inscribed in the margin was Charlie's motto, taken from one of St. Paul's letters. It read "I can do all things through Christ who strengthens me. Phillipians 4:13." At my request Charlie brought Louis Goldstein to lunch with Betty Brownell, Sister Pat and me at the Treaty of Paris in Annapolis.

We explained our plan and arranged a tour of Glen Mills. Charlie and Louie were as astonished as I had been the first time I went there at the overnight changes, just short of miraculous, made in Hickey students transported the fifty miles from Cub Hill to Glen Mills. We asked them to persuade Governor Schaefer to go see for himself, after which Don became an enthusiastic supporter of privatization. A request for bids was published, but the bad news is it was designed by the same hostile bureaucrats who wanted privatization to fail.

The first private contractor at Hickey was Youth Services International, a creation of Jiffy Lube's founder Jim Hindman. Glen Mills was excluded as a potential bidder. YSI went public and until it was taken over by another company, things did improve. Each succeeding private contractor has been less effective than its predecessor, as the bureaucrats learned how to program for and perpetuate failure. If you are interested in the Glen Mills story, read Grant Grissom's "Without Locks and Bars." Or better still, see the German language documentary "Arrested Without Locks and Bars."

In early January, 1990 my wife stopped by my Towson office and found the reception desk deserted. She opened her brief case, sat down, and started working. She answered the telephone, received visitors and made herself useful. At the end of the day she found her way back to my office, handed me a resume she thought I should see. Believing that God uses wifely intuition as messengers, I glanced at it, asking "Why do you think I should see it?" I wanted to know what she knew that I needed to know.

"If he is anything like her, I think you would hire him instantly."

"What was she like?"

"One of the most elegant, attractive and competent young black women I've ever met."

My wife had taught music at the Bryn Mawr School since before our marriage. She knew class and character better than most, so I called the number and set up an appointment.

The next day a tall, quite ordinary black man stood in my office door. In a slow, soft-spoken drawl, he said "Hi, Mr Blanton. I'm Leon Coleman. You asked me to stop in to see you."

I invited him to sit down, wondering how the lady described by my wife had settled for such an ordinary guy as Leon appeared to be. His father was principal of Edmondson High School in Baltimore, and he had come back to Baltimore to counsel his parents through a rough patch married couples encounter from time to time.

After graduating from college, Leon and his wife went to California where she worked in a talent agency, dividing up royalty payments among Hollywood stars. Leon, on the other hand, worked four years as a clerk in the Los Angeles bankruptcy court, four years in the U.S. Trustee's office, and four years as a paralegal in a large, Los Angeles law firm. His slow talking drawl was charming, masking great intelligence, wisdom and competence. My wife thought he was God-sent to help me through a difficult year. Just having him nearby was better than taking valium. He was a tower of strength.

When I first set up my law firm, I saw myself as a gynecologist, obstetrician and pediatrician for corporate persons young entrepreneurs hoped to bring into the world. After President Reagan left office, I was glad I had mastered bankruptcy reorganizations, for our economy was heading for the bushes and I had to become a geriatric specialist to avoid becoming a corporate mortician.

I suspect Leon cost me nothing. At his own expense, not being busy enough to satisfy his enormous energy, he placed ads in a newspaper soliciting Chapter 7 and Chapter 13 bankruptcy cases, which I had never done, as I limited myself exclusively to Chapter 11 reorganizations and creditor work. He met with the clients in my conference room, did the work and deposited the fees in our firm account. Shortly thereafter his wife became pregnant, so I called Al Neville, a tennis buddy and former Maryland and Colt quarterback who handled my insurance program, to make sure they had pregnancy coverage.

Leon was also a computer, savvy guy. He told me my system 36 surrounded by a ring of PC's was too powerful for my office.

"It's like having an interstate highway system all to yourself, only you don't need it because you're the only one on it."

But that happens when you take technology salesmen seriously. You always buy more than you will ever need.

So determined was I to get broad support for Glen Mills to operate Maryland's training schools I did not decline when Dick Bennett invited me to the Maryland Club for lunch. Dick was then the United States Attorney for Maryland, but he met me in a military uniform. He was a JAG colonel in my old National Guard outfit, the 29th Infantry Division, its blue/gray insignia representing Maryland and Virginia.

Dick was also chairman of the Maryland Republican party, and he wanted me to run for attorney general against Joe Curran. This posed a problem because Joe's son Max had been a friend and classmate of my younger daughter at the Bryn Mawr School in Baltimore several years before. Max, of course, was at Gilman, but Bryn Mawr girls have a bridge over Northern Parkway to the boy's campus, where they take some classes.

I listened anyway because Tommy DiBiagio, a young lawyer schooled in my office while he was in law school and later worked with Cleve Miller at Semmes, Bowen and Semmes, had sought my help in joining Dick's staff as an assistant United States Attorney. Five years of admiralty law in a city no longer a viable port had caused him to consider a career change. I asked Dick to consider him for a position on his staff, which Dick agreed to do.

A year later, Dick told me that Tommy was such a competent prosecutor he would have hired him even if I had not recommended him. I told Dick it was not my intention to help Tommy; rather, I had sent Tommy over to help him, hoping that together they could do something about the pandemic of public corruption in Maryland. Tommy was well on his way to doing just that when the Clinton Justice Department stopped him.

"Just promise me this. The next time we get a Republican president, I want Tommy to be the US Attorney for Maryland."

Dick put out his right hand, and we shook on it. I told Tommy, after President Clinton replaced Dick with Lynn Battaglia, that he was our choice for U.S. Attorney when we got another Republican in the White House. Tommy stuck it out as long as he could, but the politicizing of the office frustrated his efforts, and he could not, in good conscience, continue to be part of a system he loathed.

Neither Dick nor I seriously thought I could defeat Joe Curran. Our goal was to scare Joe, who had a substantial war chest, and deprive him of it before 1994, when Don's second term would be up, and Joe his likely successor. I told Dick I would help on two conditions: I did not want a repeat of the primary problem I had with Warren Rich in 1978, and we needed strong candidates in the counties surrounding Baltimore City. I sought his help recruiting Bob Dubel to run for County Executive in Baltimore County regardless of party.

A few days later, Dick called to say he had talked to Bob, who could not see his way clear to run. He recommended a fellow named Roger Hayden, who was a Republican President of the Baltimore County school board. He had asked

Roger to call me and set up a meeting. Roger lived not far from me in Baldwin, Maryland. He stopped by to see me one Sunday afternoon and we talked for four hours.

I wanted to know what he knew about Baltimore County politics, and to tell him the things I thought he needed to know to be successful in the general election. His opponent was the Democrat incumbent, a bright and attractive young man who had erred greatly and alienated those who were his principal supporters. I thought he was a sitting duck.

Roger was not the neophyte I had thought he might be, and I called Dick and told him that I could live with Roger as a running mate. Not having a lot of time to devote to politics, my campaign would have to rely upon organization in the heavily populated center of the state. Strong candidates for county executive in Baltimore, Harford, Anne Arundel, Howard and for County Council in Carroll upon whom I could depend for support were essential to a creditable candidacy.

The Democrats were having a fund raiser at the Timonium Fairgrounds, and I went, primarily to tell Tommy Bromwell what I had been asked to do. Tommy encouraged me to do it, not because he distrusted Joe, because he did not. It would be better for the process if I were the Republican nominee rather than someone like Melvin Perkins who had made a career filing for offices no sensible person would seek. I also needed to let Joe Curran know I was to be his opponent in November.

I told Joe I was responding to my party's call for aid, a duty imposed on me subconsciously, I supposed, while taking a typing class. Joe laughed, and we agreed to talk about issues and qualifications only, avoiding personalities. I told him my younger daughter warned me not to get her in trouble with Max, and if I did I would be the proverbial "dead meat". We parted as friends, and remained so.

I dutifully filed for the Republican nomination for Attorney General, and did little else. The press received me favorably, as they always had. I called on the Republican National Committee and set up a lunch at the Capitol Hill Club, next door to their office. They had three possibilities for campaign manager, all of them named Mark. I took their resumes home to review.

The most highly recommended was Mark Rivers. He lived in Connecticut and he had been running a gubernatorial campaign in the mid-west. He had climbed out of his swimming pool to answer a telephone call, slipped on the deck and fell through a glass-topped table, severely injuring his right hand. While he recuperated, the campaign replaced him, and he was sufficiently recovered by mid-September to take my campaign. I called him and made arrangements to meet him in New Jersey to get acquainted.

Mark was energetic, smart and determined, just what I had been told he was. We agreed upon his compensation, for a nine-week engagement, beginning the week after Labor Day and continuing through the general election in November. In the meantime, I gave him my resume and a piece published in the Sun about my campaign. My recollection was that the headline called me "a party-switching lawyer" although I had been a Republican since 1964. The text, after referring to the poor quality of Republican candidates in general, said this time the party had "trotted out a real professional." Since Choco and I were still doing a lot of trotting on the hills behind my house in the Long Green Valley I was encouraged.

When Mark arrived in Baltimore, he wanted to stop by the house and meet my wife. She liked him immediately, and offered him the guest's quarters for the evening, rather than sending him on to the Holiday Inn on Cromwell Bridge Road, where he and I had planned on his staying. Mark was going to have office space within my law firm in the Alex Brown building in Towson, not exactly the place for a political campaign, but just right for the campaign we planned to run.

We hired Mark Hagood, a former Virginia legislator who had just returned from the G-7 meetings in Houston. My old friend Jack "Shorty" Surrick agreed to help as a volunteer. Mark Rivers would concentrate on strategy and earned media, Mark Hagood on events and fundraising in the Washington suburbs and Shorty would go with me from place to place throughout the state as we campaigned.

I hated fund-raising, and I would not do the things Hagood told me I had to do if I wanted to be attorney general. My duty was to offer myself: if the public didn't want me, it was their loss and my gain. When Harry Hughes complained in 1966 about having to meet a contributor in the sauna at a health club, I pulled out my checkbook, asked Harry how much money he needed to win his campaign, and wrote him a check.

Mark Rivers decided to substitute "smoke and mirrors" for the real thing when Hagood left the campaign a month later. He purchased some old-fashioned mercury thermometers and mailed them to every reporter—newspaper, radio or television in the state—suggesting they could use them to keep track of the hottest political race in Maryland. The party's candidate for Governor had so little support his wife was running with him as his lieutenant-governor candidate, as she had four years earlier.

I was scheduled for a radio interview in Westminster on primary night, and we were due to arrive at the Shepherds headquarters in Rockville in time for some photographs and party unity stuff. Mark wanted to meet them and find out how well Mark Hagood had done in spreading our story around Montgomery County. Initially, Mark Rivers took it upon himself to handle Prince Georges County. We were not providing living quarters to Hagood, and it was convenient for him to work from his home in Virginia. He was a Robert Redford look-a-like, and I thought he was just right for the DC suburbs.

Like the proverbial man who came to dinner and stayed, Mark Rivers had Estelle's blessing to stay in the guest quarters indefinitely. I rarely saw him, and we left notes and assignments for one another on the staircase. His hand was healing well, and he often took a morning swim while I was having breakfast. I never did know what he was doing in Prince Georges County, but every now and then someone would grab my hand, say how glad they were to meet me and admit their enthusiasm was predicated on the gutsy things I was doing there. As curious as I was, I never found out.

Shorty Surrick and I were sent out on missions from the Eastern Shore to Western Maryland. We had a radio-telephone installed in a new Ford Taurus I bought from Sherwood-on-the-Shore to use in the campaign. It replaced my old Mercedes 450SEL, which had been totaled one dark and stormy night in early August in front of the entrance to Goucher College. Rich Evans had taken me to an Oriole game and I was hoping he would point for me as he had for Carter, McGovern, Mondale and Dukakis, as 1990 was not a presidential year. The rains came in the middle of the first inning and never stopped. Cars were flooded out on North Charles Street as we passed them heading back to Towson. It was still pouring at eleven when I made a run for my car. I drove a few blocks when I saw a lake in the middle of Dulaney Valley Road. Not wanting to go through the water, I slowed down to get a better view of the depth and width of it, peering through the rivulets of water cascading down faster than my windshield wipers could brush them off. Suddenly and with great force my car was struck from behind, rendering me momentarily unconscious.

When I awoke the rain was still coming down. I got out of the car to see how the people in the other car were doing. But there was no other car. My engine was still running, so I got back in the car. When I got home, I called the police and reported that I had left the scene of an accident. They had heard nothing and seen nothing, absolved me of liability and told me to call my insurance company. My car was totaled, and I used the check they gave me to buy the Ford.

Fall was a great time of year to campaign in western Maryland, and Shorty and I spread my message about the social and economic consequences of changing the way we treated juvenile delinquents. It was a message that astounded those expecting a right-wing conservative to advocate harsh treatment and brutal consequences. It caught the attention of those who interviewed me, and we were often invited back for televised interviews. It was beginning to work. We actually carried Washington County in the general election.

Shorty elected to drive and let me play with the telephone. We were between Cumberland and Hagerstown, where I had talked to the Exchange Club at lunch, and we were on our way to a Hagerstown television studio. Mark urged us to hurry back to Towson as soon as possible, because local television was clamoring for my views on a prisoner release fiasco that had broken over Joe Curran's head.

A program designed to relieve prison overcrowding added good time from all sentences served by a convict to reduce the time to be served in the current sentence. That is why, if you wondered, why those convicted of attempted murder and armed robbery are sentenced to twenty years and serve eighteen months. As a result, unsavory characters were being released early, and one of them, harboring a death wish, had cruelly murdered some teenaged children on the eastern shore. We also received calls from state employees outraged by the policy, encouraging us to pursue it. They were eager to help us.

The author of the opinion was working for Sandra O'Conor, the alleged Republican States Attorney for Baltimore County. Joe would not release the opinion to me or the press. I called Sandra and asked her for a copy. She refused. Her voice filled with moral indignation as she defended her employee, angrily shrieking "He's a good kid. He has a wife and family. I'm not going to let you destroy him."

Who did she think I was? All I wanted to do was read an opinion that was costing the lives of innocent citizens, to see whether it was what we had been told it was. There was no way I could debate Joe—who was taking the blame for what his assistant had done anyway—without reading the opinion. Did Sandy seriously believe I wanted to relieve Joe of the blame? I signed opinions as an assistant attorney general I did not approve of, because I had written them one way and the deputy or the attorney general edited my work before signing, often reaching a result opposite to mine, just as Judge Kern often did when I submitted draft opinions to him.

Joe had antagonized automobile dealers in Maryland, and they were supporting my campaign with a fund raiser at the Towson Sheraton. I needed something to say, and the one thing I had learned in campaigning so far was that Joe was well liked by everybody. No one had said anything bad about him, and it was unlikely that they would.

My standard theme, when asked about Joe, was "He's a nice guy. Everybody likes him. They like him because he never says 'no' to anybody. That's what's wrong. There are a lot of people Joe should be saying 'no' to. There are a lot of state agencies he should be saying 'no' to. Instead, he lets them do things they should not do, simply because he is a good guy, he's liked by everyone, and he likes being liked."

There was also some egregiously bad advice he had given to the State Pension board about buying out the retirement obligations owed to state employees, which was costing the employees dearly. In the boom years of the 1980's, Louie Goldstein had closed out state pension investments shortly before the stock market crash in October, 1987. The fund was awash in money, and state employees were told they could withdraw their money and roll it over to an IRA tax free. They could under the law as it existed in 1986, but not after the way the law was changed by the Internal Revenue Code of 1986.

Employees who were ill-advised withdrew sums as much as $800,000 each, rolled it over to their IRA, only to discover that penalties for excess contributions to an IRA and excess withdrawals from a retirement plan resulted in the loss of as much as one-hundred twenty percent of the total they received. It was a disaster, and the state was moving quickly to contain it. It was excellent campaign fodder talking to public employees, and I found myself called upon to exploit another flaw in my opponent's armor. But there were some things we did which annoyed him more.

No one in Maryland seems to understand that the attorney general has no law enforcement responsibility other than in very limited circumstances. Prosecution of crimes is the job of the elected states attorney in each county unless the criminals are elected officials, in which case the State Prosecutor for petty matters and the United States Attorney for serious stuff.

Steve Sachs ran for Attorney General in 1978 as if the attorney general is a prosecutor because it makes the public more interested in the race. When I explained this to Mark, he wrote and recorded an ominous sounding radio commercial that grated on Dennis Sweeney's nerves, and as Joe's campaign manager, Dennis negotiated with Mark to get it off the air. We wanted a debate badly and he promised us one if we pulled it.

We ran the commercial on radio early and often to signal that we were serious about waging an aggressive campaign. So when our budget for this part of the campaign required the commercial to stop running, we pulled it. There never was a debate. Joe and I saw one another but twice in the entire period between the primary and the general election. The media no longer insists on debates. Politics is now all about sound bites, and that is as far as the media's interest extends. There are no debates, no speeches, no confrontations. Unless, of course, you create them, so that is what Mark did.

There were several candidate fora where Joe and I were scheduled to speak. Inevitably, Joe always showed up after I had left, whether accidentally or intentionally. I saw him once at West Friendship. I had the crowd to myself for most of the evening. As the hall emptied, I decided to leave. As I walked out the door, Joe was walking toward the building. I called "A bit late, Joe. Everybody's gone home. But don't worry, I told them what a nice guy you are."

"I bet you did." he replied, and went inside the almost empty building. Later, Joe's campaign insisted this was the debate they had promised us for taking our commercial off the air.

I was scheduled to be interviewed by the Afro-American the next morning. I was promised fifteen minutes. When I started talking about Glen Mills and my hope of actually educating youthful offenders rather than putting them in cages, I got an extra hour of their time. Making this point was what I was getting out of the campaign, and my party was interested in making Joe spend his campaign war chest.

We started airing our "Fight Back" commercial, and we dumped enough money in the bank account before filing the pre-election report to worry Joe. He committed all his money to a last-minute, eleven day blitz on the airways. All we could do was shut our eyes and ears and let it wash over us.

I had a press conference on the eastern shore. Shorty was busy reviewing video clips, Leon Coleman was running my office, so he volunteered his lovely but pregnant wife to go with me. The press present that day were all women, anxious to have fun at the expense of a pro-life, pro-death penalty Republican running against a pro-choice, anti-death penalty Democrat. Mrs. Coleman defended me so well their antagonism turned to interest. She was a remarkable lady. It helped that a number of the women attending were also African-American. We believed we had made our mark, and when I made my Glen Mills pitch to them, they were intrigued.

I had great interviews and pushed my Glen Mills points with newspapers in the Washington, D.C. area, picking up several endorsements. I met with the Washington Times editorial board, led by Tony Snow. When the interview was over, Tony mentioned Davidson College. I did not realize Tony was also a Wildcat, but I was glad he had done enough homework to be aware of my background before the interview.

I think Tony was disappointed a right-wing Republican was talking like a bleeding heart liberal, which is what Pat McDonough was calling me on WCBM. Yet, George Tyler and Bob Thieblot, Baltimore lawyers who were my closest political friends, told everyone I was somewhere right of Attila the Hun, a phrase they picked up from Bill Swisher, the Baltimore City states attorney, who had said that about me in 1978. It was so far from the truth we laughed about it, but my friends liked repeating it. When you tease a lot you get teased a lot.

Compassionate conservatism was not invented by George W. Bush. Richard Chaney's wife Lynn was active in Maryland politics. Helping people help themselves so they can in turn help others is what motivated me. Restoring human dignity and promoting self-reliance will prolong the Republic. Massive government programs to keep the people dependent upon government will destroy America just as surely as it destroyed the Western Roman Empire.

On the Thursday before the general election we had scheduled television coverage for the farmers market in Towson, and Joe Curran was to receive an award from an environmentalist group on Federal Hill. We moved the television event to the Inner Harbor, where I talked to tourists happy to be on television but unable to vote on Tuesday. Spotters on the hill called down to let me know Joe was out of his car and on the way to receive his 'atta-a-boy.'

A call to my headquarters in Towson released a flood of previously prepared press releases by telefax to the radio, television and print media that I was going to interrupt Joe's ceremony to force the debate he had promised us but never delivered. A third call moved two automobiles to block Joe's limousine so he could not get away. With everything in place, I walked up Federal Hill as the media arrived in force.

Joe began to suspect something was up. A throng of television cameramen and microphone were moving toward him. In the midst of that throng, a handsome young man, a smile on his face, thrust out his right hand to shake mine.

"Hello, Mr. Blanton. I'm Martin O'Malley."

"I know who you are, Martin. Glad to meet you."

Over his head, I saw Joe making a run for it. When I tried to move, Martin and three very large muldoons began dancing with me, moving in front of and beside me no matter which way I turned. As Joe hurried to his car, I called after him.

"Joe, call off the muscle so we can talk. The election's Tuesday. People need to know how we stand before they vote. You promised a debate. Let's have it right now. Everybody's here. We owe it to the public."

Joe did not respond. When he was safely inside his car, Martin pulled the guard. I walked over to the car in the midst of a jungle of microphones and cameras filming away. I had an impromptu press conference, a one-sided debate with my opponent sitting inside his blocked vehicle reading his 'atta-a-boy.'

Michael Marr's teen-age son, Eric, often drove me to political events. Mark, who teaches classes in practical politics, asked Eric to collect samples of every piece of campaign literature being passed out by attendees and their supporters. Eric, who died tragically in his twenties, was a strikingly handsome teenager whose driving skills left much to be desired. It was not that Eric was reckless. It was lack of experience in the traffic and weather we encountered.

On the Saturday night before the election, my telephone at home began ringing and did not stop. Ronald Shapiro was host of a television interview program and he invited Joe Curran to be his guest. This was seen as a violation of the doctrine of fairness, and my supporters were complaining loudly to me and to the station. I called WMAR and asked to speak to the manager. I was told he was not there. I asked where he was, but I was told they did not know.

"Suppose the station caught on fire. Would you be able to notify him?"

"Under those circumstances, I could find him."

"Well. I suggest you find him now, because I have people so angry they are threatening to burn your station unless you make amends for your conduct tonight."

The next morning Eric was going to pick me up for a full day of campaigning. We turned the WMAR problem over to Shorty Surrick, ex WBAL, to resolve. WMAR offered to let Shorty write and record a sixty second spot which they agreed to air a specified number of times Sunday evening and during the day and evening Monday. Eric and I stopped by WMAR when we finished our schedule. Eric and I arrived about five o'clock, and after several takes Shorty was satisfied with the result.

Eric, in the meantime, had understandably fallen head-over-heels in love with a beautiful young lady named Mary Beth Marsden who was then a WMAR anchor. A kind and gracious lady, she had spoken to the young man patiently waiting, melting his heart. On the way out of the station, he asked,

"Do you think I am too young for her?"

Unwilling to pour cold water on his ardor, I said, "Intelligent women prefer younger men. They tell me it makes them easier to train."

Having spent an hour trying to charm her, Eric was considerably relieved. He asked if he had my permission to call her. I told him he may, but it might be a good idea to make sure her husband was not at home before he dialed. He was crestfallen.

The results on Tuesday were actually better than we expected. We had done what we set out to do. Joe spent his entire war chest on unneeded media. I had pushed the Glen Mills story from Hagerstown to Easton, and everywhere in between.

Roger Hayden won in Baltimore County, and we also elected a Republican sheriff in Baltimore and Anne Arundel. We picked up state delegates and a senator or two as well. Our party was poised to score in 1994.

Mark endeared himself to my family, and returned to New England with our blessing. He has stayed in touch and his skills in public relations were recognized when he was hired by a large international company. He promised to come back if I was interested in running for Governor in 1994. I told him to stay where he was, as I reverted to my role as consigliore and tried to sort it out.

I wrote Joe a personal note, thanking him for adhering to the commitment he made prior to the election. He in turn, wrote back, telling me he thought my party had made a great choice and that we had run a good campaign. He was not alone in that view. The day after the election I was doing some research in the Baltimore County Bar Library, and Bob Murphy came over to shake my hand. He had enjoyed watching me and Joe slug it out.

"For a while I thought you might pull it off." he said, laughing as he recalled the outrageous radio commercials we ran and our attack up Federal Hill.

"Yeah, but all I was asked to do was to take Joe out of the gubernatorial race in 1994. I think we did that."

We did, but Martin O'Malley, his son-in-law, had his eye on the office, and he got even with me in 2006 by defeating Bob Ehrlich's bid for a second term.

Within a few years, Bob Murphy died, and Estelle and I saw Helen and their daughters at the reception following the service at the Cathedral of Mary Our Queen. Two old friends from the Attorney General's office, Judge Alan Wilner and Judge Lawrence Rodowsky, spoke at the funeral. I remembered Tom Finan's prediction at his farewell party at the Emerson Hotel in 1966. Looking out over the dedicated band of lawyers that constituted his little law firm, he had predicted he was looking at a future Governor, an Attorney General and a few judges of the Court of Appeals. Both of the speakers were then on the Court, they had also been there that sad night in 1966 to hear Tom's prediction. We were burying Tom's deputy who had been the Chief Judge of the Maryland Court of Appeals when he died, a position Tom Finan was appointed to fill the very day he died.

The new Courts building in Annapolis is named after Bob. Tom's failing was that he hired scholars instead of politicians. If we had been more skilled politically than we were, Tom would probably have won in 1966. And if he had, his 1966 prophecy might have come true. How different our national history might have been had we all been what Tom hoped we were and what perhaps we should have been. Mea culpa. It breaks my heart I let him down more than any of the others.

"Shut up, Ed, I don't care what you think. I want to know what he thinks."

"And so you shall, soon enough. But I already know you don't care what I think. If you did, you would be in your second term in the United States Senate, and Ellen Sauerbrey would be finishing her second term as Governor of Maryland."

Conversation with Helen Delich Bentley,
February, 2001

Governor Robert Ehrlich

When the Clintons moved into the White House in 1993, the Maryland Republican party was looking for some one to run for Governor the following year. Tom Clancy had been active in the 1990 campaign, appearing at fundraising events for Republican candidates throughout the state. In early 1994, I was invited to the Frederick County Lincoln Day Dinner in Walkersville, where Tom Clancy was going to speak.

Mindful of Louise Gore's advice never to go anywhere alone when you are a politico, I called Rick Geritz to see if he could go with me. His mother was Don Schaefer's secretary and she arranged Maryland Day festivities for the Governor every March 25th. I had met Rick when he testified as a witness in one of my cases. He could not go, but suggested I ask his roommate, Patrick Jamison, who was a great fan of Tom Clancy.

Patrick, like Rick, was a graduate of St. Mary's College. He was also a member of the Maryland State Police SWAT team. When not swatting, he was an investigator for the Attorney General, he was interested in politics, and I was interested in having him as a running mate in 1994. He cross examined me on issues, posing theoretical situations for me to resolve. I decided to take him to political club meetings, fund raisers and state Republican Party conventions just as I had done with Bob Ehrlich a few years before.

Tom Clancy had a serious case of foot-in-mouth too often, which is almost always fatal politically. We were at Marwood when he told me he was not going to run. Louise told me it was my time, and Patrick suggested we lock up a number of billboard locations throughout the state and plaster them with signs proclaiming "Coming Soon. Blanton and Jamison."

To those who may not know, Blanton's is an expensive Kentucky aged-to-taste bourbon, sold in a velvet case, poured from a multi-faceted diamond shaped bottle, sealed with a metallic jockey on a racehorse affixed to a cork. Jameson is an Irish whisky, less expensive than Middleton's, the standard sold in a finished wooden box, but Jameson is more widely known.

I began to think seriously about actually running. I took Patrick out on the campaign trail for a few weeks to see how he managed in a crowd of strangers. He was a good campaigner. At an event near Ocean City, he worked his generation and I worked mine. When we met in the parking lot to go to our next event, some young girls came over to talk to me. I asked what I could do for them.

"Please run for Governor." they said, looking somewhat embarrassed. Not having talked to them that afternoon, I asked them why. Their response was unanimous. "We want to vote for Patrick."

Pat had that kind of star quality about him, a trait I always looked for in the lawyers I hired to practice with me and without which one is wasting time contending for political office in the age of the sound bite, motivated voter who can not see beyond the outside of a candidate. The voters go for eye-candy like Mitt Romney if it can think fast enough to repeat mantra like one liners. There are no debates in Maryland so candidates no longer need to be able to think.

What I found, when looking closer, was that Ellen Sauerbrey, minority leader in the House of Delegates, wanted to run for Governor. The Democrats were almost certain to nominate Parris Glendenning, a double-dipping "professor" at the University of Maryland who moon-lighted as Prince Georges County Executive. He was drawing two public salaries, vested in two healthy state-funded retirement pensions, going for the hat trick by getting elected Governor and picking up a third. I could not wait to get him in my sights.

Maryland had not elected a Governor from the DC bed-room counties within memory. Mickey Steinberg was Glendenning's chief opponent in the Democrat primary, and he was a Baltimore man through and through. I liked the way things were beginning to look, and I wanted to test the depth of disgust felt by the people of Prince Georges County toward their pricey leader. There was more than a little detestation.

Robert Neal, a former legislator from Anne Arundel County, was elected Anne Arundel County Executive in 1990. We had campaigned at some of the same places in 1990, and we had good things to say about one another. He was also showing some interest in running for Governor. There was always the possibility of a candidate from Montgomery County, but Louise would not have pushed me if anyone she knew was interested. Nor was I hesitant about having two candidates in the Republican primary from Baltimore County.

As much as I liked Ellen Sauerbrey, her husband Will had never forgiven me for taking Bob Ehrlich's side in 1986. He was openly hostile and physically threatening at political events. But three, that was too many, and the closer we came to filing deadlines, the more it looked like Ellen and I would have Congresswoman Helen Bentley to contend with as well.

Dick Bennett was running for Attorney General. Our initial choice for the United States Senate got cold feet, and I could smell victory if I could persuade Helen Bentley to take his place and run for the Senate. I did my best, even stalking her once or twice, to persuade her of the merit of a strong team running together statewide.

President Clinton's popularity was in the pits, and Newt Gingrich, the Georgia Congressman who took the seat of my college classmate T.K. McDonald, who died on KAL 9, published his "Contract with America." Bob Ehrlich, just as I had suggested, signed on to run for Congress in Maryland's Second District the day after Helen Bentley filed for Governor.

Bob Neal and Helen Bentley were slightly left of center while Ellen and I were both conservatives. We could not afford to split the conservative vote unless both Bob and Helen remained in the primary. But Bob went to the spring convention of the Republican Party in Cumberland and announced that he would no longer be a candidate for Governor. He later left the party altogether, and became a Democrat in fact as well as theory.

I do not know why he decided not to run, but I suspect Helen Bentley's involvement. She learned to play hardball so well when she was in Congress I no longer knew her. With the three of us, all from Baltimore County, Helen would win. Ellen and I met for breakfast at the McDonald's in Jacksonville, Maryland, and I told Ellen I was so disgusted with Helen I was leaving that afternoon with my wife and daughter for Istanbul, and when I got back I was going to put my heart and soul into her campaign. My friend Cleve Miller, his wife and daughter, were going with us.

Before I left I asked my sister Millie to go to Ellen's headquarters, roll up her sleeves, and block Bentley at every turn. My sister's strength is radio talk show, where she comes across as innocent as a dove and as sharp as a scorpion at just the right time to score big. My children urged her to start an "Ask Aunt Millie" website to publicize her incisive comments. It would have been an excellent anti-dote to progressive acceleration toward permanent decline, but the Drudge Report and Fox News now have that market.

When I returned from Turkey, Patrick and I were seated on either side of Ellen at a political dinner at the Turf Valley Country Club. She asked me if I had changed my mind. Ellen, the biology teacher who nosed out my ally John Shoup for the House of Delegates in 1978, was prosaic, and there was nothing she needed more than an attractive and intelligent running mate to draw young people to her cause. I nodded toward the tall, darkly handsome, all-American alpha male sitting beside her, and said,

"Patrick was going to be my running mate. I'm not going to run. He is my gift to you. Having an intelligent young state policeman with star-power at your side, given the public's concern about crime, is just what you need to win the general election. If I'm not in, you will win the primary, about that I have no doubt."

Ellen ignored the Consigliore's advice and chose an older, retired state policeman who become a lawyer and married the politically active clerk of the Circuit

Court of Howard County. When the votes were counted in September, Ellen had trounced Helen decisively. Helen refused to congratulate Ellen, would not shake her hand, slapping it away when offered. She called a press conference a few days later and endorsed Glendenning. The Baltimore *Sun* gleefully published a picture of her and her staff, touting Helen's betrayal as the clincher for their choice, the triple dipping, mush-mouth professor. I vowed she would never again win another election in Maryland.

Because of Helen's determination to thwart a conservative Republican candidate, the party selected a former Senator from Tennessee, then living in Annapolis, to run for the Senate. Mr. Brock's fortune was made selling candy. He did well enough, but it is difficult to run against the man who is not there, and Paul Sarbanes, brilliant and hard working as he is, is always beneath the radar.

Paul had been in the Senate for a long time, and he might not have run at all if Helen had been his opponent, as they both relied upon the ethnic vote in Baltimore. When I needed to talk to Paul, he hosted me in the Senate dining room. He had a rally at The Crease in Towson which I attended, and he made a stirring speech, the first time I had ever heard him speak in person. I congratulated him and suggested he should concentrate on personal appearances and avoid television, where he comes across, just as Nixon did, as weak and ineffective. We trusted one another, just as Steny Hoyer and I do, for the three of us had worked together in the Legislature in the 1960's doing the hard work *Time* magazine attributed to Agnew.

In 2002, when Bob Ehrlich resigned his seat in Congress to run for Governor, Helen rushed to get her old seat back. She appeared as a guest at a private dinner I was attending following a session of the Baltimore Council of Foreign Affairs. She asked our guest, a German general, why the United States needed NATO, an organization she disliked because of her partisan Serbian roots. President Clinton had just sent troops to Kosovo. Having warned him earlier in the evening about Helen's Serbian bloodline, I answered for him, while he gathered his thoughts.

"NATO is an albatross history hung around our neck to keep us from doing what is right and just."

"Shut up, Ed, I don't care what you think. I want to know what he thinks."

"And so you shall, soon enough. But I already know you don't care what I think. If you did, you would be in your second term in the United States Senate, and Ellen Sauerbrey would be finishing her second term as Governor of Maryland."

Prior to the November election, Ross Pierpont urged Ellen to hire Pinkerton guards for a number of polling places in Baltimore City where odd things had happened before. Most of the polling places were in predominately black precincts, and Ellen was timid about cries of racial intimidation. State law permits a candidate to have watchers and challengers at every polling place. In retrospect, had Ellen listened to Ross she might have won the general election in 1994. Instead, she lost by about five thousand votes, and the margin came from the very precincts pinpointed by Ross. With Patrick at her side she would have won.

She did not consult me when she took her contest into the Courts acting on the advice of the Republican National Committee, which sent in some New Jersey lawyers to represent her. Later, when their case was in serious trouble, I received a call to meet with Ellen. I could not get there as fast as she thought I should, so the case was tried without my help. As deficient as the Maryland judiciary has become, it still needs something other than theory to decide cases. It's called evidence.

In 1998, she was back with a new running mate and a more liberal stance and lost badly to the incumbent Democrat. The Legislature, frightened by her near-victory at the polls in 1994, had enacted a ten percent income tax reduction, reducing the top rate from five percent to four and a half percent over five years. Joe Curran was still Attorney General, and they were not told part of the law they passed was unconstitutional. Judges of the Maryland Court of Appeals confessed at oral argument that they did not understand taxes, so they had to defer to the Comptroller to tell them what the law passed by the Legislature means. The people of Maryland are enthralled, deprived of the rule of law by the incompetence of the Court they rely upon for preservation of their rapidly dwindling liberty.

Twenty years of work by the Republican Party in Maryland to increase representation in the Senate and House of Delegates was wiped out by Ellen's defeat, and the loss of representation could not have come at a worse time, because reapportionment following the 2000 census cost the party two seats in the United States Congress in 2002. That forced Bob Ehrlich to run for Governor, something he may not have done if his district had not been gerrymandered out of existence.

In 1998 I attended events sponsored by the Republican clubs in Baltimore County, hoping to move forward the careers of several young legislators who looked promising. At a Ken Holt event I met Michael Steele, who was running with Ellen for Comptroller. Michael was a lawyer from Prince Georges County. As I shook his hand, I said "Michael, I have heard nothing but good things about you."

Smiling broadly, he replied, "Oh! I guess you must have been talking to my mother."

Michael had a future in the Republican Party, and I was pleased four years later when Bob Ehrlich chose him as his running mate. The triple-dipping Parris Glendenning was Governor for eight years, and for the first time since being admitted to the bar, Maryland had a Governor I did not know personally. But Don Schaefer was elected Comptroller in 1998, so there was at least someone I could talk to on the Board of Public Works.

In January, 2002 Elizabeth Brownell and Sister Pat Hangis and I met with Don, still trying to end the institutionalized child abuse at the Hickey School. We urged him to pull the contract of the company running the School. Youth Services International had been acquired by a Florida company which brought in employees who were rude to Sister Pat, and things were almost as bad as they were before privatization. We had not yet succeeded in having any input to the RFP, although we had volunteered to help write it at no charge.

We asked Don to seek a refund of money paid for services not provided, and to insure that the next RFP issued was not written by people in the Department of Juvenile Justice, who seemed determined that privatization fail. The Department however, was the special province of the lieutenant-Governor, Kathleen Kennedy-Townsend, who was running against Bob for Governor. Don told us that he could not do anything until after the election because the head of the department responsible for Hickey absolutely adored Kathleen, and he would view anything done at this time as politically motivated to hurt her chances of winning in November.

So another year of institutional child abuse was the price to be paid for political expediency. To my surprise, Don, by body language, voice inflection and a twinkle in his eye telegraphed his support for Bob Ehrlich. I did not tell Bob as I was not sure until after the inauguration in January that Don would go public with his views. Like a lot of people in our generation, character was more important than party to him, and that was why the United Christian Citizens launched Don's political career in the 1950's.

Although I often stopped by Bob's headquarters on LaSalle Road in Towson to read position papers and drop off campaign contributions, the only time Bob and I had a chance to talk during the campaign was at Chip Lewis's house in Monkton.

"So I guess you really are in this thing," I said. Bob nodded affirmatively and asked,

"What do you think of Tommy DiBiagio as U.S. Attorney?"

"Pleased, of course. If you had anything to do with it, I'll hug you right here in front of everybody."

Bob and Tommy had roomed together as our guests at the National Debutante Cotillion at the Washington Hilton in November, 1985, a swanky, three day fund-raiser for Children's Hospital in DC. Otherwise, Bob and Tommy were not acquainted.

The spring convention of the Republican Party was held at the Towson Sheraton, and Bob addressed the delegates at the Saturday morning session. I was sitting beside Kendel and Drew, who was absorbed in the political process. I wondered if Bob, at the age of five, was like-minded, for he was the most focused young man I had ever met, his every action, word and thought directed toward his long-range goal.

Bob was enthusiastic, long before Ronald Reagan ended the cold war, about Solzhenitzen and his "Gulag Archipelago". He gave me his books to read, and I found them devastating to the Soviet system. He had come a long way since 1986, and he was an accomplished and confident young man. He told the convention he would win and he did. As the enthusiastic applause of the delegates subsided, Bob hugged his wife and shook my hand. I told him how proud I was of him, and asked, "Bob, what is it worth to you for me *not* to tell Kendel about the first Republican convention you attended?"

"Oh, no, Ed, you wouldn't do that, would you?"

"Not everything, of course, but there were some things I think she would appreciate knowing."

He smiled again, and said "Yes, she might."

A few months later I was sitting on the sofa in his campaign headquarters reading his juvenile justice proposals when Mickey Steinberg, who opposed Parris Glendenning in 1994 for the Democrat nomination, walked out with two other men, carrying mailings and campaign material. I looked up, caught Mickey's eye, and he turned back, grinned and extended his hand. I stood up to take it, and said, "Glad to have you aboard."

He didn't say a word but the grin on his face spoke volumes. It is a good thing that Maryland Democrats hold grudges, for without them, Republicans would never win.

The next time I saw Bob was election night at the Hyatt Hotel in Baltimore. He stepped down from a chair he was standing on while being interviewed by a WJZ newsperson on election night to greet me and Mac McLure and accept my congratulations on his election as the first Republican Governor of Maryland since Spiro Agnew in 1966.

Other than recommending lawyers for appointment to judicial vacancies, I adopted the same approach I had taken with Harry and Don —I would not abuse our friendship by seeking anything from them for anybody. Bob only took my advice on judicial appointments twice, and when Bob and I were sitting back to back at a meeting of the Federalist Society in Baltimore in late 2009, the lawyers at my table were openly critical of the Democrats he appointed to the bench.

Friends on his staff told me Bob left judicial appointments to his wife and Jervis Finney. Jervy was part of the Shriver firm, and he and I had adjoining boxes at the fall steeplechase races at Shawan Downs. When I asked Jervy about it, he denied it, and so did Bob, who insisted the appointments were all his doing. It would have helped if we had been able to blame them on someone else.

We kept up a personal correspondence, avoiding any policy talk, primarily because I disapproved of almost every thing he did. He appointed others whose careers I had helped to positions of responsibility and I often saw them on the nightly news. Chris McCabe was at Human Resources, Al Redmer was Bob's Insurance Commissioner, Jim Ports at DMV, Dick Flanigan at Transportation, Steve Kreseski as Bob's Chief of Staff and Jervy Finney as Legal Counsel. When I saw them misrepresented and misquoted on newscasts I cringed.

The most flagrant case was that of Tommy DiBiagio. When he was an assistant United States Attorney, working under Lynn Battaglia, we frequently had lunch at Paulo's in Harbor Place. When he became U.S. Attorney, we moved to the Oregon Grille. I thanked him for taking the job, hoping he would uphold the high traditions of that office set by Leon Pierson, Joe Tydings and Steve Sachs. And yes, even George Beall, whose lot it was to prosecute Vice-President Agnew.

Because there is no prosecutorial function for the Attorney General of Maryland, and rarely an effective State Prosecutor, political corruption goes unpunished unless the U.S. Attorney acts. As far back as my memory goes the office had an exemplary reputation. Joe Tydings used it as a springboard to the U.S. Senate and Steve Sachs to Attorney General of Maryland and ultimately as a candidate for Governor.

Tommy had no political aspirations. I told him that we were wasting the office, because the Republican Party in Maryland had no bench, and we needed candidates with visibility and name recognition. He was adamant that he would serve one term only and return to private practice the day after the 2004 election. He feared for his wife and children, and I worried he only took the job because I wanted him to have it.

Within weeks he convinced me the Federal Bureau of Investigation was staffed by bureaucratic incompetents. For eight years, promotions in the Bureau were determined on the basis of political loyalty and political correctness. The agency had no imagination and no work ethic. Political corruption in Maryland, rooted in single party dominance flourishing with the blessing of a complicit press, was immune from attack unless whistle blowers came forward.

The U.S. Attorney's office became less effective because during Steve Sachs's tenure the lawyers working there became civil service employees, with all of the mind-numbing inertia such status engenders. They can not readily be discharged for incompetence or inaction. They have an "us-versus-the-boss" mentality, no loyalty, and if the boss tries to crack the whip to make them earn their pay, it is the boss who is pilloried by the press. This is what I heard about it from federal judges.

The only "headline" prosecutions Tommy was able to complete resulted from leads developed, not by the FBI or the lawyers on his payroll, but, believe it or not, by *Sun* reporters. And yet it was the *Sun* and its sister television station that falsely accused Tommy of seeking to further his political ambition when he urged his staff to complete its work before he resigned following the November election, the date he had selected to return to private practice regardless of the outcome of the Presidential election in 2004.

Tommy and I met at the Oregon Grille in early January 2005. I was delighted to see him revert to the happy, fun-loving lawyer I had come to know in the 1980's, one I thought I had lost forever. The grin on his face spoke volumes. It was the first time since he went to work for Dick Bennett in 1990 that I had seen him truly happy. He acted as if the weight of the world had been lifted from his shoulders. His loyalty to me exacted too high a price, and I apologized to him for the hell I had put him through.

As we left the restaurant, someone grasped my arm. My friend, client and neighbor Elizabeth Shea Miller, was there with three of her friends.

"Ed, aren't you going to introduce us to your famous friend?"

"Of course, Betty. Tommy, this is Elizabeth Miller. If you ever run short of money, take her to Pimlico. She can pick winning horses better than anybody I know."

Betty introduced each of her friends, all of whom grasped Tommy's hand and offered words of encouragement. Betty had been a member of the Maryland Racing Commission and had trained race horses at Merryland Farm. I succeeded her as President of the Long Green Valley Association in 1976. Tom thanked them for their kind words.

One case Tommy had hoped to finish languished in the office more than five years after he left. One of the lawyers the Justice Department insisted he keep on his staff was actually running his wife's restaurant from the Federal Court House, only showed up in the morning and was never seen in the office after lunch. Civil Service is our undoing.

In 2005, Estelle and I accepted a dinner invitation to the Governor's Mansion in Annapolis. We were greeted by Drew, who was playing on the lawn. As we went inside, someone directed us toward the sun room where two dozen people were gathered around a portable bar. When no one we knew materialized, we wandered back through the otherwise empty house. Kendel nodded as she passed through a room where we were examining some oil paintings Pat Hughes acquired when Harry was Governor.

We found our place at one of four round tops set up in an otherwise empty room. I began to wonder if Parris had stolen the furnishings Pat spent years collecting. We did not see Bob until after dinner, when Kendel urged me to push my way through a crowd surrounding him and say hello. I declined, having a life-long aversion to anything that smacks of a queue.

In January 2010, I invited Bob to lunch at the Center Club, hoping to persuade him not to run for Governor again, but to run for the Senate instead. Barbara Mukulski had been there forever, and I hoped she might not run if she had a well-known opponent. I assured him Martin O'Malley was bright, intelligent, quick and aggressive, but in my judgment obnoxious in the extreme. Debating him would be deadly. He exudes a charm to those who don't know him well that is appealing. I saw it when he blocked me on Federal Hill in 1990.

"Besides, Bob, this flood of resentment is aimed at Washington, not Annapolis. It will help you in a Senate race; it won't mean a thing in the Governor's race."

I followed our meeting up with a three page letter summarizing the things he had said and done that would undermine his credibility. He quickly responded. I had told him that his Democrat "friends" in the Legislature had set him up.

"How did they do that?"

"Democrats raise taxes people don't know they are paying. They raise income taxes, and when Joe Voter gets his pay check, he doesn't blame the Governor; he blames his boss for not paying him enough. They raise sales taxes, and when voters buy something that costs more because the tax went up twenty-percent, they don't blame the Governor, they blame the merchant for gouging them.

But here's what they did to you. They raised the fee for automobile tags fifty-percent. Annually when I write that check for $180 instead of $120, I blame you. Every March, when I send in my franchise tax, I blame you because the fee increased from $100 to $300 on your watch. And yes, the Board of Public Works sets the state's portion of the real property tax, because that is the only way the state can balance its budget. They happily let you raise that as well, knowing they could cut you off at the knees when you ran for re-election."

Bob insisted "fees are not taxes," and Martin used footage of Bob saying it ad nauseam in his commercials, mouthed by people who were trying hard to restrain their laughter. It undermined Bob's credibility and raised doubts about his intelligence. He lost the 2010 election by a much wider margin than he lost in 2006. What I feared would happen in January happened in November.

Bob Murphy in 1966 said "the people of Maryland get the government they deserve." But they have no choice, for they are kept in ignorance by the print and electronic media. I know a free press is necessary to shine light in dark places. There is no tradition of doing that in Maryland, however, and the knee jerk reaction of the reporters is to assume the worse. Competent people avoid politics like the plague, and it is our undoing.

The media never treated me badly. Even when they endorsed my opponent, they said nice things about me. When Tommy and I left Betty Miller and her friends at the Oregon Grille in 2005, he told me how much better the world looks when your every move is no longer suspect. I knew exactly how he felt, because I had once been there myself and vowed never to go back. The "gotcha" attitude motivates the media and guarantees poor government, for sensible people will have none of it.

"If the facts you allege are proved at trial, I have to let them stay in business so they can afford to pay the judgment you will get."

Judge Cypert Whitfield,
June, 1993

"Judge Waldron made a finding of fact that these parties decided to shoot the race horse. He made the finding based upon his conviction that the parties believed the company was not earning profits and that it was better to close it down and cut the losses as opposed to continuing to operate."

Judge Cypert Whitfield,
June,2000

The Loss of the Law

Never having been and never wanting to be a judge myself, I urged judicial appointments on Governors Tawes, Hughes, Schaefer and Ehrlich, and more often than not, they responded favorably. And just as often, those I recommended demonstrated their worthiness to sit in judgment.

I found the bench in some Maryland counties woefully inadequate, but it was not until after I retired and retained lawyers when I needed them that I realized why and when things began to go so terribly wrong.

A case in the Circuit Court of Harford County involving my client Elbert Bruce Greer was the beginning. I met Bruce in the late 1970's when he and his general manager, James Wilson, encountered a problem small business men face when starting out: the employees have to be paid weekly, the customers take a month or two to pay for the work the employees do, and governments insist the income taxes, FICA and Medicare premiums withheld from employees wages and the employer's matching contributions must be deposited weekly. Federal and state governments not only demand payment in advance but assess penalties and charge interest if the payments are late. Jim and Bruce, like most start-ups, quickly fell behind in their tax deposits.

Financing government on the backs of small business began during World War II to pay for the war. Work and labor done is not billed until it is finished, and contractors delay paying their bills as long as possible. It's called managing cash flow. Employers must also pay federal and state unemployment taxes ranging from two to six percent of payroll, the amount of the latter being set by each state depending upon the demands made upon it by the unemployed.

I write this in the midst of an unprecedented economic malaise perpetuation of past policies have exacerbated. You have to have money, and lots of it, to make money. And like the Egyptians requiring more bricks from the Israelites with less straw, the state and federal governments, by adhering to World War II emergency funding policies, foster prolonged jobless recoveries.

Extending unemployment benefits sounds like a kind thing to do, but it puts a heavier burden on employers when payroll taxes go up to pay for it, discouraging calling people back to work. If you subsidize unemployment, you get more of it. If you tax employment, you get less of it. Government does not understand this because governments are run by politicians, and good politics is bad economics.

As Jim Wilson testified fifteen years later, "we kept pushing and pushing and we finally pushed through and began to make a lot of money." After the stagflation of the Carter years was banished by the Reagan revolution, Greer's business not only prospered, but grew so fast he and Jim employed their sons in various aspects of the business. This was Bruce Greer's undoing, for his sons and Jim's did not like each other.

Jim's son, Scott, began working for Greer before he went to college, and his pay and his schedule were adjusted so he could earn a degree at Towson University. They saw Scott as a polished young man who could run the business for them when they were ready to retire. They brought him a box at Camden Yards and a country club membership and put him in charge of sales. It became difficult to staff all of the jobs he sold from Bel Air, which is where their principal office was. The commute for workers from their homes to Bel Air and then from there to the job sites wasted time and gasoline.

Jim's son-in-law, William Russo was hired as a financial officer. Purchasing agents at Ryland and other large area builders were of the same age as Scott and Bill. At Oriole games, on the golf course, and at social gatherings—all paid for by Bruce—the ties that bound the sellers and the builders to Greer's drywall empire were forged. Jim Wilson was promoted to general manager and he was paid the same salary as Bruce. In fairness, Jim was a good business man and Bruce was not. But together, they were a good team. But no good deed goes unpunished, for as Judge Kern warned me, people are never as honest as you think they are. The problem was too much trust on Bruce's part and too little knowledge of tax accounting on Jim's part.

Jim's salary and bonuses were an expense of the entity that paid them, Bruce's were not. Because the entities were taxed as subchapter S corporations, withdrawals in excess of base salary to Bruce were treated as dividends and were not deductible as expenses. To equalize the payments to both men, the accountant charged a management fee to the four corporations and paid Jim through a management payroll company. The management fee reduced corporate profits to a tax loss on its income tax return.

In 1989, Jim and Bruce set up a branch office in Sykesville, Maryland to service builders west of Interstate 83 as well as those in Howard and Montgomery

Counties. They would each own half of the stock. To achieve economies of scale and eliminate duplicate effort, the jointly owned company would not bid jobs east of Interstate 83, and G&L Drywall, wholly owned by Bruce, would not bid jobs west of Interstate 83.

As G&L's general manager, Jim had authority to borrow money, to hire and fire employees and to decide which bills to pay and when. His lawyer set up the new company, which he named Interior Masters, Inc. He sent his son to Sykesville to handle sales and his son-in-law to be chief financial officer. Jim transferred computers, furniture, scaffolding, inventory, vehicles, employees and customers from Bruce's wholly owned G&L to the new company in exchange for the stock issued equally to Jim and Bruce. Both men were directors of the new entity but neither worked there.

The customers of the new company knew Jim's son and son-in-law but they did not know Jim or Bruce. In addition to his salary, Jim got fifty percent of the profits from Interior Masters and ten percent of the profits from G&L. Ignoring the imaginary boundary of Interstate 83, Scott and Russo went after all of G&L's business. When the sales manager in Bel Air realized Scott was undercutting his bids on jobs east of Interstate 83, he complained to Bruce, who, in turn, complained to Jim.

Sales made from Bel Air declined as those in Sykesville increased. In 1992, Bruce met with me, John Owen, who handled their employee benefits, and Sam Shriver, a business consultant I relied upon, at a Bel Air restaurant and asked us what he should do. We recommended he either sell his stock in IMI to Jim and his sons or close the company down immediately.

Bruce attended the Interior Master's Christmas party in Sykesville in December, 1992. He testified the party "died" when he entered, and he sensed that he was as unwelcome as Marley's ghost in Scrooge's bedroom.

In January Jim asked Bruce's accountant to runoff a preliminary financial statement for Interior Master's as of December 31, 1992. Jim wanted the financial statement recast without booking the management fee, because he knew the company was making money and the subchapter S tax return, after deducting the fee, showed a loss.

As every tax lawyer knows —but few other lawyers or judges do—profits of sub-chapter S corporations are taxed on the returns of the stockholders as dividends. The purpose of the management fee was to create a loss for tax purposes of the individual tax entities by transferring the income to the company that paid salaries to Jim and Bruce.

There was not a judge or a court auditor in the Circuit Court of Harford County who understood this. They all insisted the business was unprofitable, unaware tax equity mandated that the company's tax return had to show a loss if Jim was to avoid being taxed on Bruce's share of Interior Master's income.

When Bruce asked Jim why he wanted the financial statement recast, he said it was because he knew the company was making money and the statement had to be wrong. Jim repeated that, under oath, at trial. Bruce, who was too far from the daily operations to know, told Jim to "go up there and find out why it's losing money" and either "fix it or close it down."

Jim went to Sykesville and told his son he was fired and invited him and Russo to his house for breakfast the next morning, having decided it was time for him and Bruce to part ways. And since he didn't want to be out on the street without a job, he —just as corporate managers of America's publicly traded corporations also do —stole IMI assets, erecting a fence topped with barbed-wire around its offices, warehouse and garage housing its fleet of vehicles and posting an armed guard to keep Bruce away. To the Harford County bench, that was a prudent and sensible thing for Jim to do, and what any good businessman would do. Maybe the Black Panthers were right in 1971, and anyone who makes a profit is a thief.

Scott called the customers and said they were closing Interior Masters as of Friday and opening up on Monday as J.W. & Sons. He asked if the jobs could continue without interruption next week, and to a man they all said they could. He later testified he got "one hundred percent of them." A week later Jim told Bruce, 'You aren't going to like this, but I have opened up as JW.' He cleaned out his desk and went to Sykesville, never to return. Bruce got in his car, drove to Sykesville, and found the Interior Masters offices, vehicles, equipment and supplies surrounded by a chain link fence with an armed guard at the gate. He could see his business and his vehicles behind the fence, but he was not allowed inside.

For four months I tried to persuade Jim he should buy rather than steal Bruce's half-interest in IMI, but Jim had no interest in paying for something he already had. Being unaware at the time that most lawyers and judges in Maryland no longer know the difference between law and equity, I filed an equity action in the Circuit Court of Harford County against Jim, his sons, JW and Interior Masters, seeking appointment of a receiver and an accounting from all five defendants for the property stolen from Bruce.

We asked the court to enjoin use of assets belonging to Interior Masters by JW. Only the use of the G&L vehicles was enjoined, because, as Judge Whitfield put it, "if the facts you allege are proved at trial, I have to let them stay in business so they can afford to pay the judgment you will get."

Defendant's motions for summary judgment were denied by Judge Maurice Baldwin. At a pre-trial conference, Judge William O. Carr suggested that the case be bifurcated, meaning we would have a trial on the issue of liability, after which the issue of damages would be referred to the Court Auditor for a preliminary finding, from which either party could take exceptions. The trial judge could then make an informed judgment as to the fair market value of the stock, which was the legal standard for damages in cases like this.

The case came before Judge Waldron in November, 1995. There was no dispute of fact at the trial. The defendants freely admitted, almost boastfully, how skillfully they had managed things. They put on about twenty minutes of defense designed solely to explain why they collected IMI's accounts receivables and deposited them in a JW account, contending they wanted to make sure IMI's suppliers were paid. The suppliers, understandably, saw no difference between IMI and JW.

The trial ended on the morning of the third day, and Judge Waldron said he would render an opinion "after lunch." When we returned to his court room that afternoon, he said he had to hold the matter "sub curia."

A year later, Bruce was desperately trying to stave off putting G&L into bankruptcy. There was no word from the court. Another year passed, and I finally wrote Judge Waldron a letter urging him to give us a decision one way or the other.

The Maryland Constitution requires judges of the Circuit Courts to render decisions within sixty days of the trial, and the Court of Appeal to file written opinions within ninety days of oral argument. But the Court of Appeals long ago decided the Maryland Constitution is advisory, not mandatory, and the Maryland judiciary is exempt from its provisions.

Judge Waldron advised he had written a forty-seven page opinion, and he would release it as soon as he found time to edit it. Yet another year passed and my client's situation was beyond desperate, so I complained to the Judicial Disabilities Commission, which did absolutely nothing. Three months later, Judge Waldron issued his opinion and signed a three-page decree.

He found that Jim Wilson and Bill Russo had violated fiduciary duties they owed to Interior Masters, converted the assets of the company which employed them and ordered them to account to Interior Masters for the amounts they owed. He also recused himself, acknowledging in so doing he could no longer be trusted to render a fair and unbiased opinion, undoubtedly because I had dared complain of his three year and three month dereliction of duty.

Judge Waldron did not understand that IMI no longer existed, having been swallowed whole by JW. Judgment was to be entered against the defendants—but in who's favor he did not know or say—for the amounts due after which the court auditor was to determine the fair value of IMI's stock on January 15, 1993. If Wilson did not agree with the value determined by the court auditor, the 'corporation' was to be liquidated and the assets divided equally between Jim and Bruce. Clearly, I had won the case, but I had three problems with the vagueness of the decree.

There was no Interior Masters. In whose favor was the judgment against the defendants to be entered? There was no dispute as to the minor adjustments Judge Waldron ordered made to the 'corporation's' balance sheet before its fair value was determined, because the parties stipulated the numbers. Incredulously the clueless Court Auditor decided the net value of the minor adjustments to the balance sheet was the fair value of the stock. So inane was this result that both parties filed exceptions.

The exceptions were heard by Judge Cypert Whitfield, before whom an expert witness testified that the Auditor had failed to do what the Court ordered him to do. He had not determined the fair value of the stock but simply netted some insignificant adjustments to a six-year old balance sheet to which both parties stipulated. The difference was $33,500 and the auditor said that number, less his fee, was the fair value. The expert also testified, without any rebuttal, that the actual fair value of IMI's stock, using standard business appraisal methodology, was $5,200,000.

A rapidly failing Judge Whitfield, the same judge who allowed IMI to use all of the stolen assets except the vehicles in 1993—on June 28, 1999, his last day on the bench—denied the exceptions and sustained the Auditor's determination. Judge Carr, who inherited Judge Whitfield's unfinished work, entered judgment in favor of Jim Wilson, who lost the case, against Bruce Greer, who won the case, for $16,500 with interest from January 15, 1993. The defendants who were found to have committed fraud were allowed to keep what they stole, and Greer, from whom they stole it, was ordered to pay Jim half of its value.

Nothing is more settled in equity than the rule prohibiting a wrong doer from profiting from his wrongdoing. It has been etched in stone for nine hundred years. Judge Carr's order is the equivalent of requiring a murdered man's estate to pay the murderer the value of the victim's projected lifetime earnings. A bar and bench dominated by trial lawyers schooled to prosecute and defend crimes and litigate torts might understand that is wrong. It is highly unlikely, however, that even the best lawyers and judges we now have know what equity is. It's no longer taught in most law schools, but in 1958 it was taught in the first year at the University of Maryland law school by a Federal judge.

Before I realized the law schools no longer taught law, I thought the young lawyers I hired were intellectually challenged. I now know it was because the law schools stopped teaching law in 1960 when the critical legal studies faculties captured Harvard and Stanford law schools and the rest of American law schools, except fewer than twenty holdouts, quickly followed suit. Law schools now teach how the law works, but they don't teach what the law is.

The Greer case was an equity case, and although equity has existed since Becket established it during the reign of Henry II, the only lawyers and judges who even come close to it today are those who specialize in divorce. Decrees—like orders entered in equity cases everywhere —always remain subject to modification. Once the jurisdiction of a court of equity attaches it continues until complete equity is done. Equity has yet to be done in the case of Bruce Greer and Jim Wilson, the Circuit Court of Harford County still has jurisdiction and it still has the power to correct the injustice it wrought. But the judges don't know it because they are post 1960 law school graduates. Their knowledge of the law is limited to what their computers spit out.

Recall my earlier story about the brief I was asked to write setting forth the views of the State on Maryland at the request of Chief Justice Warren when a decree *pro confesso* was erroneously entered against a law student imprisoned for defending the honor of his wife. Divorce like the Greer case is an equity proceeding.

We filed a motion to have the order of July 9, 1999 set-aside on the basis of fraud, mistake or irregularity. Judge Carr denied the motion because Wilson had elected not to pay the value of the stock to Greer but to have the 'corporation' liquidated and assets divided between them. Judge Waldron did not specify what he meant by the word "corporation" and Judge Carr did not bother to think it through. As far as he could see the assets were the funds owed by the defendants to Interior Masters, based on the accounting adjustments Judge Waldron ordered in his decree. He ignored altogether the successful business IMI/JW was. He ordered Bruce, the victim, to pay Wilson half of the amount Wilson and Russo owed the receiver the Court failed to appoint. Had a receiver been appointed, he could have recovered the money from the defendants and divided it equally between Bruce and Jim. Instead, Judge Carr ordered Bruce, the victor, to pay Jim, the loser.

On appeal, Judge Waldron's legal conclusions with respect to Scott Wilson and his failure to impose a constructive trust on the assets of the defendants; the correctness of the Auditors determination of the fair market value of Interior Masters' stock; and Judge Carr's failure to set aside the order of July 9, 1999 were assigned as error. The judge who wrote the opinion had been Parris Glendening's campaign manager. He did not decide or even discuss any of the issues raised on appeal. His unpublished, per curiam, two-page opinion adopted Judge Waldron's opinion and decree verbatim.

A petition for writ of certiorari to the Court of Special Appeals was denied. The petitions are read by second-year law students who earn credits for graduation by doing the job the judges are paid to do. Never having been taught any law, they have no idea what they are reading. But they do give the judge for whom they work a list of questions to ask at oral argument, making it appear that the Court has actually read the briefs.

Back in the Circuit court I immediately filed a motion to have a receiver appointed and the decree, adopted by the Court of Special Appeals, enforced. I caught an airplane to San Diego to attend a meeting of the National Lawyer's Association, of which I am a member. It was formed by the law schools which still teach law. I wanted to review this disgraceful episode with like minded lawyers, and my former associates, Blake McFeely and Doug Grinnell.

Doug was his ever buoyant self, progressing from marathons to iron man competitions. I congratulated Dee on having left him the same delightful person he was when I first met him by the fireplace at Peerces. Doug is a successful tort lawyer in California, he was educated at Pepperdine, one of the few law schools in America that still teach law. It was funded by Mellon/Scaife money, clients of Nick Shriver's firm where I learned lawyering only after I had been taught law. Blake also graduated from law school in 1960, when law schools still taught law.

Having confirmed my thoughts with the two best lawyers yet alive, I undertook, without success, to convince endless panels of three judge courts in Baltimore and Harford counties that the decree adopted verbatim by the appellate courts in Maryland had never been implemented, and they still had the power to correct the injustice. They were baffled, and to my amazement, so were the litigators in the best law firms in Baltimore I asked to pursue the case after my retirement. The blank looks on their faces betrayed their ignorance.

The point of this story is that you need to be aware that we are no longer ruled by law. Law as it existed when I was born is as dead as the recently deciphered language of the ancient Hittites who defended Troy from the Greeks. And my reference to the classics is intentional, to remind you that the Roman Empire fell, not to Barbarians climbing over the walls, but when its remote central government no longer had the means to enforce its complex regulations.

As a Ford Fellow at Vanderbilt in 1954 I had the good fortune to know Dr. Charles Calhoun Provine, President of Ward-Belmont College in Nashville, one of the first private schools to be destroyed, intentionally, by the disciples of John Dewey, spokesperson for progressive educators who saw the American public school system and our reverence for the common law of England as the principal obstacles to the adoption of socialism in America. Dewey was a professor of Education at Columbia, as was, incidentally, the political mentor of President Barack Obama, the terrorist William Ayers.

Dr. Provine advised me to research the creation of the Shipping Board by the United States Congress during Woodrow Wilson's first term in 1913. Because Wilson attended Davidson for a year and later as President drove to Baltimore to hear Dr. Harris Kirk's sermons at my church, I delved into the Congressional Record in the Joint University Library in Nashville.

There was an epic battle fought by heroes like Hector and Achilles on the floor of the United States Senate. The outcome was tragic. It was then and there America lost her way. The soul of our nation instead of the beautiful Helen was the focus of the battle. The Senate sergeant-at-arms arrested members and drug them back to the Chamber to vote just as Achilles drug Hector's body around Troy. The doors were locked in all-night sessions, with members sleeping on cots and talking until they dropped from exhaustion. Giants from the pages of American history thundered at one another on the Senate floor.

We adopted the income tax and direct election of senators. Worse, the government, which until then only undertook necessary projects no sane businessman would touch —like the Panama Canal and the Alaskan railroad —could now build, own and operate merchant ships in competition with private shippers. Why was there no American fleet? Charles Dana's "Two Years Before the Mast" gave rise to government control by regulation which drove ownership abroad, which, in turn, created a need for transport under the American flag in time of war.

Today the need to protect us from "terrorists" is the justification for knuckling under to Orwellian surveillance from satellites, x-ray machines in airports and on the streets, with Google monitoring every click of our keyboards under contract with the government.

The shift in 1913 was momentous. Before, government could only do what business refused to do; afterward, government could do whatever *it decided* business did not do well. Government's power to regulate is the power to destroy just as the power to tax is the power to destroy. Government's regulation of health insurance passed because no lawyer remembers the Supreme Court long ago decided insurance was not interstate commerce. Yet, insurance commissioners in all fifty states are there for all to see.

Professor-President Wilson had a stroke trying to impose an idealistic new world order practical men knew would lead, not to democracy but to totalitarianism. Roosevelt picked up where he left off in 1933, failed miserably with the economy and died of a stroke too late to see the United Nations come into existence in 1945. But by 1950, John Dewey's disciples had control of the public schools and certification authority over private schools and colleges, including the law schools , the latter under a committee of critical legal studies professors appointed by the American Bar Association, which operates like the NEA dictating employment terms which must be followed if law schools are to retain their certification.

The obstacles to imposing socialism have been removed. History is no longer taught in the public schools and law is no longer taught in most law schools. To Teaching Assistant Obama's credit, he has never hid his motivation or his objective. He can do so without fear because he knows it is too late to stop him.

As a lawyer, military officer, economist, political scientist, and historian, I can tell you where it is going. But you already know. Follow Athens and the wealth of its client states in the Delian league. Her democracy was so short-lived and the end so horrific, our founding fathers, predominately Freemasons, eschewed anything remotely approaching it. They opted for a republic, following Rome's example, and designed it to prevent escalation to Empire. Rome started out badly as an empire, improved under the Antonines, but fell victim to bureaucratic zeal and the need to feed and entertain 600,000 idle citizens in their midst. Roman legions depended upon aliens and client states for manpower, as does our military today. Look it up in Gibbon.

The election of emperors in Rome passed to the legions, just as public employees and those who control their unions select the executive and legislative branches of our state and national government. SEIU, NEA and AFL-CIO, backed by well-healed bosses of bygone unions control the outcome of urban elections, getting out the vote, putting up the signs, and working the polling places.

The experience of three millennia teaches that democracy degenerates into oligarchy and oligarchy leads to military dictatorship. Pericles was followed by Alexander and Cicero by Caesar. The crowds in the streets of Athens and London foreshadow scenes now being repeated in the streets of America. Lest we forget, as recently as the 1930's, General Douglas MacArthur's cavalry charged into the Potomac flats to drive out World War I veterans lobbying for a government bonus.

Where there is no justice, discontent flourishes, then builds and explodes into violence. It is not a question of if; it is a question of when. I might not see it, but my children will. My grandchildren will reap the whirl-wind, and I write to warn them and you.

"I need your help, and it will require some state money"

"Well, you are out of luck. We don't have any."

"Think of it this way. There isn't enough money in the world to buy Central Park in New York City. Yet, a hundred and fifty years ago, courageous city fathers, the Governor of New York and Frederick Law Olmstead bought that land, without which New York City would not be livable today... If we have to sell bonds to get the money, the Cromwell Valley should be part of the Gunpowder State Park. We need to buy it while it is still affordable. It already connects with the Loch Raven water shed and the huge acreage the Hickey School owns on Cub Hill Road. If we do this, it could well be your most lasting legacy."

Conversation with Governor Schaefer,
March, 1992

After Hours

The house in which I live in Maryland was here when Maryland was a colony, built on land granted to the Gittings family by Lord Baltimore. Much of my *pro bono* time as a lawyer was devoted to the preservation of farm land and open space in Baltimore County, beginning a few years after I moved to Long Green Valley in 1965.

Baltimore County had purchased a tract of land bordering Long Green Creek on Hyde's Road to erect a high school, oblivious to the fact that we and most of our neighbors send our children to private schools. It would have been an environmental disaster, for the run-off from the parking lots would have killed the native brown trout in the Long Green creek and increased the flooding at its junction with Rattlesnake Run at the intersection of Long Green Road and Long Green Pike, a usual occurrence with a heavy rain. Long Green Valley sits on a limestone slab atop the Long Green aquifer, an underground river flowing between the Gunpowders. Long Green Creek flows into the Big Gunpowder below the Loch Raven Dam straight into Chesapeake Bay.

The Long Green Valley Association was formed in 1972 by Elizabeth Shea (Betty)Miller, who then lived at her Merryland Farm in neighboring Haystack Valley, and the Deford family, who own land on both sides of Long Green Creek, where Boordy Vineyard is now located. Meetings were held in Betty's house overlooking the Merryland Farm race track.

My success opposing an expansion of a Baltimore Gas and Electric facility on Long Green Road brought me to Betty's attention, and she invited me to attend meetings of the Association. As pro bono counsel to the Association which opposed any further development in the area between the Gunpowders, Harford Road on the east and Manor Road on the west, we challenged spot-zoning changes between zoning cycles, encouraging political candidates who shared our views and opposing those who did not. Members appeared in large numbers to speak against zoning changes that infringed upon the fading rural beauty of Long Green Valley.

When I was a young lawyer with Nick Shriver's firm, I had secured 501(c)(3) status from the Internal Revenue Service for the Green Spring and Worthington Valley Planning Council, predicated upon the Council's performing a governmental function, i.e. planning for future growth undertaken by private citizens at their own expense. The Council had retained the McHarg Group in Philadelphia to prepare a development plan they donated to Baltimore County as a working document.

Fortunately, in 1955, Baltimore County had already adopted the most restrictive zoning in America to protect unique farmland similar to the limestone based Middleburg area of Virginia, middle Tennessee and Kentucky. Although Councilman Eugene Gallagher during his service in the County Council was helpful, we quickly recognized that zoning is temporary, subject to political interference by the council or bureaucratic favoritism in the county government. Constant monitoring of every government action is essential, or all can be lost over night.

Farming still clung on tenaciously in the Valley, with two horse farms with race tracks, five herds of cattle, a herd of sheep as well as crop-farming, an orchard and the vineyard. Our first big step was taken when the County at our urging created an agricultural preservation district in the valley floor. We also persuaded the County to transfer the Hyde's Road school site to the Parks Department. That backfired when Jim Smith administration paved a huge parking lot and the run-off from the pavement killed the trout.

In 1982 I succeeded Betty Miler as President of the Association, and we moved our monthly meetings to Boordy Vineyard. Julia Randall, then poet laureate of Maryland, lived in one of the old mill houses beside Long Green Creek on Hartley Mill Road, a Currier and Ives neighborhood with bridges so narrow but one car can cross at a time over the rapidly cascading stream splashing over the rocks making its way down to the Big Gunpowder.

Julia and Beth Hartline conceived the idea of having the valley recognized as a national historic district. Mac MacLure, a young lawyer in my firm, researched the law. We formed Historic Long Green Valley, Inc and petitioned the government to give it 501(c)(3) status. Money was raised by contributions from members and volunteers contributed their services. We hired James Wollon to help us and at his direction, Kathy Gabriel and Denise Shapiro, working with Julia and Beth took pictures of every house more than fifty years old within the boundary. They converted the pictures into slides, inventoried them and sent them with our application to the Maryland Historic Trust.

We compiled and published a history of the Valley and achieved our purpose. No federal funds could be spent to change any infrastructure in the Valley, be it roads, bridges, or schools. It was some protection, but not enough. Incursions by outsiders and dreams of wealth by insiders continue to threaten the valley with rezoning and development, and the Association continues to fight them one by one.

As the environment became more of a politically correct thing to do, there was recognition at various levels that conservation should be encouraged by grants and tax advantages, both to keep farm land from becoming too expensive for farmers to buy and to preserve the family farm from burdensome estate taxes that would be owed if farm land was appraised at its development value instead of its current use.

More and more family farms were being broken up by the need to raise cash to pay taxes when a family member died. Anti-development easements were encouraged, and after I was succeeded as President of the Association by Rob Deford, I became active as Vice-President of the Long Green Valley Conservancy, a project Catherine Ebert, the new owner of Prospect Hill, began on her own. Together we re-wrote the Conservancy's application for grants from the State's open space program to buy conservation easements from local land owners.

The Conservancy, as a 501(c)(3) organization, could also accept donations of easements for which the land owners got substantial income tax deductions and qualified for lower estate tax valuations on land permanently conserved for agricultural use or limiting future development to preserve open space.

The School Sisters of Notre Dame maintained a retirement home for members of their Order on Glen Arm Road on a 560 acre tract of land zoned RC-2 and RC-5 located beyond the hills behind my house. When the School Sisters later decided to sell the property to the Presbyterian Church, I was counsel to the Committee of the Presbyterian Church in Baltimore. The Long Green Valley Association appealed to Gene Gallagher, our councilman, to oppose any effort to rezone the property. Because of a conflict of interest, I turned that problem over to Betty Miller and Julia Randall.

The Church wanted to expand the existing building site to accommodate the Glen Meadows retirement community, and a compromise was reached in which the number of buildings authorized by the zoning of the entire tract could be clustered around the existing buildings, permitting the Church to proceed with the purchase, while preserving five hundred acres as open space for agricultural use in perpetuity. The County Council approved the bill, and, it was thought until recently that the property was permanently preserved. The Church now apparently has a different idea.

That was, however, the first of four major steps we took to protect the Valley. We had learned that we had to fight our battles as far from the Valley as possible, in order to put potential developers on notice we were serious about preventing any expansion beyond the urban-rural demarcation line on the Planning Board's maps.

During Governor Schaefer's second term, John Howard represented a developer interested in building a large planned community in the Cromwell Valley. He invited me to his office to see his client's plans. His associate, Rob Hoffman, was shepherding the project through the planning and zoning phases in Baltimore County, and from past conflicts, John knew he would have a problem with the Association and he wanted to open discussions at an early stage.

Two of the major farms in Cromwell Valley were to be purchased, and one was already under contract. Judge Jenifer's widow still lived in the valley in the large house they once shared. She came to an Association meeting to seek our help. A committee was set up to oppose the zoning requests, but with one farm already under contract I decided a more urgent approach was needed.

Estelle and I were attending a black-tie reception at the Center Club for The Family Tree, a child abuse prevention organization founded by the Towson Exchange Club, and when I saw Governor Schaefer there, I told him I needed to talk to him. A few days later I drove to Annapolis, climbing once more the familiar marble stair case in the State House to the Governor's office. Arriving a few minutes early, I sat in the ante-room under massive oil paintings of men I knew well. The state policeman at the Governor's door was nodding off again, and there was an eerie silence as Governor Tawes, Governor Agnew, Governor Mandel and Governor Hughes looked down at me, far better looking in oil than in real life. A recognition of mortality swept over me, as if I were sitting in a mausoleum.

When Don bid his visitor good-bye he called me in. I began by telling him I needed his help but it would require some state money.

"Well, you are out of luck. We don't have any."

"Think of it this way. There isn't enough money in the world to buy Central Park in New York City. Yet, a hundred and fifty years ago, courageous city fathers, the Governor of New York and Frederick Law Olmstead bought that land, without which New York City would not be livable today. Long before you get to the Loch Raven High School, while still heading southwest on Cromwell Valley Road, you can see the high rise buildings in Towson looming above the trees. If we have to sell bonds to get the money, the Cromwell Valley should be part of the Gunpowder State Park. We need to buy it while it is still affordable. It already connects with the Loch Raven water shed and the huge acreage the Hickey School owns on Cub Hill Road. If we do this, it could well be your most lasting legacy."

I clearly had his interest. He said he would see what he could do, and he picked up the telephone and called Torrey Brown, head of State Parks, to make an appointment for me to meet with him. He also called the Director of Juvenile Services and told her to arrange the transfer of hundreds of acres of the Hickey property to the Department of Natural Resources, linking Cromwell Valley with the Gunpowder State Park.

I volunteered to talk to Roger Hayden, who was then Baltimore County Executive, to see if we could get the County on board. Don told me not to bother, he could work that out and he would take care of that as well. Exactly how he did it I do not know, but Cromwell Valley is now a Baltimore County Park. The County's insatiable appetite for paving park land to provide parking continues, despite the State's frantic effort to save the Chesapeake Bay. Mineback Creek flows through the Cromwell Valley into the Gunpowder below the city's Loch Raven Dam.

Mrs. Jenifer told me when the owner of the farm under contract realized development could be avoided, she cancelled her contract, refusing to say how much it had cost her. She admitted it was a lot, but it was worth it.

As the twentieth Century waned, I saw an advertisement for a foreclosure sale on Hoffman Orchards where I often rode my Tennessee Walker, Co-Ed Strolling Pine, a/k/a Choco, through the blossoms in the spring. Lew Hoffman warned me not to let Choco eat the grass under the trees because the spray he used on the apple trees washed off when it rained and the concentration in the grass might be fatal. Choco seemed to know that, having never shown any interest in it, preferring the view from the hills. He liked to stare down into the valley watching the cars move along Hyde's Road several miles distant.

Once an airplane flew past us, and the pilot shouted a friendly greeting as he sailed down below us to land at Phil Albrecht's landing strip on the valley floor. Choco acted as if looking down at an airplane was an every day occurrence, but before he died in my arms one cold January morning, he had traveled with Boumi Temple all over the east coast, climbing the steps at the Philadelphia Art Museum like "Rocky," crossing the bridges into Pittsburgh, cantering down the Washington Mall under the cherry blossoms or crashing through the waves in the Atlantic ocean, wherever the Shrine annual convention was held and the Boumi Temple Mounted Patrol competed.

Fearing an auction of the orchard would put it in the hands of a developer, I formed a limited partnership to buy the orchard and lease it back to Lou, rescuing him from money-lenders who were exacting heavy interest charges Lew could ill afford to pay. Cathy Ebert put the Conservancy behind the effort by participating as an investor. Initially I planned to borrow most of the money from the Mercantile Bank, for the head of their mortgage lending department was on the Association's board.

Cathy Ebert suggested I apply for a loan from the Maryland Enviromental Trust, which, in turn, suggested we apply for a larger, interest free loan from the Board of Public Works. After I completed the grant applications with the help of one of my law clerks, I was hospitalized in 2000 with esophageal cancer and Cathy attended the meeting in Annapolis, persuading the Trust and the State to participate.

I asked Jim O'Connor, one of Doug Grinnell's friends, to handle the settlement for me, and we ran the checks from the Trust, the State and our limited partnership through his trust account to pay off the loans Lew had against his property. Lew, whose health was also failing, had agreed to pay rent on the property equivalent to the interest we would owe the Mercantile and he signed a lease agreement with the limited partnership to that effect at settlement.

As soon as our partnership took title to the land, the development rights were conveyed to the Maryland Environmental Trust. Lew had an option in his lease to buy the farm back, and I resigned as a trustee and vice-president of the Conservancy when the partnership instituted litigation to collect the rent, terminated the lease and sold the farm, subject to an easement that restricted development. Of all the efforts I made to preserve the Valley, this is the one I regret, although it was successful and wildly profitable to the members of the partnership.

Betty Miller invited me to lunch one day to talk about the sad state of Merryland Farm. She had owned the farm for many years and later ran it for the man who bought it from Danny Shea's estate. He later donated the farm to Baltimore County and took a tax write-off based upon the fair market value of the farm. The County leased the farm to a tenant who had trouble paying the rent and maintaining the farm's many buildings and fences, including those surrounding the race track, which were in such poor condition Betty thought it dangerous to run horses on the track.

As far back as the early meetings of the Association, farmland in Baltimore County was too expensive to buy and devote to farming. Betty believed Baltimore County would have to sell Merryland for at least $5,000,000. When I told her that was not the case, she poured me another glass of sherry and said, "Tell me why I'm wrong."

"To begin with, it has been a while since the farm was given to the County, and limitations have probably run on any challenge to the deduction on the donor's tax returns. More importantly, it was the donor's intent, when he gave the farm to the county, that it be preserved and maintained as it was when it belonged to you and Danny."

"The thing that troubles me is that Jim Smith might sell the farm to a developer, and that would be the end of Haystack Valley. How can we prevent that?"

"Go back to the county and suggest they record conservation easements on the farm to the Gunpowder Conservancy or the Maryland Environmental Trust. Based upon my experience with Hoffman Orchards, that would reduce the value to something in the neighborhood of $4,000 an acre, which would permit someone to buy the farm from the county for use as a horse farm. If you can persuade the County to donate the proceeds from the sale to the Conservancy for use in purchasing additional easements from farmers in the Valley, it would be a "win-win" for everybody."

Betty picked up her pen and asked me to go over it again, and she made notes of the steps that needed to be taken. She asked me what she could do if they refused. I suggested she not give them a choice. She should insist that, as the person who arranged the gift to the County in the first place, she had the moral right and responsibility to see to it that the donor's wishes were carried out.

The County took part of her advice, but instead of devoting the proceeds of the sale to preserve open space they kept the money. The new owners repaired the farm and young horses are being schooled there by a prominent Harford County horseman. When Betty died in 2007, there was an old-fashioned wake at Merryland that began in early afternoon and continued through the evening. The band played jazz music and romantic pieces from the thirties and forties.

Rich Evans's mother was an Edelen, and her family was from the Haystack, which begins in Glen Arm and runs northeast almost to Harford County. Much of the floor of the valley is still in large farms, and those not farmed by the Dietz family are part of the Foard family's Valley View Farms. Rich's father was an intelligence officer during World War II, dead under mysterious circumstances on the day the war ended.

Rich's older brother had served in the Dandy Fifth with me, and Rich had lived with Betty in her house at Merryland when he was a young man. The last time I took her to the races at Shawan Downs he found a golf cart he used so Betty could visit Wally Lanahan, who had helped me as a young lawyer when he handled a private placement of securities for a corporate client. She told me when she married Danny Shea she knew so little about horses the only way she could tell which horses were theirs was she recognized the groom leading them onto the track. Every horse we bet on that day won his or her race.

Saying good-bye to Betty in the barns and out-buildings that had been so much a part of her life was a satisfying experience. It was stewardship well done. The buildings were in excellent shape, the race track was fenced and painted, looking as it did when I first visited it in the early seventies. Rich spent the day with Estelle and me, recalling hilarious things Betty did and said. She loved life, and life is less lovely without her.

Betty was a great source of information about everybody, but guarded it carefully. As the personal representative of a friend's estate, she retained me to defend her in a dispute in the Harford County courts, and we were both amused as the testimony unfolded. At the end of the first day of testimony, Betty rolled her eyes as we left the court-room, and said, "Stay tuned for the next exciting episode."

When I think back, it is clear to me that I set out to be a lawyer hoping to do it with a servant's heart, helping my friends with wise advice and leadership in the political world and securing justice for them in court. But politics has nothing to do with who is best qualified to serve, and the law has nothing to do with justice. Candidates are sold like soap, and the candidate with the most money and savviest advertising agency wins, unless time and fate intervene.

The Courts exist to settle disputes, and that is what they do. Judges are interested in clearing their dockets as quickly as possible and doing it in such a way there is little likelihood a reversal on appeal making them look bad. If they err, the important thing is not that the error be corrected, but that it is buried so thoroughly in the Court of Special Appeals certiorari is impossible.

I failed in both of the things I set out to do. My goals were as hopeless and unobtainable as King Chanute's effort to sweep back the tide. What I did not set out to do but what I did as an after thought I find at the end of my life brings me the most satisfaction. We preserved over five thousand acres of land in the Long Green and Haystack Valleys. My legacy is the house I preserved, Long Green Valley and perhaps another valley on the Pacific coast.

Rob Deford interned at the Stags Leap Vineyard in Napa Valley. When I was in Newport Beach in 1983 working on my anti-trust case against Beckman Instruments, Doug Grinnell introduced me to an exquisite Gamay wine from Boordy vines planted at Stags Leap in Napa Valley. When the Vineyard's owner attended a fundraiser for Young Audiences in Baltimore, he visited Boordy and

Rob asked me to meet with him to explain how we had saved Long Green and Haystack Valleys from development.

We spent an afternoon in my office and I outlined what I just related to you, and just as Betty Miller did when we talked about Merryland, he made notes of the steps to be taken: an Association to litigate and hold the local politicians accountable and developers at bay; a tax exempt entity to create a historic district; another tax exempt land trust or conservancy to hold permanent conservation easements; and limited partnerships to buy threatened land, conserve it permanently and sell it for uses compatible with open space activity. This must be done with an educational outreach to landowners and legislators and an aggressive law firm to back it up.

Land is forever and we do not own it. We use it for a time and pass it on to others. Avondell has a remarkable collection of original building, including a multi-level icehouse, a smokehouse and an outside kitchen. We hold it in trust for those who come after us. It is comforting to sit by the fire in the library on a winter night, knowing people sat there during the French and Indian War. We hope they will love it as much as we did, and when they ride their horses on the hills above the valley they will still be able to trace the path of the Maryland Hunt Cup last run in the Long Green Valley in 1899.

"Now my days are swifter than a runner; they flee away, they see no good, they pass by like swift ships, like an eagle swooping on its prey."

Job Ch.9: verses 25-26

In Retrospect

Josephine Tey's novel of the same name postulates that history is "The Daughter of Time." As a student of history and a dabbler in historical novel writing, I know we judge our leaders not by their approval rating when they leave office, but by looking back at the time and events of their lives and putting their actions in the context of the time in which they lived.

Making a mark is vanity, a grasping at the wind. Nothing lasts forever and most of what we do is momentary. Few among us achieve our wildest dreams, finding a comfort level somewhere between our hopes and the limitations imposed by time, place and the circumstances we face daily. But we all hope we made a difference to somebody.

Shakespeare wrote of the tide in the affairs of men which must be seized—like a surfer seizes the wave at its crest—to ride on to whatever it is you hope to do. We can never be sure the destination we seek is the one we want. They are not necessarily the same. The impostor "success," if Kipling will allow me to borrow his word for it, is impossible to reach because more is never enough for those who seek it.

For me and those who supported me it was political influence or position. For others, it is celebrity or completing a task, curing a disease or climbing a mountain, exploring the depths of the sea or the far reaches of space, before time runs out and we pass into the world beyond time. For the young men I was given to mentor—mostly lawyers and judges but not all of them—I pointed out that the goals which motivate all of us are subsets of love, power and knowledge.

One may seek a university degree because it provides knowledge and influence. It might make her more attractive to a mate, more worthy to be loved or more respected by peers. Another may seek to become a CEO, because it gives him power, wealth and approval from others. Still others pursue love in all its manifestations, including sexual conquest, which some seek, or pretend to seek, to the exclusion of all else.

My thesis was that whatever the goal may be it was set too low, and if attained, it does not bring joy but dissatisfaction. The goals we set for ourselves fall short of the ultimate goal we were created to seek. Rene Descartes described a 'God sized hole' in every human being that only God could fill. God is all knowledge, all power, and all love. When we set our goal short of the ultimate, achievement does not bring the love, joy and peace we sought. Only God can give us that and most of us don't know that and far too few of us find it.

We don't seek God because we don't trust God. We fear He will take the fun out of life, failing to remember that life is a gift we are meant to enjoy. God made us and knows all that the flesh is heir to, if I may borrow another line from Shakespeare. We forget He knows our temptations and has promised us a way out so that we may be able to bear them, a consolation for which I thank St. Paul.

This memoir is not about the search for meaning in the events of my life or the meaning of life itself. Far more competent observers, blessed with the solitude imprisonment or philosophy affords, have addressed that mystery. See Frank's "Man's Search for Meaning," set in a concentration camp but one of the more beautiful books I have ever read. When my law office was in Heaver Plaza, I was having lunch in the restaurant there with a client whose wife was terminally-ill, and I recommended he read Frank's book. A stranger at a nearby table, as he was leaving, put his hand on my client's shoulder and said "Listen to your lawyer. Read that book."

Life is about choices, and every choice has consequences, for us and those around us. The foreseeable consequences are not nearly as important as the ones that are unforeseen. I agonized that my meeting Blake McFeely for lunch in 1966 was responsible for Spiro Agnew becoming Vice-President and Gerald Ford and Jimmy Carter later becoming President. If Harry Hughes had gone to the Senate in 1968, America may have avoided the Carter presidency. But then there might never have been a President Reagan just as Barack Obama might never have become President had it not been for the failures of the Bush dynasty.

After I committed my life to Christ on May 17, 1981, I invited Watson Pindell to meet weekly in my law office with the Towson committee of Christian businessmen. Watson played football at Johns Hopkins in the 1920's, wrote a book positing the late-in-life conversion of Abraham Lincoln, and spent most of his life teaching younger men to know God. He challenged me to find five things God prepared in the book of Jonah. I found four mentioned specifically —the whale, the plant, the worm and the storm; but there was no fifth thing prepared by God anywhere in that short story of love transcending disobedience, a very comforting thought I might add.

Watson pointed out that the fifth thing God was preparing was Jonah's heart to bend to His Will. He also taught me the brothers of Joseph, jealous of his favored status, sold him into slavery, thereby saving Joseph's life and his extended family as well. What the brothers meant as evil, God turned to good. The good was far off, and before it came, Joseph suffered, just as all of us do throughout our lives. Nobody gets out of life alive because God is preparing us for whatever follows.

Suffering and pain are gifts from God which come to us as we make our way through a three dimensional world blocked fore and aft by time, perhaps ultimately merging with it as some have suggested. Paul Brand in his "Fearfully and

Wonderfully Made" describes the look of sheer pleasure on the face of a leper when first he feels pain. Pain warns us to be wary.

It was Mother Teresa who explained to President Reagan after he was shot that suffering is a Divine calling. Pope John XXIII made it clear in his dying days he wanted us all to see that he, like us, was a man called to suffer and die. It happens to saints. Suffering precedes death as surely as pain precedes birth. Both are a beginning.

Joseph achieved responsibility as an intelligent youth graced with a moral compass who sought to do what he believed to be right. Sold by his brothers into slavery he became his master's overseer, arousing lust in the eye of his master's wife, refused her advances and was cast into prison and adjudged guilty of a crime he did not commit. Joseph remained steadfast to his convictions in the imperfect world in which he found himself. We were both placed close to those in positions of power, and he probably thought at times as I have thought that there is no justice.

The world we live in is far from perfect. It's not supposed to be yet. The lesson I learn from this is we are all interconnected in ways we can not even begin to imagine. Our every word and action, no matter how insignificant and inconsequential it may appear to be, can have far-reaching consequences to the farthest corner of the planet.

At Roger Hayden's Dundalk campaign headquarters in 1990, I introduced my wife to a student I flunked in math. He told her something I said to him, but I did not remember saying, caused him to turn his life around. He was master of my Masonic Lodge and shared with David Connor's father, my first boss, in raising me to the third degree, in 1973. Words remain in memory and change lives, whether it is for good or bad we can not yet tell. Remember Herodotus's tale of Croesus, who hoped Solon would acclaim him the most fortunate man who ever lived. Solon declined to please him because Croesus was still alive and neither had any way of knowing what calamity might—and in the case of Croseus did—befall him before he died.

When my cousin Al Herndon died, his wife Callie—who took forever to fix dinner the night before my bar examination in 1960—asked me to read at his funeral a few passages from the Bible which were his favorites. One was the admonition from the prophet Micah as to what God required of us —"do justice, love mercy and walk humbly with God." My cousin did that well, I try to do it still, and I commend it to you. Remember the parting words given me by Judge Kern in 1962, as he assured me that people are never as honest as you think they are but they are always kinder than you think they are.

I became a lawyer because I wanted to achieve justice. My goal was a sub-set of the ultimate. I did not know that until 1981. Justice is something only God can achieve, because only God knows our hearts. So I write to urge you to be merciful to those who fail you, for I am one of those who did. I now know that I need mercy far more than I need justice. In fact, I've bet my life that God's mercy will spare me His justice.

Author's Biography

Ed Blanton was born in North Carolina and educated in the public schools of North Carolina and Maryland. Upon graduating from Davidson College with a BS in Economics and Business, he received a Ford Foundation Fellowship to Vanderbilt University, where he received a Master of Arts in Teaching degree jointly bestowed by George Peabody College for Teachers.

After two years as an army staff officer with the 11th Airborne Division in Germany, he attended law school at the University of North Carolina (Chapel Hill) and Stetson, receiving his LL,B from the University of Maryland and earning the highest score awarded on the Maryland bar examination in 1960.

After clerking for a judge in Washington, D.C. for two years, he practiced corporate law with a prominent Baltimore law firm. Graduate legal studies were later undertaken at Georgetown, New York University, Villanova, Harvard and Pepperdine Universities.

As an assistant attorney general, he drafted landmark legislation, working with and advising six Maryland governors, state and national legislators, officials and judges. A more detailed biography appears in Marquis's *Who's Who in America* and their *Who's Who in the World.*

www.PenorSword.com
Penors Word Press, Inc

Made in United States
Troutdale, OR
11/03/2026

56852529R00137